Inner Critic
∞
Inner Success

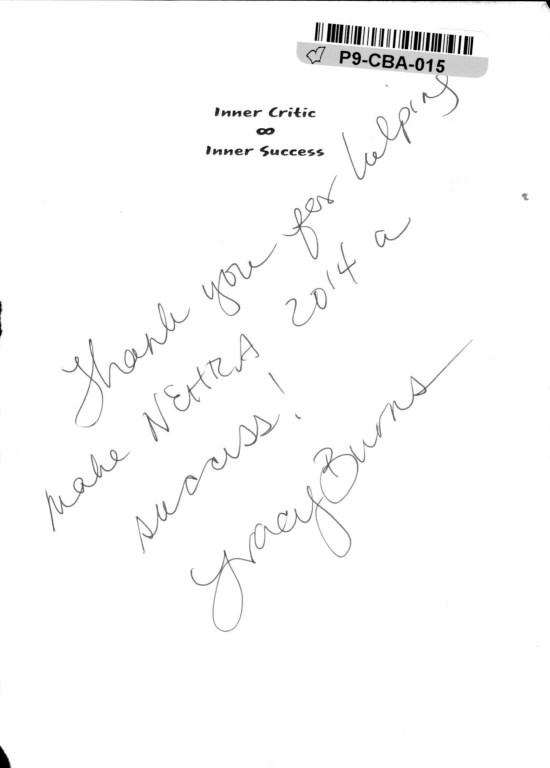

Thank you for helping
make NEHRA 2014 a
success!

Tracy Burns

STACEY SARGENT

INNER CRITIC
∞
INNER SUCCESS

CLAIMING YOUR SUCCESS
WHILE TAMING *the* CRITIC

Three-G Publishing
SEATTLE

Three-G Publishing
Seattle, Washington
stacey@innercriticinnersuccess.com

Cover design by Braid Creative, braidcreative.com
Interior design by Dorie McClelland, springbookdesign.com
Author photo ©Mallory MacDonald, mallorymacdonald.com

ISBN: 978-0-615-89705-9

Dedication

To God.
Thank you for your Love and Grace. For this book, I say the prayer
you've heard so many times, "God may all of your love flow through
me and out of me as thoughts, words and actions so that those
around me smell the fragrance that is You."

To Merrill Chertok.
Thank you for the idea, it has changed my life.

Contents

Gratitude

To My Clients.

I want to express my deep gratitude for each and every person who has allowed me the honor of being witness to their life and learning as I've coached, facilitated, designed and spoken with you. There is a passage in the book Gilead that resonated inside my soul as I recognized its truth:

> When people come to speak to me, whatever they say, I am struck by a kind of incandescence in them, the "I" whose predicate can be "love" or "fear" or "want," and whose object can be "someone" or "nothing" andit won't really matter, because the loveliness is just in that presence, shaped around "I" like a flame on a wick, emanating itself in grief and guilt and joy and whatever else. But quick, and avid, and resourceful. To see this aspect of life is a privilege of the ministry [of being a coach] which is seldom mentioned.
>
> —"Gilead" by Marilynne Robinson

Each of you have been a glowing light, full of divinity, beauty, angst, challenge and hope. One of my biggest hopes is that I have used your wisdom in good stead, that it may help others. Thank you for your stories, your honesty, your candor, your laughter, your tears, your trust, your commitment, your presence. You are part of every cell, artery and vein of the body of this book.

Introduction

Why, Why, Why?

Why Me? I'm a Master

For eight years, I enjoyed huge success as a Program Manager, Consultant and Director of Strategy in the software and high-tech industries. However, by 2004 I was no longer enjoying myself. In fact, I was suffering from chronic migraine attacks. I had no idea what was wrong with me. I thought I had it all—a great job at a status company, a six figure salary, a beautiful home. But something wasn't right. Every day I'd get up and think of a reason not to go to work. And then I'd go to work.

I thought maybe I just needed to switch to a new team, so I jumped to a different one. Yet, lo and behold, nothing changed. By now, my migraine attacks were so debilitating I was missing work, which made me feel even worse. To top it off, while I was moaning about my job, my best friend's husband was wasting away from cancer at just 34-years-of-age. Relatively speaking, I had nothing to complain about, but I couldn't help bemoan the utter lack of life in what was supposed to be a good life.

While I was attending the Microsoft Women's Conference that September, I learned that Casey (my friend's husband) had passed away. I was in a state of numbness as I looked up at the slide introducing the session. I don't remember what the subject was, but I'll never forget being struck by the title beneath the presenter's name: "Coach and Facilitator." The words elicited a momentary flutter of excitement in an otherwise grim day. I leaned over to my friend and colleague Samantha and whispered, "I've always dreamed of doing that." The futility of an early death and the flutter of a dream combined to shed a whole new light on my situation. "Life's too short Stace," I thought as I sat there. "Don't spend it feeling miserable . . . and stuck."

After the speaker, Mitch Shepard, concluded her talk, I plucked up the courage to introduce myself, ask for her card and invite her for coffee. I wanted to learn how I could become a "coach and facilitator." Mitch told me about the graduate program she attended and suggested I try it out. "Try it out?" I asked, confused. I mean, I couldn't just quit my job and go to school to "try it out." It was too big a risk. "Besides," an inner voice berated me, "you could never do that. You could never be good enough to be a coach. You don't know enough about anything to help anyone."

When I relayed to Mitch that quitting my job wasn't an option, she suggested I do both—keep my job and go to school. If I didn't like the course, I could just quit and stay with my job, reasoned Mitch. This was a foreign concept to me: simply to try something—in defiance of my Inner Perfectionist, who demanded I finish everything I start, and to do it perfectly.

I decided to try trying. It got me over my commitment bump and I applied to graduate school. Surprisingly, I was accepted, and started that January.

For four months, I worked full time and pursued my Master's degree in Applied Behavioral Science from the Leadership Institute of Seattle at Bastyr University. I was in both heaven and hell. I loved what I was learning (heaven), I was certain I was the worst student in the class (hell), and when Monday morning rolled around, I'd feel sick at the thought of having to go to work (hell). I mean, truly sick, with near-constant migraines and nausea. I was popping so many pills just to get through the work day that I began having tremors.

One day, one of my fellow students (who's since become a firm friend) pulled me aside and asked why I didn't just quit my job and use my savings to "invest" in my education.

"That's insane!" railed a voice in my head. "Who would do that?

"You work at Microsoft, one of the biggest, most awesome, status companies in the world!" chimed in another. "You make great money! What kind of idiot would quit a job like that?"

"You've been incredibly successful in this industry," reasoned a third, "why would you want to jeopardize your stellar track record?"

My Inner Critics were on a roll . . .

"No sane person spends her life savings to pursue some no-guarantee dream just because it's fun and she enjoys it!"

"There's no way you'll make it in that industry."

"You'll bomb, you'll be bottom of the class, everyone else is bound to have way more talent than you."

"You know software development and high-tech; you have no idea how to do leadership development and coaching."

"Besides, if you do this, your dad is gonna lose all faith in you. And he'll be right! You'll end up broke, with no savings, no job, and no house. And the only reason you bought that house was so you could have a dog. So you're gonna lose Bella, too."

"Not to mention, who do you think you are to deserve happiness? You should just shut up and appreciate what you've got. There are lots of people out there who are worse off than you—they're making less money, and they're even more unhappy."

"And those headaches? They're not that bad. You're just being a wimp."

"So what if you're sick and in pain? Just get your lazy butt out of bed and go to work."

So that's the deal. I know the territory of the Inner Critic only too well. I know how vicious the voices in your head can be. I know how hard it is to get clear on what makes you feel happy and successful and excited to get up out of bed in the morning. I know how scary it is to take the risk when you don't know how—or if—it's going to work out. Man, do I get it!

I often joke that I'm a Master Inner Critic, something equivalent to a Black Belt level in martial arts, but the reality isn't so funny. I have been my own worst, most cruel, most contemptuous critic. Every pivotal moment of my life, every time I've been on the brink of victory, the sweet smell of success has been poisoned by the bitter sound of my own internal "naysayer" voice.

They say the best addiction counselors are recovering addicts and I'm a "rational" success addict. I'd spent years numbing my emotions and suffering tremendous doubts while scoring hit after hit of "conventional" success. I was one of those people who would race back to her office after a meeting, slam the door shut, cover her face with her hands and say, "Why *didn't* I say that in the meeting?" Or, "Why *did* I say that in the meeting?" I questioned every move I made, while mentally chipping away at my own self-esteem.

I'd enjoyed the highs of my high-tech career but when it no longer challenged me, I became less and less satisfied, and more and more apathetic. I was living someone else's idea of success, and it was literally making me sick.

Yes, I know how bad things can be, but I know that it gets better, too. The very act of enduring those horrifying Inner Critic moments has fueled my success as a coach. Not only can I relate to other people's self-doubt, but I know how to pull them through to the other side. I've been there. I am familiar with your pain. And I know how to help you—both to diminish the impact of the Inner Critic and to get clear about what Inner Success looks and feels like. The result leaves you with no other option than to take the risk that moves you one step closer to that which you crave in every cell of your body.

It is possible to live a life of spectacularly satisfying Inner Success while managing those nasty Inner Critic doubts and fears that crop up along the way. I'm living proof of the possibility!

Why This Book?

Wolfgang Amadeus Mozart, Virginia Woolf, Nicole Kidman, Steve Jobs, Virginia "Ginni" Rometty. What does this seemingly disparate bunch have in common? Success? Sure. But also struggle—by way of critical inner voices that threatened to paralyze them with fear, sabotage their efforts and deter them from stepping into greatness.

But their Inner Critics did not paralyze or sabotage them, nor eclipse their greatness. Not because they found a way to silence the voices of doubt—but because they found a way to **manage their critics while moving toward success**. Ginni Rometty did not wait until her self-doubts were conquered before she took the jobs that would eventually lead to her selection as the first female CEO of IBM. Rometty knew she must *live with and learn from* those Inner Critics in order to attain success. Nicole Kidman has spoken of the voice inside her head that tells her she can't act. In spite of that voice—perhaps because of it—she has an Academy Award that proves otherwise. Both Wolfgang Amadeus Mozart and Virginia Woolf struggled with near-crippling self-doubt throughout their lives. Yet, they are widely considered the greatest composer and novelist, respectively, of their generations. That's the irony of the Inner Critic—it can drive you to the brink of madness, but it can also be a vital source of information about what really matters to you. Thus, your Inner Critic can reveal where your personal source of success lies.

Ginni Rometty learned to balance doubt and success

While speaking at Fortune's Most Powerful Women Summit, Ginni Rometty, CEO of IBM, shared the moment she realized the importance of pushing past self-doubt while moving toward success:

"Really early in my career, I [was] offered a big job. And I can remember [my] reaction. I said, 'You know what? I'm not ready for this job. I need more time, I need more experience and then I could really do it well. I need to go home and think about it.'

I went home that night and told my husband, and he just looked at me and said, 'Do you think a man would have ever answered that question that way?'

What [it] taught me was you have to be very confident even though you're so self-critical inside about what it is you may or may not know. And that, to me, leads to taking risks.

And when I say "success" I mean what success looks like in *your* words, on *your* terms. These high achievers didn't limit themselves to others' definitions of success; they created their own personalized version. Steve Jobs was adamant that beauty, one of his deeply held core values, was critical to the success of Apple. He bucked industry and business standards, defied a hoard of external critics, kept his focus on beauty in design, and re-vitalized a company many had written off as a joke when he created the iPod.

Critic and success are not mutually exclusive. They are in fact interrelated. To understand one, you must become familiar with the other. To achieve one, you must find a way to manage and mine the other. And to be able to do that, you need to understand and engage *all* aspects of your intelligence: the rational, the emotional and the physical.

However, in the business world the motto is, "Check your emotions at the door." The problem with this motto is that people *have* emotions. You would never check your arms and legs at the door, nor would you check your thoughts and ideas at the door. Why then would you be expected to check your emotions at the door! Pretending it's any other way has dehumanized the workplace and given birth to a workforce that's more stressed, anxious, depressed and dissatisfied than at any other time in our history. Mental health benefits constitute *the* fastest growing costs facing companies today! And we've lost the connection to how smart and full of wisdom our bodies are.

I know because I see it first-hand. I'm a Leadership Coach. Clients working at companies like Amazon and Microsoft hire me to help them map out their "success." We start out talking "business," which is to say a rational, conventional vision of success. But once the door's shut and we *really* start talking—digging down to how they really *feel* about what they do, what *motivates* them to succeed, and the *doubts and fears* that come up along the way—the emotions bubble to the surface. They're *dying* to talk about how they feel!

I coach my clients to activate and capitalize on the massive tool that is their emotional intelligence. I help them use their body as a source of vital information. By connecting the dots between all these seemingly disparate things—feelings, emotions, thoughts, ideas, shaky hands, fast heartbeat, fears, failures and successes—they emerge not only as better leaders, but also happier, more satisfied, less stressed human beings. I call *it whole-person intelligence* and it's the kind of approach that belongs back in business and brings life back to work.

My vocation is incredibly rewarding. There's nothing I love more than seeing clients smile as they finds their way back to a place of ease and joy in their jobs. My one regret is that I can only coach one person, or one team, at a time; I know there are hundreds of thousands of people out there who are **desperate to feel human** again. That's why I wrote this book—to reach those I can't coach and help as many people as possible find their way back to a life that feels meaningful, joyful, and successful.

Why This Book Is Different

This book straddles the worlds of business and self-help in a way that's bursting with smarts yet is full of soul. It's a guide to finding the sweet spot in life where you can hold both success *and* doubt in a way that feels actionable and spacious instead of pointless and stuck.

This book does not promise to rid you of your Inner Critics and self-doubts. Rather, it asks you to dive right into the center of them in order to find valuable insights you can use. This book helps you capitalize on the dynamic and powerful relationship between critic and success. With attention and awareness, you'll become adept at seeing the dynamics of how success and doubt play off each other on a day to day basis. You'll begin to transform that negative Inner Critic voice into a beam of light that spotlights your most cherished hopes, values and strengths. You'll begin to use the light of this knowledge to tame the taunts of your critic while reminding yourself *why* you're doing what you're doing, as you continue to move forward toward your vision of success. You'll become so grounded in your strengths *and your doubts* that, like Jobs, Kidman and Rometty, you too will have the power to forge ahead, beyond the inevitable voices that tell you, "You're an idiot. You don't know what you're doing. You'll fail." You may even wink knowingly as you sail on by these inaccurate messages.

Why This Work Is Critical . . . At Work

My almost decade-long process reflects the most updated thinking in business leadership: that the job of a leader is to generate trust, and that the job of a company is to motivate and engage their employees with their greatest strengths. These goals are achieved on an *emotional* level—not a *rational* one. It is no longer acceptable to mutter the tired corporate mantra, "It's not personal, it's business," because emotions are very personal—and they have significant influence and impact on the bottom line.

Is it any wonder that research-professor-turned-author Brené Brown—whose TED talk on "vulnerability" went viral? She tapped into a visceral hunger to connect at an emotional level—and is now being asked to speak at business conferences around the world. From entrepreneurs to major corporations, businesses are starting to wake up to the dollar value of her message.

In Brown's book, *Daring Greatly*, she shares what Peter Sheahan, CEO of ChangeLabs, says about the high impact shame, fear, and doubt have on the bottom line. According to Sheahan:

"The secret killer of innovation is shame. You can't measure it, but it is there. Every time someone holds back on a new idea, fails to give their manager much needed feedback, and is afraid to speak up in front of a client you can be sure shame played a part. That deep fear we all have of being wrong, of being belittled and of feeling less than, is what stops us taking the very risks required to move our companies forward."

Yes, it may seem radical to suggest there'll be no innovation, no creative thinking, no new markets identified if we don't overcome fear. But the reality is people *do* doubt themselves and they *are* holding back in some way. I hear about it in coaching sessions all too often. What if we unleashed all that untapped potential?

What if we felt more connected to, satisfied with and engaged in the type of work we do—because it's truly aligned to our personal definition of Inner Success? How much more energy and passion would we devote to our work? What impact would that have?

While Brené's awareness came via time in the trenches of research, mine came from being in the trenches of the business world. As a leadership coach, I've had the privilege of working with thousands of people from all backgrounds, operating at all levels within large corporations like Microsoft, Amazon and Raytheon, fast paced start-ups like Moz and BigDoor, and associations and non-profits. My clients trust me; they know I was once one of them. I speak their language. I get it. I get business, I get how that world works, and I get what it's like being on the other side of the wall—the side where you don't talk about your feelings. But they are talking about their feelings—only, they're doing it behind closed doors. They're talking to me. And boy do they have a lot to say!

- They're talking about the challenging dynamic of finding true success despite their inner doubts and fears;
- They're talking about the pressure to have all the answers, all the time;
- They're talking about wanting to be more authentic, more themselves;
- They're talking about the insecurities that hold them back;
- They're talking about wanting more than the kind of success their company maps out for them; and,
- They're talking about wanting to find meaning—in work and in life.

In this book, I share how I've helped them do that. I wish for all of you to experience the results I've witnessed: the way a client's face softens as they're reminded just how truly successful and awesome they. How they smile oh-so-sweetly as they slip inside a success story that plays to their absolute greatest strengths and fits them like a glove. *This* is what compels my clients to be better leaders, to take the risk of bringing up that crazy-sounding idea that ends up becoming a business game-changer and to start letting go of the thousand-doubts-a-day that make them no fun to be around when they get home to their families at night.

This is life work. It is the process of creating your own spectacular definition of success, while competently and compassionately dealing with the doubts that crop up along the way. My clients tell me they experience dramatic change not only in their jobs, but in all areas of their lives. When you explore anything at this level, you can't help but operate at a whole new stratosphere. It sticks with you. You can never return to the old ways of doing things. And that's why my clients keep bringing me back.

In this book I share what I've seen, heard, taught, and learned as a leadership coach, a businesswoman and a human being; that we all have an Inner Critic *and* an Inner Success story. When you trust yourself to combine your smarts *and* your emotions, you'll be using all of your intelligence and operating at your *most* successful. It's precisely in those moments when you're *most* overwhelmed by doubt and fear—yet you act anyway in alignment to your own definition of success—that you'll appreciate the challenge and feel the exhilaration at the same time.

Why This Work Really Matters

In the end, you'll have the ability to stay firmly rooted in **what really matters** to you **no matter what**. You'll be in possession of practices that empower you to mine and manage the doubts that will inevitably show up as you continue to redefine and evolve to new, more expansive visions of success that reflect who you are and what matters to you now—not five years ago, not when you were in college, but in this moment. Bottom line: the life you are navigating will feel more spacious, compassionate, vibrant, profound, joyful and ease-filled.

Life is a process, and so is this work. Is it easy? No! Can it be done? Yes! Does it work? Absolutely!

Will life hold more meaning and satisfaction? Yes, because you'll no longer be skipping across the surface of the water, afraid to look down, afraid to get your feet wet. You'll have dived deep into the belly of the beast and faced what makes you feel successful *and* what immobilizes you through fear. You'll have the skills to take advantage of both sides of that amazing brain of yours—the rational, thinking side and the emotional, feeling side. And like a true warrior, you'll have come out the other side with the courage and the grace and the resilience to keep moving forward no matter what life throws at you.

1

This Is How We Roll

"Three seemingly small changes have made a huge impact on my life," Kimiko told me during our last coaching session together. I'd asked her to summarize what progress she'd made during our work together. "I'm much more aware of how I'm feeling and how this drives what I do. I constantly ask myself what others might be feeling, and why they might be saying or doing what they're saying and doing—beyond the actual business at hand—and I address both in my response. Lastly, I have a much better sense of what I'm really good at. I simply don't question it anymore."

I couldn't have been happier for Kimiko. I'd been coaching her (and her entire team) throughout a year-long leadership program. She's a brilliant, highly influential Director of Programs at a Fortune 100 firm. Kimiko faces the same dilemma confronting most business leaders I coach: the desire to do excellent work, to make an impact and to feel good about what she does—in the face of obstacles, challenges, self-doubts and Inner Critics.

Kimiko had given one hundred and ten percent in coaching. She'd been open to learning, changing and improving, and she'd seen the profound results of her investment. These are the moments that cement the knowledge that I'm doing the right work, what I call the "work-love-of-my-life"—which fills me with gratitude. I offer this book to you with the hope that you, too, will learn how to take advantage of all the valuable resources I share, including what your Inner Critic can teach you about finding a very real, very meaningful definition of success that works for *you*.

If you do, you'll experience an incredible bonus—what you'll learn will benefit *all* areas of your life. This is expressed in a saying that I love: "How you do anything is how you do everything." In other words, if I sent you out to tackle a ropes course with your coworkers as part of one of those corporate team-building exercises, behavioral science tells me you'd approach the course in the same way you'd confront a challenge at work or deal with a crisis at home. Why? Because the common denominator is *you*—you're the one showing up in all three places: work, home, life.

So it is with the lessons in this book. You get to take them with you everywhere you go. And, considering you'll be hanging out with yourself for the rest of your life, isn't that worth the investment? My goal is that you earn a serious ROI on yourself!

Let's Get Real

This book does not promise easy answers; it's not filled with quick and simple five-step recipes for a critic-free life. I'm a coach, and my job is to believe in the capacity of my client—you!—to find your own answers. Don't expect me to hand you any one-size-fits-all solutions on a silver platter. Besides, we both know those don't work in the long run don't we!

What this book does promise is a process for managing those moments in life when you're called upon to redefine your vision of Inner Success and manage the Inner Critics that will inevitably show up along the way. **You won't find *the* answer; you'll find *your way*.** Not my way—yours. If you want someone else's way, go buy a book where you can read that author's answer for you. However, if you want to find the way that fits like a glove and sticks with you throughout all of life's changes, challenges and curve balls, then continue reading.

Getting the Lay of the Land

In this chapter, I'm going to lay the groundwork you'll build on throughout the rest of the book. I'll explain the foundational tools you'll be using, break down some key terms you may not be familiar with, and introduce you to the concept of Emotional Intelligence, explaining why it's integral to both Inner Critic and Inner Success work.

You'll notice that a multi-layered infinity symbol appears frequently in the book. This is the logo for my business, Connect Growth and Development. I chose it because it represents the dynamic relationship, or flow of energy, that exists between concepts that initially appear to be polar opposites—such as Inner Critic and Inner Success.

In our journey together we'll use the infinity spiral in the same way—exploring two parts that are related. Starting with the left curve for the Inner Critic: I'll help you name your critics (chapter two), de-mystify and tame their potency (chapter three), and dig deep into the valuable data hidden underneath (chapter four). Then we'll take a big step back for a panoramic view that offers eye-opening new perspectives on your critic stories (chapter five). At that point, you'll be armed with incredibly useful information that will allow you catch your critic early and zap its energy before it has a chance to zap yours.

Chapter six is the turning point of the book. Here, at the epicenter of the infinity spiral, we'll reveal your Divine Flaw—the powerful link between Critic and Success. (Remember, in this book, success is just a label I use for whatever makes your life feel satisfying, joyful and vibrant.)

Next, we'll explore the right curve of Inner Success, starting with some core-strengthening moves that will give you the stamina to complete your journey (chapter seven). Together, we'll ground deeply in the how, when, where and why of those moments in which you've felt *most* successful and proud (chapter eight), and get clear on the energizing strengths that make you feel like a superhero (chapter nine). By chapter ten, you'll be ready to write your living and authentic masterpiece: a personalized, meaningful, up-to-the-minute definition of success that defines the life you want to live, both in the moment and that's headed in the forward direction the feels right inside. Now you've done the inner work, it's time to ensure you've got the outer support crew in place. In chapter eleven we'll focus on work it takes to be surrounded by the people who will help you stay aligned to your success and fight the critics when they show up.

Lastly, in chapter twelve, we arrive back at the epicenter of the infinity spiral, this essential energy flow, to talk about how to cultivate a life-long practice that will keep the energy moving and alive. This is where you put together the tools and resources that fit for you—and how you'll practice them daily to strengthen and maintain the good habit of keeping your success top of mind and the critics in the background.

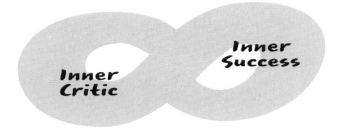

Throughout your journey, I want you to think of me as your coach, challenging you to dig into the work as well as cheering you from the sidelines. I'm grateful for the opportunity to partner with you as you grow, evolve and find more meaning, ease, joy and success in life.

Inner Critic and Inner Success—It's Like PB&J

Critic and Success may seem like an odd pairing, but just like peanut butter and jelly, you'll be surprised what a natural fit these two make. Contrary to what other authors will tell you, it's my belief that you can't simply flip a switch and "get rid of" the Inner Critic. I believe that as you develop your capacity to reduce its power over you, you can become an I.C. Master (earning Black Belt status). Similarly, I believe that success isn't static and that it's human nature to experience new desires, give birth to new goals and update your vision of Inner Success. And guess what happens when you do? A new Inner Critic pops up! Your Inner Critic and your Inner Success are related in a dynamic relationship.

You'll discover that your Inner Critic has an incredible amount of valuable information about what you care most about. And getting super clear on what you care about leads to your authentic definition of Inner Success. Conversely, as soon as you get Success clearly in your sights, you can bet your Critic will show up—packing a whole lot of firepower.

Rather than view one (I.C.) as an impediment to achieving the other (I.S.), you'll start to see the relationship as a flow of energy, and you'll learn how to manage it so that you will be flowing **towards Success and away from doubt**.

Speaking of which . . . People often ask why I devote as much time to the Success side of the flow as the Critic side. It always amazes me how eager they are to talk about their fears and their doubts, but they're too squeamish to talk about their successful and proud moments. When it comes to our jobs, most of us are all too familiar with the *how*—how we're falling short—but few of us pause to consider the *why*—why we do what we do—until it's too late. Most of us tend to neglect the *why* until we're so deep in the struggle to keep up, and so far underwater, that satisfaction and meaning have long since disappeared from view.

I'm hearing more and more clients lament, "What with the hours, the challenges and the politics, I don't know if it's worth it anymore. I mean, what am I doing this for? Why I am sacrificing all this time away from my family? It's not like I'm curing cancer." Not even the most "successful" are immune (and by successful, I am thinking about how our society defines the term). I recently had the CEO of a multinational company tell me, "You know, I'm beholden to all these people who all have their own agendas: the shareholders, the board, the investors. I'm under so much pressure to perform, perform, perform—every quarter. If we're not up, we're down, and I feel like my head's constantly on the chopping block. Sometimes I wonder if it's worth all the stress, anxiety and pressure."

The reality is that today, one million Americans skip work due to stress. I've noticed a major uptick in the prevalence of Imposter Syndrome, a.k.a. the Inner "Fraud" Critic. As soon as I hear someone question *why* they're doing what it is they are doing, I know they're close to burnout. It's only a matter of time before they quit or, if that's not an option, they stop giving their best effort because on some level they've already decided it's just not worth it anymore. This is the most defeating struggle I witness—staying in a job that makes you unhappy; losing the ability to muster your best efforts, energy and talent; and then suffering even more debilitating self-doubt. Shower. Rinse. Repeat. This vicious cycle kills people's spirits and it pains me to witness them in that place, especially when I know that I can help them.

In her bestselling book, *Lean In: Women, Work, and the Will to Lead*, Facebook COO Sheryl Sandberg advocates an immediate start in focusing on these difficulties:

> Internal obstacles are rarely discussed and often underplayed. Throughout my life, I was told over and over about inequalities in the workplace and how hard it would be to have a career and a family. I rarely heard anything, however, about the ways I might hold myself back. These internal obstacles deserve a lot more attention, in part because they are under our own control. We can dismantle the hurdles in ourselves today. We can start this very moment.

It's those internal barriers—fear, doubt and uncertainty, as well as a loss of meaningful success—that hold people back. And while Sandberg is addressing women, my experience leads me to conclude that this applies to men and women. I want you to know what those barriers are and then *choose* if you want to keep them or not. Either way, I'm totally cool. If you want to keep that barrier up because it's right for you, fabulous! Paint a mural on that wall and own it. But if you don't, then let's Berlin Wall that son-of-a-gun till it's a tiny pile of rubble.

As a coach, I'm not married to what choice you make. But I want it to be a clear one, and I want you to say yes or no from the core of your being because only then will you hold yourself accountable.

The New 80/20 Rule

By the way, not knowing the answer to the question, "What makes me happy?" doesn't give you a free pass from taking action! A good eighty percent of my clients don't know what would give their lives meaning and most believe they have to wait until they figure it out *exactly* before taking action. They'll tell me, "I can't make a change because I don't know what I want to do." Well, guess what? Most people don't know what they want to do! As a coach, I know this to be true because I see it all the time. Most of us think everyone else has it figured out. That's just the Inner Critic talking; *everyone's* like you. Think of it in terms of the 80/20 rule: eighty percent of people don't really know what they want to do; only twenty percent do. And of those, only some are actually doing it, because going after what you want takes courage. But everyone I know who's done it says it's worth it. The inner work activities in this book create a guide to figuring out what your success is—whether you achieve it at work or home.

Start with Self: Working from the Inside Out

When working with clients, my focus is always in this order . . .

1. Self
2. Team
3. Organization

While some coaches take a different approach and start from a larger, organizational perspective, I've always believed that the most powerful starting point for growth and change is within the individual. That is why this book has the title, *Inner* Critic, *Inner* Success. Together, we'll be working on *your Inner* Self.

However, after doing all this deep internal work, you'll notice a ripple effect. As you change, people around you will change, too. While it's absolutely true that you can't change others—you can only change yourself—it's also true that you can alter your interactions with others by altering how you show up in the world.

I didn't always believe that to be true, especially when it came to my family. I wanted *them* to change, dang it! However, I've seen unequivocal proof that as I've changed, it has drastically changed *how they relate to me*. So, in a sneaky way I guess I have changed them! But I did it by focusing on myself first.

I'm often asked the question, "Well, what do you do about *outer* critics—*other* people who are critical of *you*?" My response is the same: the most powerful place to affect change is within. When you work on your inner "stuff," outer critics won't trigger you nearly as easily. That isn't to say that working on your *relationships* with other people isn't essential (my second order of work is team after all). Skills such as interpersonal communication and the ability to give and receive feedback are vital in today's global economy—but maybe that is the next book, *Outer Critic, Outer Success* perhaps?

The Learner's Mindset: Managing Expectations

As you progress through the book, constantly remind yourself that you're in *learning* mode. Whenever you're learning new attitudes and behaviors, it goes without saying that you should not expect perfection. (But then again, if you're reading this book you may well be a perfectionist!) Your primary goal here is to learn about yourself, to build your awareness and to pay attention to what's going on inside you as you do the activities and practices. You'll make mistakes, suffer Inner Critic attacks, and feel uncertain about defining your Inner Success—and that's totally fine. In fact, that's how you learn.

Even if you catch your mistake—for example, "I was an idiot in front of my boss"—hours after the fact, that's ok, too. The point is you *did* catch it. And guess what? You have a chance to get a mulligan (a.k.a. a "do over") tomorrow. You can go back and have another conversation with your boss about the project and this time, you can do better. Next time, you might catch your mistake two hours after the meeting. One day, you'll catch it *in* the meeting. And eventually, you'll catch yourself in the moment—and get to choose whether or not to do things differently. That is learning.

Foundational Tools

You're going to encounter a lot of applied behavioral science and coaching language throughout the book, so treat the following section as a little primer—so there's no surprises, question marks or frown lines later.

Emotional Intelligence (E.I.) Primer

It drives me *crazy* when I hear people say, "It's not personal; it's strictly business." Your thoughts and your emotions are inseparable from you, who you are as a person. You're a package deal. You take your thoughts *and* your emotions to work, and everywhere else for that matter. It's physiologically impossible to separate the two. Besides, your emotional brain processes information up to 80,000 times faster than your rational brain—why on earth would you want to shut down that kind of an asset? That would be like developing a sprawling, 100-building campus and then saying, "Eh, we're not going to use *those* buildings," (pointing to 80 odd units).

Learning to understand and utilize your emotions empowers you to become your absolute best. There's a ton of published research (in books such as *Primal Leadership, Emotional Intelligence 2.0, The Happiness Advantage, Drive,* and *Working with Emotional Intelligence*) suggesting that your emotional brain has much greater influence over your attitudes, behaviors and actions than your rational brain. One of my favorite passages in Jonathan Haidt's work on the subject is, "Human rationality depends critically on sophisticated emotionality. It is only because our emotional brains work so well that our reasoning can work at all." Our emotions are necessary! Most people have a vague understanding that Emotional Intelligence (E.I.) is important, but they don't know much about accessing and applying it.

Emotions Rule, and Why That's a Good Thing. In his book, *The Happiness Hypothesis: Finding Modern Truth in Ancient Wisdom*, Haidt uses the analogy of an African elephant to represent our emotional brains, and the rider sitting on top as our neo-cortex or rational brains. Imagine this pairing of elephant and rider ambling slowly along a path when all of a sudden someone jumps out of the bushes and pokes the elephant in the side with a pretty pointed stick. Good luck to the driver now! As the elephant rampages through the jungle, just about all its passenger can do is hang on until the elephant calms down. So it is when your emotional brain is triggered—as your emotional self takes off and runs wildly through the jungle, you and your rational brain will do well just to keep up!

When I share this analogy, clients often get ticked off initially—because they want to be bigger than the elephant and they want to have more power over their emotions. But when it settles in, they gain a visceral understanding of just how big, powerful and deserving of respect their emotional (a.k.a. limbic) brains are. Now, your emotions aren't *always* running wild (although we've all felt that way at times, right?). Nevertheless, they are very strong. So why not tap into that fantastic asset? Ultimately, my goal is to see you create a fantastic partnership between both your emotional and your rational brains.

" '*What can emotional intelligence do for me?' In the context of the work environment, emotional intelligence enables three important skill sets: stellar work performance, outstanding leadership and the ability to create the conditions for happiness.*
—*Chade-Meng Tan,* Search Inside Yourself: The Unexpected Path to Achieving Success, Happiness (and World Peace)

Check Your [Rational] Brain at the Door. It's impossible to have a thought without an emotion, but it *is* possible to have an emotion without a thought. Yet we're taught to value thinking and devalue feeling. How often have you been told to "check your emotions at the door?"

But think about it: why would you want to do that? How many of you have been at a meeting where a colleague passionately pitched a new idea or a new product? Could they have sold the team on that idea without getting excited? Would you really prefer that your employees not excitedly argue a point that could mitigate some major risk? Of course not! So when people say, "Check your emotions at the door," what they *really* mean is, "Check the emotions *I'm uncomfortable with* at the door." The thing is, emotions all come from the same place. You can't command people to bring some—and coat-check the others.

How can any business hope to motivate and engage their employees without appealing to their emotions? How can any advertising campaign connect with a customer without eliciting an emotional response? Why is it people leave a manager not a job, or regret leaving their team most when they move on? Emotions are key to motivation, connection, desire and performance. It no longer makes any business sense to push this fantastic asset under the table.

"Sharing emotions builds deeper relationships. Motivation comes from working on things we care about. It also comes from working with people we care about. To really care about others, we have to understand them—what they like and dislike, what they feel as well as think. Emotion drives both men and women and influences every decision we make. Recognizing the role emotions play and being willing to discuss them makes us better managers, partners, and peers. —Sheryl Sandberg, Lean In: Women, Work, and the Will to Lead

One of Google's master engineers, Chade-Meng Tan, writes about the power of E.I. in his book, *Search Inside Yourself,* "Based on my team's experience teaching at Google and elsewhere, I am optimistic that emotional intelligence is one of the best predictors of success at work and fulfillment in life. . . . With the right training, anybody can become more emotionally intelligent."

If you want to read more on E.I., Travis Bradberry and Jean Greaves' book *Emotional Intelligence 2.0* is an outstanding primer. I highly recommend Daniel Goleman's tome, *Working with Emotional Intelligence*, for those looking to take a deeper dive into the E.I. pool.

Now, don't get me wrong—I absolutely love my own rational brain and my client's vast cognitive skills. But I want to advocate expanding into what I call "Whole-Person Intelligence." This endeavors to add emotional intelligence and body wisdom to the rational, cognitive intelligence. This powerful trio gets you access to all your assets, intelligence and wisdom, allowing you to bring the best of all of you forward. I'll explain more about E.I., and add the body element into it.

The main components of E.I. I use the following four-quadrant matrix from Daniel Goleman's, *Primal Leadership: Realizing the Power of Emotional Intelligence*, as the framework for teaching how to understand and apply emotional intelligence.

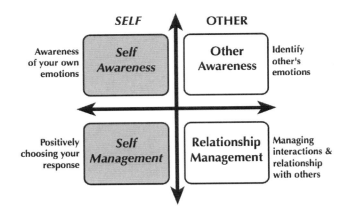

Self-awareness is the skill of identifying your feelings. Most experts agree there are four basic emotions—mad, sad, glad, and afraid—of which everything else is derivative. While some people argue for a fifth (surprise) and others for a sixth (shame), for the purposes of this book I will stick to the four basic emotions. Of course, there are lots of different words used to describe these core emotions and many degrees of intensity for each one.

To build your E.I. skill (Whole-Person Intelligence), I'll pepper the following three "E.I. Builder" questions throughout the book:

1. **What are you feeling?** Regularly checking in with your emotions will help you become adept at quickly identifying how you're feeling—mad, glad, sad or afraid, or another descriptive word related to these. This sounds like, "I feel disappointed."

2. **What are you thinking?** It's important to build your ability to distinguish between thoughts and feelings, which we often confuse. Thoughts originate in your cognitive, rational brain and usually take the form of assumptions, judgments, perceptions and stories. This might sound something like, "I'm a loser, I should have done better delivering that presentation."

3. **What's your physical reaction?** I want you to start being receptive to the information your body sends to the brain when you experience emotion. I used to have no idea this connection existed; thus, I never figured out that being miserably unhappy was triggering my migraines. But now I know better. Now I recognize my physical reactions as a key piece of the puzzle, telling me how my experiences, decisions and environment are impacting my body—and therefore me. A physical reaction might be your throat feeling tight, becoming less vocal, or nervous foot tapping.

Self-management is the ability to use self-awareness—of your feelings, thoughts and body responses—to make intentional choices around what to do with the information. Up to this point, most of your responses were dictated by habit or by your auto-pilot default setting. But now you'll see how improving your ability to self-manage gives you a broader range of choices around how to behave and act. To help build your self-management capabilities, I'll pose the following questions:

1. What choice do you want to make based on what you're feeling and thinking right now (your self-awareness)?
2. What behavior and actions are best suited to this situation?

I don't cover the last two components of the E.I. matrix as deeply in the book, but for all the Perfectionists reading this, I'll briefly explain them.

Other-Awareness indicates how good you are at picking up on what other people are feeling in the moment.

Relationship Management is the art of combining your self-awareness, self-management and other-awareness in order to have more effective and efficient relationships with others.

Ben transformed his relationship with his boss just by boosting his E.I. Whenever he had to deliver bad news—for example, that a project was behind schedule—Ben would bombard his boss with all the minute details around why the project wasn't as far along as it should be. As you can imagine, it didn't help.

I coached Ben to become aware of how he was feeling in these meetings:

"I feel nervous and anxious; I'm afraid."

He also started to track what he was thinking:

"I'm gonna get fired if we get behind one more time."

"My boss is gonna realize I have no idea what I'm doing. I'd better tell him everything."

Needless to say, Ben was experiencing some funny sensations in his body, too:

"My stomach's doing flip-flops."

"I start talking and can't seem to stop."

Ben came to realize that his thoughts increased the intensity of his feelings and he'd get lost in the clutches of anxiety. Once that happened Ben would start talking incessantly to try and explain his way out of it. After Ben became aware of what was happening internally during these meetings he began to self-manage. He started "catching" his nervous moments—noticing his belly flops and short attention span (physical responses)—which gave him an early clue that he was about to start chattering. Instead of reverting to his default autopilot mode, he would give his boss a short, concise update he'd prepared before the meeting. And like all hard work, Ben's practice paid off. Nowadays, he makes a smarter choice when he gets nervous—because he's *aware* of being nervous!

"*Self-awareness is not about discovering deep dark secrets or unconscious motivations but rather it comes from developing a straightforward and honest understanding of what makes you tick. —Travis Bradberry and Jean Greaves,* Emotional Intelligence 2.0

Self-awareness and the bottom line. Bradberry and Greaves found that 90% of people who score high in self-awareness are considered top performers. But it's not just about being a top performer or a bottom performer. This book is about being able to achieve your Inner definition of Success *while* experiencing Inner Critic attacks. Those of you who develop a high degree of self-awareness will be better able to control your I.C. so that it doesn't hold you back. And this will pay dividends across all areas of your life. I see E.I. as a leverage point to making you successful, period—whether at home or at work. Leverage is about honing in on those skills that will have the biggest bang for your buck. If you're going to invest your precious time and effort I want it to pay off *everywhere*!

Coaching 101:
As a coach, I believe that my clients already have everything they need to figure out the solutions themselves. My job is to help nurture their self-understanding, self-awareness and self-knowledge, so they can recognize it and engage their own capabilities. It's a vastly different role than that of a manager, mentor or teacher.

"*If he is indeed wise he does not bid you to enter the house of his wisdom, but rather leads you to the threshold of your own mind. —Kahlil Gibran,* The Prophet

If I were coaching you, we'd be sitting down, having a face-to-face conversation. I would ask provocative and challenging questions based on what you'd tell me. I listen to your responses and then repeat back to you what I've heard you say. Inevitably, you'd say, "Wow! That's brilliant! How did you figure that out?" And I'd remind you that I'd simply repeated back what you'd told me. The insight *always* comes from the client.

It's important that you understand I'm never going to tell you what to do. Obviously, we're not engaged in a "live" conversation—trust me, I *wish* I were there chatting with you right now! But I will be presenting you with a bunch of coaching-style questions that will lead you toward *your* answers. In order to maximize the benefits of this process, I suggest you "mirror" the live, interactive coaching experience. You can do this in one of two ways.

1. Journal your responses to my questions, then read aloud what you've written (in lieu of me repeating it back to you). You may want to take a break between journaling and reading, or you may want to role-play. By that I mean actually go sit in the "coach's chair" and play Stacey—put your coaching hat on and "listen" as you repeat your words back to yourself. As you do, I want you to practice what I call "deep listening"—listening not only to your words but to your body language, your tone of voice and your energy, so you can determine the emotions and feelings underlying the language. The words you say are the *content*—everything else is *context*. My intention is for you to increase your awareness of both the content and the context—learning from your words and body language.

2. If you're just not into journaling or you're more of an extrovert who prefers to talk things through with someone else (like me!), you might use the questions as a basis for a conversation with a trusted

friend or colleague. Remind them that their job is not to give advice or feedback, but to step into the role of a coach who listens deeply and paraphrases back what they've heard you say. No more, no less.

Ask insight-inspiring questions. Another foundational element of coaching is to ask questions I describe as "challenging and provocative." These are questions that challenge your way of thinking and get you to consider how you might think differently or see things from an alternate perspective. For example, let's pretend you're Ben and you're telling me about that meeting with your boss when you had to explain why your project was late. Let's say you told me you felt your boss was disappointed in you. The first question I'd ask is, "Are there any other possibilities about how your boss was feeling?" Of course there are! Get the drift?

Get super specific. A third fundamental aspect of coaching is to get super clear on your language and meaning. For example, if you told me your goal is "to become more strategic," I'd ask you to be more specific about what "more strategic" means. How do you *think* of the word "strategic"? That is, what assumptions, judgments and perceptions do you have around the word? How do you *feel* when you're being strategic? I'll ask you to drill down (getting more and more specific) into your own language in order to get super clear on what you mean. As you do, you'll start to "hear" yourself with a lot more clarity and awareness.

Three key questions. There are three primary questions I ask every coaching client as we begin working together:

1. **What does success look like?** In other words, what's your goal? What do you want to look differently at the end of the coaching engagement (or in this case, the book)? And how can you reframe your goal so it becomes a success statement? For example, your goal of: "I want to stop getting so angry in meetings," becomes the success statement: "I want to be more influential in meetings."

2. **Why does that matter?** I mean this in two ways: why does that success statement or goal matter to your job/work/business and why does it matter to you personally? The latter is frankly the more important of the two because you generally only do the work required to accomplish a goal when you are *personally* motivated. The answer to this question usually boils down to elements of your core (values, identity, feelings). You might tell me that, from a business point of view, you want to convince more partners to use your tools and products. But I want to know why it matters to *you*. From a personal point of view, it might matter because you care about doing high-quality work, which relates to an underlying core value of integrity. Will you be more motivated to act now that you're aware your integrity is on the line? Absolutely!

3. **What do you need to change or learn in order to get there?** In order to change something that isn't working, you'll usually need to learn a new skill, learn to stop doing something you've always done, or learn to apply an old skill to a new situation. Using the above example about getting angry in meetings, you might reply, "In order to change how often I get triggered and become too aggressive in meetings, I need to learn how to manage my emotions."

You'll notice I didn't mention anything about creating an action plan or a task list in any of the above examples. I'm not a fan of task lists. Instead, I prefer that you focus on changing and learning new attitudes (the way you think about something), behaviors (the actions you take), or both. In order to change, learn=and grow, you have to get clear on what you want, why it matters and what needs to be different. Meaningful change is rarely accomplished via a task list. If it was, diets would always work and we could just hand a checklist to those troublesome (or, annoying) people at work and they'd behave better.

When my clients answer the above three questions, they pretty much know what needs to happen next. They don't need me to assign them a task list. I help them get specific and clear about what they think and how they feel—then and only then do they do the *real* work that achieves a change in attitude and/or behavior. Real change is a dynamic process that requires your constant attention and attunement. There's no quick-fix task list. But you knew that already, didn't you?

Sharing Your Story

While the focus of this book is internal (that is, *Inner* Critic and *Inner* Success), I want to take a moment to talk about the importance of sharing your stories, learning and experiences with *other* people.

In the first hour of my Inner Critic workshops, I ask everyone to write down their primary Inner Critic message on an index card—then they mingle and exchange "cards" as part of a cocktail-free mixer. I allow enough time for each person to circulate with at least five different people, and read five different cards. The reaction is always the same: initial horror; ultimate relief. Without fail, when I ask how people found the experience, they tell me, "Wow. I can't believe it. I've read all these index cards and I realize I'm not the only one who feels this way. It's such a relief to know it's not just me!"

When we share things about ourselves, particularly our struggles with our critics or how we crave to lead a more successful, meaningful life, several things happen . . .

- We realize we're not the only ones—everyone's dealing with something.
- We feel seen and witnessed and acknowledged for who we are.
- We benefit from the emotional release of sharing something out loud with another person.
- We feel more connected and more human.
- We oftentimes get a new perspective on the issue or situation.

Oprah says that in three decades of interviewing, the biggest lesson she's learned is that people just want to be seen and acknowledged for who they really are. It's the same reason why I believe Brené Brown's first TED talk became such a sensation—generating almost nine million hits after it debuted in 2010. Her message—that we all have fears, doubts and vulnerabilities, and that talking about them takes the sting out of the stigma and allows us feel more connected to each other—clearly resonates. In her book, *The Gifts of Imperfection*, she writes,

> Shame keeps worthiness away by convincing us that owning our stories will lead to people thinking less of us. Shame is all about fear. We're afraid that people won't like us if they know the truth about who we are, where we come from, what we believe, how much we're struggling, or, believe it or not, how wonderful we are when soaring (sometimes it's just as hard to own our strengths as our struggles).

I wholeheartedly agree. In my experience, people can be deeply uncomfortable sharing their stories—especially their triumphs and successes. But in the end, they find the experience of doing so incredibly valuable and validating.

Sharing stories and experiences—both positive and negative—is the main process by which my coaching clients learn, grow and achieve their goals. It's the same with groups and teams. As a facilitator, one of my most important tasks is to create a safe space so people can have meaningful conversations and connections. I achieve this by having teams do some of the very same activities in this book, and then have them share the results with each other. When people share their stories, the energy in the room is transformed and a deeper sense of trust and respect is rooted (the secret sauce of high performing teams).

Throughout the book, I'll be assigning lots of activities and exercises. While it's perfectly OK that you do them on your own, I'd really like you to talk through at least some of them with someone you trust or, better yet, a group of confidants. Real inner work is only accomplished when you share your story. You will not be as successful in this work if you do it all on your own.

As an encouragement to you to open up and reveal your vulnerabilities, I share many of my own personal I.C./I.S. stories and those of my clients. I've changed names and certain identifying information to protect their privacy. Nevertheless, you can be assured that their stories are very real. I believe that reading about other people's struggles and successes will show you just how "normal" these moments are and that, like me and my clients, you are not alone.

Let's Roll!

As you begin your journey, I'd like to share what Alex told me in his closing coaching session. "I no longer feel constantly under water and so far behind," he said, referring to his biggest breakthrough. "I still practice my success moments every day. Instead of constantly moving the goal post, I now stop to appreciate just how much I actually accomplished. I spend way less time hammering at myself. As a result, it seems like I've got way more time and energy now to think bigger. Oh, and I'm a lot happier."

You'll hear more of Alex's story later. I expect you'll experience some of the very same challenges he endured. And I hope you'll experience some of the very same breakthroughs he enjoyed. I deeply hope that you, too, will feel more capable, more clear—and way happier!

2

Meet the Cast of
Inner Critic Characters

Bet you didn't know you're a walking Broadway production, did you? Yes, residing inside your head is your very own "cast" of characters. Now, I don't mean that you've got dissociative identity disorder a la the iconic film *Sybil*, or *The Three Faces of Eve*, I mean that there's a plethora of voices, guides, and what I like to call "committee members" at your disposal to help you navigate through your life experiences. One might have the ring and tone of an encouraging Teacher who steps forward when you're pitching that new idea at work. Another might take the form of a Guardian who warns against taking that short-cut when you're out for your post-dusk run. Yet another voice might take the form of the Elder presence you sense when taking ownership of your strength, wisdom and power. In the context of this book, the cast of characters I'm referring to specifically is a group I've labeled the Inner Critics—those nasty, negative, limiting voices that hinder, rather than help.

When I use the word "inner," as in, Inner Critic and Inner Success, I'm talking about your inner landscape (i.e., your feelings, your thoughts and your mental model)—in other words, how you perceive the world. Surprisingly, everyone has a different mental model, which is what drives us crazy when people don't think the way we think.

The Inner Critic is a negative internal voice(s), a critical message(s) or any way in which you're hard on yourself, limit yourself or hold yourself back. There are as many Inner Critics as there are people plagued by them. But having worked with hundreds of clients—and battled my own Inner Critics—over the years, I've come to believe that most people are dealing with one of six classic types: The Perfectionist, The Driver, The Pleaser, The Fraud, The Saboteur, and The Comparer. Characterizing your Inner Critic is an extremely useful exercise. Giving it a name and an identity helps to separate it from you, and to see it merely as a part of who you are—not all of who you are.

Let's take a closer look at each character. As I flesh them out, see if any resonate with you. Perhaps several do. You might even identify with some combination of all six. For example, I've got a quintessential Perfectionist and Comparer, but I also have less intense relationships with each one of the Classics!

The Perfectionist

The Perfectionist is one of the oldest, longest-running characters in the story of my life. It's her voice that tells me I must do things exactly, perfectly right. Period. Full stop. No exceptions. She's lived in my body almost as long as I have, and if she were to get her way, she'd run the whole show—dictating my thoughts, actions and behaviors. Let me tell you, this dame has the highest of expectations. She's exhausting!

Maybe you're familiar with The Perfectionist? This is the voice, belief or story that says you must do everything flawlessly—and if you don't, you've failed. It's either black or white; there's no in-between, no gray area.

You might recognize some of these classic Perfectionist zingers:

- "Sure, you did okay on that project, but it certainly wasn't your best work."

- "Maybe if you just practiced saying it a few more times, you'd get it right."
- "This presentation sucks! You need to spend so much more time on it. It's not ready."
- "That's it? That's all you got? Wow. You're so lame."
- "Too bad you didn't catch those two mistakes. I'm sure everyone else did."
- "I have to be Superman—I have to have a great job, I have to take home a big paycheck, I have to be available to my wife and kids, I have to be playful and fun, and I have to find time to work out and stay in shape."
- "I can't drop any balls—I have to be Super Manager at work, Super Mom at home and Super Cool for my husband."
- "I can't hand in this report; it's not good enough. I know my boss wants it today, but I have to keep working on it until I'm happy with it. Even if it's late."

There are varying intensities and tendencies inherent in each Inner Critic character. On one end of the spectrum, The Perfectionist drives you to do your absolute best, which can be good thing. (However, nothing you do is ever good enough, and a nagging voice will constantly remind you of that!) On the other end of the spectrum, it can create the absolute reverse: complete inaction. "Why bother?" deadpans The Perfectionist. "I mean, if you can't do it perfectly, you may as well not do it at all."

Shandra had just received a huge promotion and, in her new role, she'd be taking over a part of the business that was totally new to her. She was frantic and filled with anxiety as her Perfectionist plagued her with doubts about her ability to step up to the challenge.

- "You don't know *anything* about this business," her critic belittled her.
- "You can't meet with your team until you're up to speed."
- "Your boss is expecting a lot from you—don't let him down!"

- "You don't add any value; you're a dead weight."
- "You're gonna fail. Spectacularly."

Perfectionists are often highly successful people because of their drive to get it just right, but as Shandra's story illustrates, achievement can come at a high price. When a critical voice becomes so harsh that at best it undermines your confidence and at worst paralyzes you, then you know it's having an impact on your health, your self-esteem and, ultimately, your performance at work.

Thanks to today's unrealistic expectations and super-competitive environment, we're all being pushed harder than ever before. What with the speed of technology, a tough economy, global competition and impossibly high standards of accomplishment, not to mention the pressure to own a perfect home and raise a perfect family—it's not surprising the Perfectionist is enjoying a heyday.

(You'll learn more about how Shandra personified, demystified and disarmed her Perfectionist critic in chapters three and twelve.)

The Driver (a.k.a. The Do-It-All)

The Driver has a list of things to do and he must do them all—usually by himself (because, you know, it's just easier and better if you do it yourself!). This little critic finds value in doing everything, and believes that being busy equates to adding value. It's a challenge ever to relax or rest because, well, then you're just not doing anything!

You might discern The Driver in comments or thoughts such as these:
- "If I don't do it, who will?"
- "My boss is relying on me; I'm the only one she trusts to get it done."
- "If I don't do it myself, it won't be done right."
- "After I wrap this project, I have to send 12 emails, sew my daughter's dance costume, price-shop for a new home computer, arrange to have the car serviced, pack healthy lunches for tomorrow, fold the laundry, check my email again real quick, and then I really

should take a look at our life insurance policy . . . which reminds me, I need to schedule a check-up with the doctor."

- "Why is it that as soon as I cross everything off my to-do list, it magically fills up with 20 more items?"
- "I'll never get it all done. I'm always behind the eight ball on everything."
- "I've got to finish this project today—even if I have to stay here all night."
- "I need to perfect my golf swing by next month's corporate tournament—in addition to making my targets, wrapping up my team's performance reviews, helping my boss with his presentation, and finding the perfect gift for my wife's birthday."

Like The Perfectionist, The Driver has a spectrum. One end is the do-it-all slave driver who's exhausted by the relentless quest to get it all done, all the time, all by yourself. The other end is the "beach bum" who's paralyzed by inertia. You know, the guy with the great ideas but no execution? The gal who never takes any initiative? The Driver hammers home the conviction that if you can't do it all, then you should just give up. And—in a classic vicious circle—in giving up you make The Driver right, because you fulfill the belief that if you can't get it all done, you're worthless.

The Fraud (a.k.a. The Fake)

You get this one just by the title, don't you? The Fraud, who also answers to the name, The Fake, voices all those beliefs that suggest you don't deserve your success, achievements and accolades. Thanks to the presence of this cruel critic, you're constantly guilt-ridden and fearful—because you're dreading the day when people find out the truth: that you're an imposter. According to The Fraud, it's only a matter of time until you're caught out.

The Fraud's constantly looking over our shoulder. She specializes in messages that undermine your confidence and are designed to keep you in a state of fear and paranoia:

- "I can't believe they gave this project to me! What were they thinking?"
- "It's only a matter of time before everyone realizes I'm in way over my head."
- "I don't deserve this promotion. My team did all the work; I just supervised."
- "There's no way I can write this speech. I mean, how can I talk about my accomplishments when I've failed more times than I've succeeded?"
- "When's the other shoe going to drop?"
- "How did I get here? I'm a B+ student or maybe an A-, but I'm not an A+. I'm not worthy of this level of success. I need to work harder and faster and stronger than everyone else to prove myself."
- "Maybe if I just sit here and don't say anything, they won't realize I don't know what I'm doing."

Two personas exist at opposite ends of the Fraud spectrum. On one extreme, this critic can come across as innocently humble. I mean, it's admirable not to take all the credit, right? Isn't it magnanimous to share the spotlight—and the accolades—with your team? On the other end of the spectrum, the Fraud shows up in the form of arrogance or an over-loaded ego. After all, if you're desperately trying to uphold a persona so people don't "find out" about the *real* you, you really have to talk yourself up, don't you?

Valerie Young focuses exclusively on the Inner Fraud Critic, also referred to as Imposter Syndrome, in her book, *The Secret Thoughts of Successful Women: Why Capable People Suffer from the Impostor Syndrome and How to Thrive in Spite of It*:

No one knows for sure how long the impostor syndrome has been in existence. For all we know, the first cave artist brushed off admiring grunts with "Oh, this old painting?

Any Neanderthal could have done it." What is known is that the phenomenon is remarkably common. How common? In a study of successful people conducted by psychologist Gail Matthews, a whopping 70 percent reported experiencing impostor feelings at some point in their life.

My client Aaron was intimately familiar with the imposter syndrome. I was helping him get clear on his mid-term career goals by having him think intentionally about how he wanted his work life to look over the next two years. The goals Aaron identified included wanting a larger leadership role and being responsible for running a larger part of the business. Together, we strategized on how best to make sure Aaron's skills and talents were prominently seen by key players in decision-making roles. That's when we ran smack-dab into Aaron's Inner Fraud Critic.

It was crucial that higher-ups see the value of Aaron's contributions. Yet as we dug deeper (you'll learn these tools in chapter four), we discovered that he had a difficult time speaking up in meetings. In fact, Aaron held back—*especially* when there was a high-level leader present! Aaron's Inner Critic told him he didn't have anything to offer, that his contributions weren't of value, and that he didn't belong in the same room with anyone he perceived to be a super achiever.

Like Aaron, your Fraud holds you back by making it all but impossible to fulfill your goals and contribute your best ideas at work. Think about it: no business can thrive when its most precious asset—human talent—is convinced they're faking it. But that's more often than not the case nowadays. In this highly competitive global economy, many of us believe we've got to be smart, we've got to be competent and we've got to know the answer—all the time. Or, at the very least, we've got to look like we do. There's no room for doubt, right? Wrong! But the ubiquitous belief that you must know the answer has proved to be a fertile breeding ground for The Fraud.

The Pleaser

It may not *sound* like much of a critic, but make no mistake, The Pleaser is insidious. This harmless-seeming antagonist is stealthy. Hidden beneath the message that you must please all of the people, all of the time, is the implication that if you don't, you won't be liked or, worse, you won't be loved. This goes all the way to the root of your belief in your own self-worth. At the core of The Pleaser is the question of whether or not you're enough. "You have no value," this critic would wish you to believe, "unless you're doing something for someone else."

The Pleaser repeats a relentless playlist under the guise of a do-gooder:

- "A good person would do this."
- "If I agree to my client's request, I'm going to be so stressed out. I already have three proposals due that day. But I can't say no. They might not want to work with me again."
- "I can't say what I really think because I don't want to rock the boat."
- "I just want everyone to be happy."
- "I really don't mind doing extra work for my teammate. Besides, it won't take me long. And he'll really appreciate it."
- "My boss just asked me to finish this report tonight, but it's date night and my wife made reservations at our favorite restaurant. I can't say no to my boss. But I can't disappoint my wife. I'm toast."
- "I have to get *all* these things done because *everyone* will appreciate it."
- "It's my job to do all this for my [insert any of the following: boss, team, kids, parents, partner]."

The Pleaser persona also shows up in multiple forms that span a broad spectrum. There's the classic "over-functioner"—the person who's *always* doing *everything* for *everyone*. Another way to recognize this critic is the "martyr"—the selfless saint who gives his all, but seems to expect nothing in return (although there is an underlying expectation that he will be appreciated for all his efforts). At the other end of the spectrum, the Pleaser appears to be the very opposite—that is, a self-ish individual who never does anything for anyone. Beneath this selfish façade is the belief that it's impossible to do enough to make people like you, so why bother doing anything at all.

The Pleaser thrives under conditions where you're responsible for the welfare of others—be it children, aging parents, a sick relative, or a large team. And this Inner Critic doesn't differentiate, pushing you to work extra hard to please everyone—at work, at home, even among friends. It's an ungratifying, unhealthy and exhausting way of living.

The Saboteur

As the name suggests, The Saboteur's goal is to undermine your own efforts, hard work and brilliant ideas. Another stealth operator, this destructive pest attacks from behind, when your back is turned. You're on the brink of a breakthrough—about to step onto the podium to accept your award—and this little voice yells, "No! Come back! The light's too bright out there in the center of the stage. You'll be blinded by the glare! Come back to the shadows where it's safe." The Saboteur doesn't want you to succeed; it doesn't want you to stand in the spotlight. It wants you to be satisfied with the sidelines and with mediocrity. "Why strive for excellence?" it goads you. "You'll only fall flat on your face."

Do you recognize the Saboteur in any of these comments?

- "I know, I know, you've got that big presentation early tomorrow morning, but what's the harm in going for one beer with the guys? It'll help you relax, and you'll sleep better."
- "That proposal's shaping up to be pretty great. You can afford to take your foot off the pedal now. It's good enough."
- "Sure, you could apply for that promotion, or you could just chill right where you are and coast a little while. You've earned it."
- "Wow. Your numbers are off the charts this quarter. Better slow down or you'll end up getting employee of the month. And then you'll be expected to keep it up."
- "You really think it's a good idea to get up and speak in front of all those bigwigs tomorrow? What if you make an ass of yourself in front of all the company's key decision makers? I'd blow it off if I were you."

- "You're really going to pitch that radical idea at the meeting today? Everyone'll think you're nuts. No one's ever done that before. Why not just pitch that other idea. It won't knock anyone's socks off, but it won't get you fired either."

The Saboteur speaks from a place of intense fear—and not just fear of failure. It's more afraid of success. The Saboteur is terrified of what comes hand-in-hand with owning your greatness and will do anything in its power to stop you. As an entrepreneur, Michael struggles with a self-sabotaging voice that tells him, "There's always someone else who's got better products and marketing materials. If you can't play with the big boys, why play at all?" He becomes so paralyzed that he can't even motivate himself to make a phone call. Michael described the process this way:

Once I start going down that road, it's a spiral. Something as simple as making a call becomes overwhelming. It takes two minutes, but it begins to feel like an insurmountable task. I set up all these barriers that are totally unreasonable and inaccurate—that I don't have the right brochure, that I don't know the industry well enough, that it's a bad time of day for them. It starts out as, "I need to make a phone call" and escalates into, "I'm tearing up my business license."

The Comparer

Rounding out the Inner Critic cast is the other character that takes top billing in my life, The Comparer. This critic became more and more powerful the older, more experienced and more successful I became. In my twenties and early thirties, The Perfectionist took center stage as I built my career and worked at climbing the corporate ladder. However, as I hit my late thirties and early forties, the voice of The Comparer grew stronger. And she's brutal! No matter what the other person is saying, doing, achieving, or even how they've dressed themselves that day, they've always done a far better job than me. This voice is constantly comparing me to everyone else, and rarely do I come out on top.

Whether it's in the context of skill, talent, body image or parenting style, The Comparer says someone else—usually, everyone else—is better than you. No matter how good you are, someone else is always better; whatever great idea you cook up, it's already been done. This critic never lets you forget there's always someone else who's smarter, richer, younger, skinnier, more talented, more accomplished, more successful, better looking, with a more picture perfect family—and a nicer home! Once this tape starts playing, you feel outpaced, outsmarted and outdone—a perennially miserable and hopeless second best.

The Comparer stack ranks you against everyone, every day. Do any of these comparisons sound familiar?

- "I wish I could be that direct—he's a real pro."
- "Wow, he really brought his A-game today. I look like a loser in comparison.
- "She always comes across so much better in meetings than I do."
- "I may have more experience, but she's clearly got way more talent. She's a natural."
- "Wish I had her booty instead of my banana-butt."
- "This guy's ten years younger than me. How can I compete with his energy and enthusiasm?"
- "These people all have fancy Ivy League educations. I don't belong in this room."
- "I'm sure everyone's thinking the last speaker was way more engaging and entertaining than me." (Okay, I confess this one's borrowed from my own personal sound track!)

John works for a big name in the Internet search business. He hates it. He doesn't enjoy what he's doing anymore. But he won't even contemplate making a change. "I can't leave," he told me. "I work for one of the most cutting edge companies in the world!" In John's mind—or rather, in the mind of his Inner Comparer Critic—were he to follow his heart and take a job he actually felt good about at a less prestigious company, it would mean being perceived as less smart. For John's Comparer Critic, this would mean social and intellectual death.

Sometimes The Comparer shows up under the guise of being judgmental of others. If you catch yourself scrutinizing someone else harshly, that's The Comparer creating a false sense of safety by switching the spotlight from you to *them*.

On occasion, the Comparer shows up at the other end of the spectrum as the over-bearing jerk who's hell-bent on proving he's better than everyone else. In a desperate attempt to shut down his Inner Critic (who says he isn't good enough), he over-plays his hand in the name of proving he's at the top of the game.

Regardless of whether The Comparer is internally or externally focused, it will drag you down to an unhealthy place—a place where you're always second best. This most critical of critics holds you back from going after what you want because, after all, what's the point—someone else has already done it and they've done it better. I can tell you from experience, having The Comparer in your ear makes for a tough life.

Where's the I.C. come from?

The critic's origins stem from when you were a little kid figuring out how to survive in the world—which was made up of your family, culture, religion, ethnicity, education, and society at large. It was very useful back when you were investigating how things worked in your environment. Unfortunately, as you got older and those strategies you once employed became unnecessary, the critic voice stayed with you as nothing more than a deeply ingrained habit.

For example, you might have grown up in a family environment in which getting good grades garnered a lot of positive attention. This often shows up later in life as a high achiever (on the positive side) or as a Perfectionist Critic (on the negative side).

I grew up in a very rural culture—we lived six miles outside of a small town of about 800 people. My culture of origin left two huge impressions on me. One was gender-based: the boys did the farm work and the girls did the housework. As a kid, I hated that my brother got to drive the trucks and the tractors but I wasn't taught because I was a girl. The other impression was growing up in a rural blue-collar environment that prized humility—people respected "salt of the earth" types. I still hear my dad's voice in my head saying, "Don't get too big for your boots, Stace." These two impressions have shown up in my adulthood as negative internal voices that tell me, "You can't be the leader here—you're a girl!" and, "Who do you think you are with that big fancy education?" Now, my parents never told me anything to that effect and I'm sure they never implied it, either. It's just how I internalized the information I gathered as a child.

These very same factors have also influenced how you think about success—both positively and negatively. It's the reason why the Inner Critic and Inner Success are so intimately related. Humility, from my culture of origin, is an important positive aspect of success for me too.

Kathleen's religion and culture of origin (Catholic and Irish) placed a high value on working hard. There wasn't necessarily a particular goal in mind, just that you should suck it up, even if it meant being miserable. (In fact, the more miserable you were, the better, because that meant you worked really hard!) For Kathleen, it showed up later in life as an obsession with being busy, but without necessarily having anything to show for her efforts except for a non-existent social life, dark circles under her eyes and a complete lack of joie de vivre!

When you were a child, it made sense to operate by family rules and societal norms. And while it might still make sense, you can also update those old stories and behaviors. Think about it as exploring what's behind doors one, two and three—family, culture and religion, respectively—but instead of just one door for each, there are multiple options.

Now, this isn't therapy so we're not going to go all the way down the rabbit hole. I'll leave that work for the great therapists and counselors of this world. My role here is strictly as a coach. I just want you to be aware of where your current Inner Critic and Inner Success messages come from so you can decide which ones you choose to keep, and which ones you choose to delete.

The Committee

What's the Committee? It's the term I use for when the whole cast of Inner Critics decides to get together and throw a rave party in my head—and in my heart. It's what happens when all those harsh, nasty voices start chattering, all together, all at the same time. All six Classic Critics are each shouting their complaints and they've invited their cousins from Jersey to join in. When this happens your head spins, your heart races, you feel a heavy hand grip your heart and strangle your soul. This is the most severe form of Inner Critic attack. I call it "DEF-CON 1"—and it's nothing short of all-out war. When I've experienced my own Committee moments, the best response has been ultimate self-care which means those things that make me feel most nurtured. For me it is rest, time away from stressful activities, and with people who love me (and maybe a good book).

In the following chapters, I'll give you tools to navigate your way through this emotional war zone. For now, just picture what DEFCON 1 looks like for you, so you can recognize an attack from a mile off and never be caught off guard again!

Cast the Character

"Casting" your Inner Critics as a group of characters is extremely useful. In labeling them, you externalize them. And by getting them outside your head, you can work on them more directly. I encourage clients to flesh out their Inner Critic characters with as much detail as possible.

- What or whom do they sound like?
- Describe their posture and body language.
- Are they male or female?
- How do they dress?
- What's their tone of voice?
- What kind of language do they use?
- If they had a name, what would it be?

In workshops, I'll often have volunteers stand up and "take on" the role of their Inner Critic character.

Janine christened her principal critic Betina. When she characterized Betina, she immediately stood up to her full height, spine straight— almost to the point of leaning back with a cocky kind of confidence. Her voice was strong, powerful and assured as she spoke Betina's words. "You are absolutely not good enough to make it on this team, your work is just not up to standard," said Betina. She maintained direct eye contact with me all the while tapping her stiletto heel-clad foot to ensure her razor sharp point sank in! (Recognize her as a raging Perfectionist?) There was no arguing with Betina; she was authoritative and she knew it.

The amazing thing is that while playing the role of Betina, Janine exuded the exact kind of confidence and strength she needed to bring to her job. Betina showed Janine that she had the power she thought she lacked, but she just needed to figure out how to redirect it from a negative self-critical message to an empowering belief in herself and her abilities. Now she knows Betina so well, Janine springs into action as soon as she shows up, saying, "Oh Betina, yeah hi, I know what you're going to say, but I really don't need your negativity right now. But thanks for remind- ing me of my power. You can go now." Boom! Immediately, Janine is empowered to believe in herself and to ignore any perceived weaknesses.

As you read further, I'll explain how you, too, can shift your energy from Inner Critic to Inner Strength, and from there to an unstoppable Superpower.

The Summary Playbill

Here's a quick recap of the six classic Inner Critics that I described above:

- **The Perfectionist**: Any outcome short of perfection is failure. Or, I know I'll fail to do it perfectly, so I'm not going to do it at all.
- **The Driver**: If I don't do it all, I'm a failure. Or, I know I can't do it all, so I won't even try. Which just confirms: I'm a failure.
- **The Fraud**: I don't deserve what I have. I'm a fake, and it's only a matter of time before I'm found out.
- **The Pleaser**: I must make everyone happy or I won't be loved.
- **The Saboteur**: This is too good to be true. So I'll do something to prove it.
- **The Comparer**: No matter how good I am, there's always someone else who's better.

Which critic(s) do you resonate with? Do you recognize yourself in more than one? Maybe even all six? Don't worry, most people have multiple Inner Critics; it's actually pretty common.

And don't worry if yours don't fit neatly into any of these categories! These are the six I encounter most often in my work, but I've come across dozens—The Judge, The Victim, The Debbie-Doubter, The Poseur, The Nag, The Parental Unit, to name a few. Feel free to come up with your own custom-made labels. But do make sure to give your critic a name. Doing so establishes in your mind the idea that the critic is merely a persona—a facet of who you are. It's not all of who you are. It's just a voice—not your voice. Once you start to characterize your I.C., you can draw it out from inside your head and bring it front and center so you can face it squarely. Then you can start to explore it, challenge it and, ultimately, tame it!

ACTIVITIES

The following activities will help you do a little character sketching so you can become more familiar with the players in your personal Inner Critic cast. Follow your intuition and inner wisdom by reading through the activities and zeroing in on the ones that call to you right now. The others can be done later. This is a good section to flag and come back to at any time, as these activities can be done on their own or in tandem with any others in the book. And don't be surprised to come back later and find that things have shifted because, as I mentioned before, this is a journey, not a moment on a park bench; it's a marathon, not a sprint; it's about navigating the path, not finding the answer. . . . Okay, you get the idea; I'll stop now.

Who Makes the Cast? Who Doesn't?

Take a look at the six Classic Critics in the summary above and answer the following questions.

- Which critic sounds most familiar to you?
- Which critic doesn't sound familiar at all?
- Which critic do you dislike the most?
- Which one could you almost like?
- Is there a name you've used in the past for your critic voice—something unlike any of these titles?

Who's Lead and Who's Supporting?

Rank the six Classic Critics in order of how applicable they are to your life at this moment in time. Next to each one, write what percentage of critic airtime each one gets. For example, if I spent an hour today in critic time, maybe 40% of it was as the Comparer and 60% was as the Perfectionist.

This helps clarify which critic(s) are leading the pack, and therefore where you should narrow your focus. It's a very useful activity to come back to time and again, because the ranking can and will change according to life stage, life cycle and whatever challenges or difficulties you're facing in the moment.

For example, this is how my stack rank looks right now *after* completing this exercise:

1. Comparer—40%
2. Fraud—30%
3. Pleaser—15%
4. Perfectionist—10%
5. Driver—5%

However, when I first ranked them the order was totally different. It was only when I assigned percentages that I realized to my surprise that my Pleaser was taking up more airtime than my Perfectionist. I was also shocked to find that my Fraud was taking so much time right now. The intention of the activity is to get specific, which can provide useful information about which critic to focus on taming.

If you, too, had a big revelation in the previous activity, ask yourself the following questions:

- What strikes you or surprises you about how you stack ranked your critics and/or the amount of airtime each one gets?
- If you were to do this exercise regularly, do you think this is how it would typically look, nine times out of ten?
- What's unusual about how your stack rank looks today versus how it might typically look?
- Any ideas why that might be? Anything going on right now in your world that might be skewing things?

Character Sketch

Take your most prevalent critic and do a little character sketch. (We'll be fleshing it out even more in the next chapter, but right now we're just going to have a little fun playing I.C. dress-up.) To get you in the zone, bring your attention to a recent Inner Critic attack. Pick one that has a lot of energy and emotion to it; that will make it easier to cast. Then, answer the following questions.

- Describe your critic's tone of voice. Sound like anyone you know? Who?
- Is it male or female?
- If that voice were attached to a body, how might it look? How does it stand? How does it walk? What kind of posture does it have? What kind of gestures does it use?
- What name best fits this character?

Over the course of the next week, test out your skills of externalizing your Inner Critic. When it starts to sound off, try one or all of the following—see if they help reduce the intensity or impact of the attack:

- Acknowledge the critic using its new character name—like Janine does with Betina. Tell her you hear her, but that her words aren't needed right now.
- Picture the character in your mind, based on the sketch you did above. Put him in a different chair or location—so he's separate from you. Heck, you might even tell him to go wait in the lobby!
- Take a moment to notice her voice, picture the persona you now associate her with and notice how you feel in the moment. That's it—simply notice. In the next chapter we're going to start digging deep and exploring all the facets of this saucy broad. For now, simply bring your awareness to how she makes you feel.

Bravo! You've studied the cast and done some great awareness raising of your own most prolific inner critics. Hold onto this as we now move into a full study of these characters.

3

Know Thyself; Know Thy Critic

Self-awareness is a critical skill for dealing with all that life throws at you. In this chapter, I ask you to become thoroughly aware of and acquainted with your Inner Critic. "Why on earth would I want to do *that*?" I imagine you asking (as most people do). "Wouldn't it be so much better just to ignore this nasty voice? Or better yet, get rid of it?" I know. It seems counter-intuitive to move *towards* something that scares the pants off you and sucks all your energy—instead of turning and running in the opposite direction. But after a decade spent exploring both my client's Inner Critics and my own, I've learned that the more you know about those inner voices, the better equipped you'll be to make intentional, proactive choices about them—instead of reacting to or running from them. (Not to mention, you'll gain a ton of valuable information about your Inner Success story . . . but more on that later!)

This chapter is all about information gathering: Your goal is to learn as much as you can about yourself in and around the moments when your Inner Critic is present—because that information will help you identify, manage and catch the nasty little critter sooner. Developing greater self-awareness—i.e., leaning into instead of running from the source of your discomfort—is a crucial step towards educating and empowering yourself, and diffusing the power and the pain of the critic.

Background Radio Noise

You may or may not be aware of it, but inside your head there's a tape playing pretty much all the time. And on this tape is a bunch of messages you may not even be aware you're hearing. I liken it to background radio noise. If you're one of those people (like me) who prefers to have music playing while you work, you'll know what I mean. You've become so accustomed and attuned to the "noise" of the music, you don't really pay much attention to the songs. Chances are, if you stopped and paid attention, you'd be shocked to realize you've been listening to music you don't actually like all that much.

So it is with the voices in your head. They've been chattering incessantly in the background for so long, you may not even be aware that you're listening to anything at all, that you don't like it and that it's actually really negative.

ACTIVITY: Tune In

I'm going to ask you now to tune in completely—listen to the inner chatter with your mind, your heart and your body. Make sure you're sitting some place that's quiet, free of distractions and interruptions, and start to bring your awareness to the background noise in your head. First, just notice that the radio is on and that *something* is playing. Then, begin to pay more attention to the content—what are those Inner Critic voices actually saying? Notice the impact of these negative Inner Critic messages. Do they generate or deplete energy? Feel into the kind of energy they create. How do they make you feel? Not so good, right?

The first step toward great self-awareness is simply to start paying attention to your internal landscape. While the negative inner messages may have evaded your awareness in the past, I have no doubt that they've had a huge impact on your thoughts, beliefs and actions. When you begin to tune in, you grant yourself the power of choice. You might choose to turn the volume down to a more ambient level. You might switch to a different station playing music you like better. Or you might switch the radio off and instead turn on a playlist with your favorite tunes—music that makes you feel better over the course of the day.

Shandra was resistant to my suggestion that she "just" notice her Fraud Inner Critic. I totally get it. In business, we want action—i.e., Just Make It Stop. But Shandra had to become conscious of what "it" was before we could figure out how to make "it" stop.

She'd just been moved to a totally new business area as a manager, and she was feeling hopelessly lost—including the loss of all confidence in herself and her abilities as a leader. "I feel stupid, and useless," she told me during one of our coaching meetings. "I'm not adding any value to my team."

I gave Shandra an assignment: over the course of the following two weeks, whenever she became aware of a negative inner voice she was to write the message on a Post-it note and put it to the side of her desk. That's it. Jot down where she was and what she heard. "Then what?" Shandra asked, perplexed. "How do I stop it?" She was anxious to switch into action mode—and the Post-it note exercise didn't seem like action. Shandra didn't think that simply tracking her background noise constituted making progress toward a goal. That's often the mindset in the business world: unless the problem is solved, it's not considered action. The fix is action. Anything that came before the fix doesn't count. But we know that's not true. Competitive analysis is action, as is research and development, right? I was asking Shandra to do some research on herself so we could then come up with a plan.

Next time I arrived at her office, Shandra had a stack of Post-Its sitting on her desk. There were easily two dozen. On each one was written a message like these:

- "I don't know anything about this business"—in office reviewing documents
- "What's she talking about? I have no idea. I shouldn't be this lost,"—in a meeting with another team.
- "I can't add anything of value here,"—in a meeting with my team.
- "I'm in over my head,"—in office, reading email.
- "I don't even know my people's names, much less who they are or what they do,"—on way back to office after meeting with my team.
- "I'm lonely,"—in office.
- "Everyone's wondering why I'm here . . . why am I here?"—in a meeting with my team.
- "All I'm doing is listening; I'm not saying a word. They must think I'm a dead weight,"—in a meeting with my manager and his team.

And on and on it went—the litany of negative messages Shandra hadn't even been aware was coloring her day a dull shade of gray. She'd been hearing them all day, every day, and they were dragging her down. Now however, being that she's a quick study, Shandra had not only begun to tune in to the background noise, she'd also identified one of the main threads common to all the messages: she felt disconnected from her team. Shandra had prioritized getting up to speed in the *business* first—versus getting to know the *people* she was working with. As a result, she felt out of the loop. She'd been trying to listen and learn everything she thought she needed to know *before* offering her input but in doing so, no one was getting to know *her*, or how she might contribute to the group. And, because she hadn't taken the time to get to know anyone on her team, she didn't know what people needed or how she might add value. As a result, Shandra felt a) disconnected, b) like a fraud just waiting to be found out, and c) afraid to ask for help. This only made her feel more disconnected. (Spot the nasty spiral effect?)

It was only by slowing down and tuning into the negative voices that Shandra figured out the problem (she wasn't connecting with her team) and therefore the solution (she needed to sit down and have one-on-one meetings with all of her people ASAP). She also realized it was impera-tive that she start speaking up in meetings even though she wasn't yet up to speed. Sure, it would be risky—she might say something she judged as "stupid"—but there was no way she could prove her value, and allow her team get to know her, until she started engaging with them.

As a result of simply "noticing," Shandra totally shifted gears. It was a little scary, but she persevered, and as she did, she started to feel more connected, she accelerated sharply in her learning curve, and she enjoyed a newfound confidence in her leadership skills. Suddenly, a dull shade of grey became a warm rosy tint.

Which Comes First: The Chicken or the Egg?

In the early stages of Inner Critic exploration, most people are aware of only one aspect of an I.C. attack; usually, the negative message voiced by the critic. However, that's just one of five ways the Inner Critic shows up. To explore the others, we're going to engage the three Emotional Intelli-gence (E.I.) Builder questions I introduced in chapter one (1. What are you feeling? 2. What are you thinking? 3. What's your physical reaction?). We will combine them with two other elements (Triggers and Patterns) to investigate all five characteristics of a critic attack, which are:

- A **"feeling" or emotional response** that originates in the limbic brain. For example, "I feel afraid because I'm about to go into my performance review."
- A **"thinking" response** by way of an I.C. message that originates in the rational brain. For example, "I suck at my job."
- A **physical response** that might manifest anywhere in your body. For example, a suddenly churning stomach that sends you running to the restroom.
- A **trigger event** that provoked your Inner Critic. For example, your annual performance review, a phone message from your boss or public speaking.
- A **pattern**—that is, a specific set of circumstances that prove to be a fertile breeding ground for your Inner Critic. For example, you have

to give a presentation, *and* it's in a meeting packed with VIPs, *and* it's on a research project you've worked long and hard on, *and* this work means a lot to you. If that weren't enough, you haven't been sleeping well *and* you really, really want this meeting to go well.

This is where the mantra, "slow down to speed up" comes into play. In this chapter, I'm asking you to slow down and pay attention to all five I.C. channels. It may not seem immediate enough and you may not feel instantaneous relief. (I understand. I also want my dang I.C. to stop, like, yesterday.) Be assured, however, that you're excavating an enormous amount of information you'll then be able to utilize for the super powers of good versus evil.

Specifically, you'll learn how to . . .

- Say, "Ah-ha, the I.C. has decided to show up!"—instead of being blind-sided by a stealth attack.
- Understand exactly how and where an I.C. attack hits you so you're ready for it.
- Inventory all the ways the critic shows up, so you have just as many ways to catch it.

Now, the Inner Critic isn't linear—it's a dynamic, personal and circumstantial experience, so even though I've listed the five characteristics of a critic attack in sequential order, please know that you won't necessarily experience them in this order, nor indeed in any order.

Prior to becoming the Inner Critic master I am now, I would always notice the I.C. message (thinking response) first and foremost. I hadn't yet become accustomed to noticing what was happening in my body, my emotional brain, or my calendar! That's how it is for most people. However, it might be different for you. Your first inkling that the Inner Critic is present might be that you start to feel anxious or afraid (emotional response)—or that you break out in a cold sweat, start tapping your foot impatiently, or sit way back in your chair and cross your arms defensively (all of these are physical responses). Or you might start to feel stressed (feeling response) as soon as you get an unexpected call from your boss asking you to stop by her office (a trigger). It might be that just knowing you're about to walk into a situation that highlights all your insecurities—your annual review, for example—makes you feel all shades of nervous hours ahead of time (a pattern).

You won't always be conscious of which one comes first, the chicken or the egg (or the Denver Scramble, for that matter). What's great is you don't *have* to know! You can look at *all* of the critic components together, or start with what you notice first and then tune into the others. If you know more about your patterns or your triggers, great—start there. If you're very in tune with your body, go with that. But don't think that lets you off the hook! You're still going to work through *all* the angles. Remember, we're in information gathering mode! Think of it as R&D.

Emotional Reaction (a.k.a. What Are You Feeling?)

Some people first notice a reaction on the level of feelings and emotions. All of a sudden, you might sense your mood shift. If you find yourself suddenly feeling emotionally charged for no apparent reason, it's highly likely your I.C. is present.

More often than not, my clients have extreme difficulty tracking their feelings. I won't go into all the reasons why this is—there are plenty— but I will say that our culture doesn't value the demonstration and the sharing of feelings deemed negative or "weak." This is even more pronounced in the business world. But as I've explained in chapter one, we all experience a whole spectrum of feelings that impact us in every way, every day, everywhere we go. So, my advice is that you start to embrace your feelings, get to know them, befriend them and learn how to use them effectively.

How do you do this? Take a moment to check in and identify the feelings you're experiencing. As soon as I hear an I.C. message, (e.g., "You'll never get that project; you don't have the chops yet.") I ask myself how I'm feeling—mad, sad, glad or afraid? In the above example, I was feeling afraid—along with its cousins insecure, nervous and excited. Yes, all of them! We're complex creatures after all.

When I first ask new clients to name their feelings, they often freeze. I can't tell you how many times I've been told, "I have no idea what I'm feeling! I really don't!" Like a deer in the headlights, they get stuck in a frozen "I-don't-know" moment.

When Phoebe came to me she was desperately unhappy. At the ripe age of 42, she'd taken a job in a game design studio alongside a crop of crazy-smart college grads, and she was having a hard time relating. Her Inner Comparer Critic was beating her up about all the ways she fell short of her energetic and enthusiastic colleagues. Phoebe felt intimated and irrelevant and isolated. She was so afraid of sounding stupid that she wasn't speaking up—at all. Not only was she not bringing her A game, she wasn't bringing any game. Though her I.C. was speaking volumes in her mind, Phoebe was saying precious little in meetings, and wondering why no one was listening to her. "I feel like a dumb ass," she told me. "I've nothing to offer."

The reality is that Phoebe is one of the most intelligent people I know. And her intelligence was combined with 20 years of rich experience. But she'd taken all that intelligence and experience and knowledge and stuffed it. We needed to dig down to see what emotion was lying beneath all that stuffing so we could get Phoebe unstuck. But her mind was so wrapped up in analysis-paralysis she couldn't separate her feelings from her thoughts.

"How do you feel, Phoebe?" I asked her.

"I feel stupid."

"Stupid's not an emotion, it's more a thinking response—how your brain interprets the situation. How does it *feel* when you think of yourself as stupid?"

"It feels like everyone thinks I'm dumb."

"That's an assumption about what others think, which is also from your thinking brain, not an emotion. [Do you see how difficult it is to distinguish between emotions and assumptions/judgments/stories/perceptions? Crazy, right?]

"Ok Phoebe, close your eyes, take two deep belly breaths. Now, tell me how you feel."

"I feel . . . low . . . and lonely."

"Is low and lonely connected most closely to mad, sad, glad or afraid?"

"It's connected to sad. I feel sad."

"Sit with the sadness for a little while, Phoebe. You feel lonely at work. You don't have anyone to relate to and that makes you feel sad. Sit with that feeling for a couple minutes."

Phoebe had no idea how she felt because, as soon as she'd begin to feel sad, she'd stuff it and distract herself by going into thinking mode—that is, rationalizing and problem solving. She got busy to avoid feeling, but her sadness didn't go away. Sound familiar? Our brain's coping mechanism is to see everything as a problem we need to fix. But you can't "cure" an emotion—certainly not by thinking your way out of it. You have to feel your way out of it; you've got to "name it to claim it." Naming the emotion you're feeling reduces its hold on you (and it gives your thinking brain something to chew on by way of an answer, which helps dial down the mental gymnastics, too). Phoebe's simple acknowledgment that she felt sad and attending to that sadness meant that the emotion had less need to jump up and down and scream for Phoebe's attention.

> **❝** *There is a simple technique for self-regulation called "affect labeling," which simply means labeling feelings with words. When you label an emotion you are experiencing (for example, "I feel anger"), it somehow helps you manage that emotion. —Chade-Meng Tan,* Search Inside Yourself: The Unexpected Path to Achieving Success, Happiness (and World Peace)

If you find yourself stuck in a frozen "I-don't-know" moment (similar to Phoebe's), try one or all of the following activities:

1. Breathe:

The following one-minute mindfulness exercise will quickly dispel analysis-paralysis by dropping you down into your body so you're centered and grounded and emotionally connected.

- Sit in a chair with your spine straight, both feet on the floor and your hands gently resting in your lap.
- Close your eyes.
- Inhale slowly through your nose to the count of four, feeling your ribcage and your belly expand as you draw breath into your chest, diaphragm and finally your belly.
- Exhale slowly through your mouth to the count of four, releasing breath first from your belly, then your diaphragm, then your chest.
- Repeat each inhale-exhale eight times.
- Slowly open your eyes and bring your attention back to the present moment.

It sounds so simple, right? I mean we breathe automatically, without even thinking about it. But you'll be amazed at how effective and powerful mindful breathing can be. It's also the third component of whole-person intelligence, using our body's wisdom. Google implemented an entire program centered on mindfulness and meditation. Cheng Mae-Tang describes the benefits of it in his book, *Search Inside Yourself: The Unexpected Path to Achieving Success, Happiness (and World Peace)*.

When you can't take time out—for example, you're in a meeting—just stop and take three deep belly breaths. That alone will give your limbic brain (your feeling and emotion center) time to flush out the chemicals, and allow your neocortex (rational brain center) enough time to catch up with and process your emotions. In other words, it will afford you a quick "breather" before you respond, react or make a choice about what to do or say next. I firmly believe that if more people practiced mindful breathing, we'd have less violence and more peace . . . but I digress.

2. Name It to Claim It:

As I explained in chapter one, there are four core emotions: mad, sad, angry and afraid. Every other emotion is essentially a derivative of one of these core emotions. If you're unable to trace how you're feeling to one of these four, then use the Emotion Descriptors worksheet as a guide as you get more accustomed to naming your emotions. Scan the list and pinpoint which emotion you're experiencing in the moment.

Be aware that this isn't an exhaustive list of *every* feeling known to humankind, but it's got most of them—along with handy blank spaces for you to write your personal names for individual feelings you encounter. I encourage you to customize this worksheet to fit your vocabulary and your emotional makeup.

WORKSHEET: Feeling Words

MAD	SAD	GLAD	AFRAID
FURIOUS	DEPRESSED	ELATED	TERRIFIED
ENRAGED	AGONIZING	THRILLED	PANICKY
IRATE	MISERABLE	EXUBERANT	FRANTIC
SEETHING	DEJECTED	PASSIONATE	HORRIFIED
BETRAYED	HOPELESS	ECSTATIC	ALARMED
HOSTILE	HURT	JUBILANT	DISTRESSED
VENGEFUL	SORROWFUL	FIRED UP	FEARFUL
PISSED OFF	DEVASTATED	DELIGHTED	SHOCKED
AGGRAVATED	DISTRESSED	CHEERFUL	FRIGHTENED
UPSET	MELANCHOLY	SATISFIED	INSECURE
MAD	SOMBER	GOOD	INTIMIDATED
ANGRY	LONELY	HAPPY	APPREHENSIVE
FRUSTRATED	DISPIRITED	VIBRANT	THREATENED
AGITATED	HELPLESS	JOVIAL	WORRIED
INDIGNANT	EMPTY	EXCITED	ANXIOUS
DEFENSIVE	LET DOWN	RELIEVED	VULNERABLE
MIFFED	DISCOURAGED	CONTENT	UNEASY
ANNOYED	UNHAPPY	COMFORTABLE	CAUTIOUS

UPTIGHT	SOLEMN	PLEASED	TIMID
RESISTANT	DOWN	WARM	UNSURE
IRRITATED	SULLEN	PLEASANT	PESSIMISTIC
TOUCHY	UNSETTLED	GLAD	STARTLED
UNSETTLED	DISAPPOINTED	MELLOW	SHAKY

*Adapted from Julia West
http://sff.net/people/julia.west/callihoo/dtbb/feelings.htm
and sourced from Bradberry and Greaves Emotional Intelligence 2.0

3. Practice:

I have some clients work on the three E.I. Builder questions several times a day—not just when the I.C. is present. It helps improve their overall E.I. So, if you're game, block out a couple minutes three times over the course of the day, set the timer on your phone and jot down what you're feeling, thinking and experiencing in your body (in the notes app of your smart phone if you have one).

❝*All learning has an emotional base. —Plato*

Thinking Reaction (a.k.a. What Are You Thinking?)

Now that you've become a pro at tuning in to Radio I.C., it's time to start really listening to the playlist. What story do the lyrics tell? What refrain is being repeated over and over in the chorus? What's the subtle message of the backing vocals? What's your negative voice actually saying?

While some critic messages are pretty obvious and overt—for example, "I'm stupid and lazy"—there are other sneaky types that are much easier to miss. Examples of these include, "I should really go back to school and get a degree in that." Or, "I'm not spending enough time with my kids." These are what I call Medium Level Obvious. Then there's the Downright Sneaky. These take a lot of practice to catch. Examples include "I should really offer to help with that project." Or, "I can't ask my boss for a raise." The word "should" is a big red flag; anytime you hear the phrase "should," sit up and listen. Same with negative self-judgments like "I can't." Or, "I'm not X, Y or Z enough." You'll also know you're on to something if you catch yourself rolling your eyes or letting out a big, long sigh. (Not to jump ahead, but these are physical "body" reactions to the I.C. See, I told you it wasn't linear!) Or you might notice you get defensive and shut down completely. These are all Big Clues your I.C. is at play.

ACTIVITY: Say What?

Open your journal and write down your Top Three Inner Critic messages—by that I mean the ones you hear *most* often. Any ideas what the over-arching theme might be? Now, don't get all Perfectionist on me and get caught up trying to identify *the* theme. Just contemplate the possibilities. Right now we're just tracking it.

Outward Projection

A subset of the Thinking Reaction, Outward Projection occurs when you launch into a critical attack of *someone else*. I became aware of this while experimenting with online dating. A friend asked how it was going, and I surprised her—and myself—by engaging in a full-on attack of the process: "It's awful! It feels gratuitous! It requires too much effort. It makes me nervous, and dumbstruck. . . ."

My friend gently pointed out that perhaps the problem wasn't with online dating—perhaps the problem was with *me*. She was right. *I* was feeling uncomfortable with myself *within* dating—it was like a playground for all my deepest insecurities and Inner Critics! Obviously, simply complaining about it wasn't going to change anything. To affect change, I had to stop pushing my critics *outward* and deal with them directly—within myself.

If you catch yourself complaining about something or someone loudly and frequently, this is a giant clue pointing at something you're unhappy about within yourself.

Physical Reaction (a.k.a. What's Your Physical Reaction?)

Each time you experience an I.C. attack, it manifests somewhere in your body. Each person has their own unique auto response, which is the body's go-to coping mechanism. I always know something's up when I start to rub my fingers together compulsively. I've always done it, but I never paid attention to why or when until I started doing this work. My body knows before my brain does that I'm anxious, stressed or both (your body is always way ahead of your "thinking" brain), and it goes into comforting mode. Nowadays, as soon as I notice that I'm rubbing my fingers, I know it means I'm anxious, which is oftentimes a clue that my I.C. is about to go into attack mode—and I'll spring into preemptive action before she's even had a chance to say a nasty little word.

How does your body react during I.C. moments? Do you . . .

• Find your palms getting sweaty?
• Get butterflies in your belly?
• Blush?
• Break out in a rash?
• Get really, really quiet?
• Start scratching your head nervously?
• Suddenly become overwhelmingly tired, like someone's pulled the power cord?
• Scoot yourself way back in your chair?
• Cross your arms defensively?
• Stop making eye contact?

You may not become defensive at all—you may go on the *offence*! Instead do you . . .

• Get louder?
• Become more aggressive?
• Start using sarcasm?
• Get short? Sharp? Shrill?

Begin to notice how your body responds when under attack—or in the moments before.

Triggers (a.k.a. What Jump-Started Your IC?)

For most people, there are specific people, places and circumstances that will always "trigger" an I.C. attack. For my friend Charlize, walking inside a fancy restaurant with a new date sends her Saboteur Critic into overdrive: "You totally look fat in that dress! OMG every woman in here is way prettier! You totally should have worn the other shoes!" By the way, Charlize is gorgeous and smart and incredibly stylish.

Facilitating a workshop with a colleague who I perceive to be better than me presents a ripe opportunity for my Comparer Critic. She goes to town in full-on party mode—dancing around me and singing about how much better my partner is, how he's far superior at reading and working the room, how much more information he's picking up on, how much more experienced and/or qualified he is—all the while taking cheap shots at me. While my I.C. is enjoying her little fiesta, the real me is feeling painfully vulnerable and exposed. (Notice how I named and claimed the feeling?).

Sometimes the link isn't always that clear. Richard was perplexed as to why he'd become irritable and cranky with his team on certain days; he'd have zero patience and tolerance—and that's *not* the kind of guy Richard is. He noticed the feeling first (mad, a.k.a. irritable), and then he continued to track it. After a while, Richard noticed this only happened on days when he'd had a *big* meeting with *senior* management. Eureka! The meeting was the trigger that sent his Inner Fraud into overdrive—but it didn't come to Richard's awareness until much later, when he found himself being uncharacteristically irritable with his coworkers.

When does the lightning strike for you? What are *your* triggers? What situations tend to hook you up the most? You need to be diligent about this—you want to learn as much as you can about what can trigger or exacerbate an I.C. attack so you're ready to take preemptive action.

A triggering event often involves something that feels high stakes to you—a meeting with your boss, delivering a presentation to a big name client, being in a heated or conflict-oriented situation, having to speak in public, address a large audience, or talk to your mother. I'm not kidding about the last one—if your critic sounds anything like your mother (think back to when you personalized her in chapter two), one of your triggers is undoubtedly talking to your mother (or any family member, the people we love can often trigger our own critics)! Triggers are unique to the individual—what triggers you won't necessarily trigger your best friend. For some of my colleagues, speaking in front of a group is a hotbed of I.C. attacks, whereas I thrive on public speaking. Sure, I get nervous—but I don't go I.C. Another thing to bear in mind is that while there are many situations that might trigger your emotions, you're looking to identify only those circumstances that trigger emotions powerful enough to warrant an Inner Critic attack.

Below are examples of situations many of my clients have identified as Triggers, along with their typical I.C. messages:

- "Performance review time is a breeding ground for my inner Fraud as I prepare my self-evaluation and get ready to meet with my manager. I'll think, 'This is it. Now they'll see how little I accomplished and give me the boot.'"

- "I was presenting my latest project progress and several colleagues jumped in with questions about whether or not I'd done this or that. In situations like this I beat myself up, with 'shoulds.' Like, 'I should have thought of this, they must think I'm an idiot.'"

- "Any conversation with my Dad about finances, with my sister about how my career is languishing, or with my Mom about delaying my next trip home to visit send me over the edge. Especially my Mom. I'll tell myself, 'I wish I were a better daughter.'"

- "Parents' night at my kids' school—specifically, sitting with a group of parents discussing how the kids are getting along . . . or not. 'Holy heck,' I'll tell myself, 'Jan and Rick sound like they have it totally together when it comes to the kids' homework. Thank goodness they don't know what goes on at our house.'"

- "Going golfing with my buddies, when the talk inevitably turns to who's making how much, how big their bonuses were, who bought a new boat, etc., etc. 'No way I'm going to tell them our company couldn't do raises this year,' I'll say to myself. 'They'll start pushing me to find another job.'"

- "Heading into a meeting with potential venture capital investors is a hotbed of sabotaging self-doubts like, 'I'm sure they won't think we have a strong enough market plan, why even bother pitching?'"
- "Sitting at home, working on the marketing plan for my new business, waiting for potential new clients to return emails, waiting for the phone to ring . . . basically running out of things to do because it's too darn quiet. 'That's it,' I'll think, 'I'll never get another client. This is the year I lose everything.'"

I believe that the best way to handle change is to tell people things will change. Most of us fare better when we expect something to change; we don't like to be surprised. Knowing *when* your critic's likely to show up lets you be prepared for it—and plan accordingly. A great way to shed light on your recurring triggers is to take a page from Shandra's book and jot them down on Post-It notes. (Man, those little yellow stickies are priceless, aren't they?) Remember to track only those triggers that prompt major internal reactions. Like Shandra, you may also start to spot a pattern.

ACTIVITY: The Rubber Band

Another high-tech gadget I have clients use to raise awareness is a rubber band. Yes, it's amazing how useful office supplies can be! When Rahul was trying to learn more about when his Inner Critic moments happened, I had him use this. First, he put the rubber band on his right wrist. Whenever he first noticed an Inner Critic message pop into his brain, he switched the rubber band to his left wrist (I also have people do this to notice feelings). Rahul was pretty surprised how often he was moving the band from wrist to wrist that first couple of days. He didn't realize how much energy was going into that those I.C. moments. The simple technique of moving the rubber band, from a thinking response to a body response, helped him get tremendous awareness and information that he could use more effectively.

Patterns (a.k.a. Does This Seem Familiar?)

You've done a lot of deep work in this chapter, and you've gotten to know yourself much more intimately, which has primed you to start identifying your I.C. patterns. This is where all the pieces come together—all of the noticing, journaling and increased awareness around the *what* and the *when* lead to the *why* found in the patterns underlying your I.C. experience. When I say *pattern*, I mean the *coincidence* of a particular set of circumstances that are always in place when a particular critic shows up. For example, Richard noticed his Fraud Critic's pattern was to show up when he was interacting with leaders two or more levels above him—whether in meetings, via email or during presentations. The louder and more debilitating his critic, the quieter he became. It got in the way of what Richard most wanted to achieve (more on his story in later chapters), so it became a pattern we targeted with all our might.

Patterns can show up in many shapes and forms. Sadly they don't come with nice little labels announcing, "Hey, I'm a pattern!" Although it sure would be nice if they did. Often, figuring out your patterns doesn't happen by following a methodical, step-by-step process. I discovered one of mine—what I call "head fights"—simply by staying in research mode, i.e., paying close attention to what was going on when my I.C. was present, looking for habitual and similar thought sequences and asking more questions of myself.

I discovered I was often "fighting" with people—but only in my head. Now, I'm not a person who enjoys conflict or who likes getting into arguments; we just didn't do it in my family growing up. But it turns out I'm a champion fighter—in the safe and lovely confines of my own mind. I started to notice that I silently fight with friends—a lot. And with one in particular: Jack. Now, Jack is one of my dearest friends and colleagues—we adore each other and share a strong bond built on mutual trust and respect. Nonetheless, I found myself fighting with Jack in my head. And let me just tell you, I say the cleverest things when I fight with him. Here's how it typically goes down:

"Hey Stace, I heard you led an, um, interesting [read: not so great] workshop last week."

"Hi Jack. Yes, I did. Interesting that you heard about it, I wonder who might have passed that information along since we're usually so good at not gossiping [said in a cutting, sarcastic tone].

"Well, you know, I just wanted to see if you needed any support. I've been in the same situation."

"Oh really? You've been in my situation—a lone woman in a room full of men? You are a man, are you not, Jack? And you work with mostly male clients? I'm amazed you know what that experience is like for me! Really, for such an educated person, I'm shocked you could say this—and that you don't know it's so different to be a woman in a male-dominated world. Didn't they teach you that in Group Facilitation 101? Jack, while you're known to be one of the best in your field, sometimes you just don't know Jack. That was a hard situation for me and—while I'm sure it would have been effortless for you—that does not mean I don't know what I'm doing. OK? Are we clear?"

As you'll have noticed, Jack doesn't say much during my head fights—but I say a lot. I assume a lot. I jump to a lot of conclusions. I instantly assume the worst intentions. I go directly into defensive mode. I'm always right, justified, smart, clever—and I have the wittiest retorts and the last word.

I could say a great deal about my silent arguments, but the point I want to make here is that I finally noticed the pattern of staging fights in my head, and I started working through it. I resisted the urge to judge myself—banishing thoughts like, "I'm being a total jerk! I fight with my friends in my head. Who *does* that?" Instead, I applied the I.C. processes

I've described in this chapter. In other words, I asked myself the three magic questions:

1. What am I feeling?
2. What am I thinking?
3. What's my physical reaction?

What I learned was that my head fights almost always happened when I was feeling vulnerable—about an important piece of work I was doing, a big risk I was undertaking, and also when I felt overwhelmed with my workload. No matter what the specific circumstances, the common thread was that I felt vulnerable, exposed and at risk.

Once I identified the underlying feeling, I continued asking myself more questions:

- Why am I feeling vulnerable? Is it related to Jack?
- Is the fight relevant to how I'm feeling?
- What am I trying to avoid by focusing my energy on being belligerent?

Bingo! This last question was the key. I realized I'd adopted the pattern of head fights as a way to feel more in control during moments of vulnerability and exposure. However, the clever little ruse wasn't actually supporting me or helping me deal with the real issue—my vulnerability. It was distracting me from my feelings, but it wasn't actually serving a useful purpose.

Just like Phoebe and Richard, **I needed to allow myself to feel vulnerable**. I needed to acknowledge it, sit with it and support myself in that space—which might sometimes require reaching out to a friend for external support, or clearing some time in my calendar for activities that help me feel safe and nurtured.

ACTIVITY: Post-It

Stuck on any of the above I.C. components? Struggling to isolate your emotional, thinking, or physical reactions? Not clear on your triggers? Failing to see any patterns emerging? Well then, it's time to whip out the trusty Post-it notes!

Rather than trying to track all five elements, I recommend focusing on the ones you most readily notice—which might be the I.C. message (thinking reaction), the triggering event or a recurring set of circumstances you suspect might be a pattern. Find your easiest access point; then work from there. As soon as you catch the critic component, jot down a brief description and then set the note aside. If you can catch more than one component, great, but don't worry if you don't catch all five. Try this for at least one week, ideally two, at the end of which you'll have some rich, fertile data.

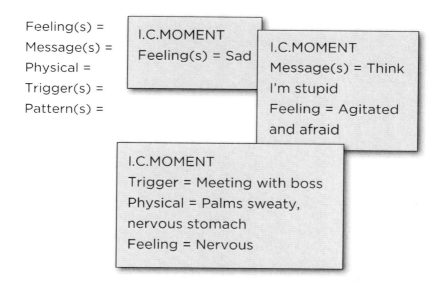

Feeling(s) =
Message(s) =
Physical =
Trigger(s) =
Pattern(s) =

I.C. MOMENT
Feeling(s) = Sad

I.C. MOMENT
Message(s) = Think I'm stupid
Feeling = Agitated and afraid

I.C. MOMENT
Trigger = Meeting with boss
Physical = Palms sweaty, nervous stomach
Feeling = Nervous

As you review your notes after "Observation Time" has elapsed, see if you can start practicing raising your awareness of the elements that *don't* come as naturally to you.

For example, Chen was pretty familiar with his critic message (thinking reaction), but he had a really tough time identifying his feelings and physical reactions. After tracking the messages for two weeks, he was able to identify two main themes: "I'm not ready to lead at this level" and, "They're going to figure out I'm not that smart"—both classic Fraud Critics. For the next week, whenever either of these messages came up, Chen tracked his emotional reaction by using his feelings worksheet to do the "Name it to Claim it" activity. He also noted the answer to the question: "Where does that feeling live in my body?" Most often Chen's feelings were "intimidated," "apprehensive," and "uneasy." He noticed these feelings manifested as tightness in his throat and a hot sensation around his neck and ears.

Almost immediately, Chen experienced two amazing results:

1. He became clear on what specifically triggered his Inner Critic: meetings with two of his peers who happened to be good friends with the CEO. Chen figured this out by noticing that's when his physical symptoms flared up.

2. By naming and claiming his feelings, the impact of the I.C. attacks started to decrease without Chen needing to do any additional work. The messages in his thinking brain didn't get nearly as loud, or last for nearly as long.

I strongly recommend you do this exercise regardless of what you know or think you know about your I.C. Like Chen, you'll be amazed what you discover when you start tracking all the elements. Nina had an equivalent breakthrough at one of my workshops. "Wow! I just learned something new!" she excitedly exclaimed as she came running over to me during a break. "I always thought I was a combo of Perfectionist and Fraud, but after doing this exercise today I learned I'm actually spending way more time as a Comparer." That's because what Nina was currently dealing with in her life was bringing up issues that provoked her Comparer Critic. By paying attention to her current critic messages, reactions and triggers, Nina updated the profile of her main critic, and in turn became way more specific in her ability to target it.

As we progress through the book, you'll start to see that your critic isn't static, it's a reflection of what's going on inside you *right now*. The challenges facing you today are likely to be significantly different to the fears that haunted you five years ago. This is why I want you to become accustomed to repeating the activities and exercises at regular intervals. Once you get that big promotion next year, and your Inner Fraud Critic resurfaces, these same practices will enable you to zoom in quickly on what's going on and why, so you can redirect all that powerful energy to a more productive use.

Bottom Line: None of the Above Come First

By now you'll understand why it's not always clear which came first—the chicken or the egg. And that's OK. You don't need to know what sparked the I.C. chain reaction. But you do need to track each stage of the chain reaction, so you can get to the underlying cause. Think of it in terms of your body: you might go to the doctor complaining of a bunch of seemingly unrelated symptoms—say, for example, a sluggish system, chronic fatigue, and skin discoloration. It's only when your doctor determines the underlying root cause of your sickness—funky bacteria in your small intestine—that she can treat and cure your body's illness and symptoms.

It's the same with your I.C. Identifying your patterns plays a crucial role in shedding light on a bunch of seemingly unrelated data—thereby isolating valuable leverage points where you can zero in on the underlying root cause. The more you understand about how your I.C. jigsaw puzzle works, the more each piece becomes an opportunity to catch your critic earlier and shift the energy to a more useful, positive purpose.

Switching from Auto-Pilot to Choice

The beauty of knowing how you typically react to an I.C. attack is that it gives you the ability to shift towards how you *want* to react going forward. That means switching from a default "auto-pilot" response to a conscious and intentional response.

For example, my typical response to a Comparer Critic attack is:

- Feeling(s) = vulnerable and nervous

- Message(s) = She's way better and smarter than me.
- Physical = hold back, get much quieter, lose the ability to make decisions on my own

After bringing my awareness to how I *do* respond during Comparer attacks, I next set my mind to determining how I'd *rather* respond. While I'd like to not feel vulnerable and nervous, I know feelings aren't something I can control. I'd also like to not have all those undermining thoughts, and while I can turn down the volume and reduce their impact (by doing the work in this book), I can't switch my brain off, either. What I can do is shift is my physical auto-response. The last thing my facilitating partner and my client needs is for me to go dark. I need to bring all of me—my skills, expertise, passion and empathy—in order to create the best, most enriching experience for everyone concerned. Despite my feelings and thoughts, I can still work towards staying engaged, being vocal, making decisions and reminding myself of what I do have to offer.

I've now not only identified my autopilot response—I've also clarified how I'd *prefer to respond*. This is the golden ticket: shifting from a reaction to an intentional *choice* to respond differently.

Now that Richard knows one of his triggers is meeting with senior management, he can work backwards. Going into a meeting, Richard already knows his I.C.'s going to show up and thanks to all the work he's done, he's prepared for it. He recognizes that he's afraid of saying the wrong thing in front of his bosses. However, instead of going into his auto-pilot mute mode, Richard tells himself, "Yup, I'm afraid. My stomach's in a knot and my palms are sweaty. But instead of shutting down, *I choose to speak up.*"

As you build your knowledge of what's happening in the moments surrounding an Inner Critic attack, I want you also to consider what other choices you have in how you respond. Take a few minutes to go back to your top three critic messages and what you've learned about them. Brainstorm three options you could do to react differently the next time it shows up.

Like Keanu Reeves, I want you to open your eyes and see the Matrix—what's real and what's not. Once you become more emotionally self-aware, and start to clock your triggers and identify your patterns, you'll begin to see things as they really are—no blue pill required! You'll be able to peruse your week's schedule Monday morning and easily point to the giant red flags. "There, there and there," you'll say. "That's when I'll see Mr. Anderson." And when he shows up, you'll be ready. And you'll choose exactly how to respond.

4

Show Me the Data!

By now, you're familiar with typical I.C. messages: "What happens when they find out I can't do this job?," "I'm not smart enough to deserve a seat at this table," "Who am I to ask for a raise?" The messages are usually quite vague—blanket statements that are generally not true. In chapter four, we'll analyze and break down your I.C. message into bite-size chunks, which will take the sting out of the critic's wickedly slashing Scorpion tail. You'll learn that blanket statements such as "I'm not smart enough" don't hold up in the court of the real world. You'll learn what is specifically true about your statement and what isn't. You'll reinforce your findings with specific, real-life examples, and you'll bolster it further with feedback from colleagues, friends and loved ones. You'll start to define what certain words like "lazy," "smart," and "quiet" mean to *you*—so they become relevant and useful.

The key to the critic-smashing tools in this chapter is to get into the details, the specifics and the data that will lead to tangible actions you can take to tame and quiet the critic. You'll uncover inarguable proof your critic is little more than a spin-doctor with no supporting substance underneath it. And, just like that, the critic will tumble from its lofty, self-righteous pedestal.

Don't Believe Everything You Think

One of my favorite sayings is, "Don't believe everything you think." It has both wisdom *and* humor. When I say this, people generally tip their heads to one side. They think about it for a minute and then comes that moment when they get it. Their heads pop back up and they laugh, but they have a bit of mystified look, too, because they've also just realized that those powerful big brains of theirs aren't as powerful as they'd always believed them to be. Worse, the brains they've put *all* their trust in—the rational parts of themselves that have served them so well over the course of their lives, and have produced glorious, all-sacred *answers* and *solutions*—are sometimes liars. Yes, I said it—big, fat, bold-faced liars . . . sometimes. The rational brain is of course incredibly useful and beneficial, too. In this chapter, you're going to learn how to harness your mind's superpowers so they are working for *you*—instead of for your critic. We're going to look at the actual data inherent in your I.C. message—the facts, Ma'am, just the facts—and test the veracity and the accuracy of its contents.

E.I. MOMENT: A word on emotional overwhelm

I want to take a moment to stress the importance of operating from a primarily rational—versus an emotional—place when doing the following activities. In this chapter you will engage that glorious, rational, cognitive, problem-solving brain of yours. And that requires you to *not* be in the grips of a powerful I.C. attack, and at the mercy of a body flooded with emotions. If that is the case, you're in the midst of an **amygdala hijack**. This term was coined by Daniel Goleman to describe those moments when you are suddenly overwhelmed with emotional sensation. The amygdala is part of the limbic system, or emotional centers of the brain, which holds the keys to those flight, fight or freeze responses built so deeply into our being. During a hijack, the prefrontal cortex (rational brain) is actually unable to respond at its peak. If you're in the middle of a hijack, with the accompanying flood of powerful emotions, your limbic system (emotional brain) is the boss right now. Please back away from this chapter slowly, turn around and go do something else until the emotional overwhelm has passed. I suggest you go take some sort of exercise (go for a run, take a walk, or bust out a dance break—anything that gets your body and your emotions moving), practice the deep belly breathing exercise from chapter three, indulge in some healthy venting with someone you trust, or delve into a hobby or activity you can lose yourself in. When you feel the hijack pass and your rational powers have come back online, come on back to this chapter.

The Truth Series

The Truth Series is a quartet of questions—which starts with a profound question from the amazing book *Loving What Is: Four Questions That Can Change Your Life* by Byron Katie—then continues with other questions that are an incredibly powerful way to break down your Inner Critic message and separate fact from fiction. You're going to dig into the data of your critic's wearisome words and unravel what's true and what's not by asking the following questions:

1. **Is it *one hundred* percent true?**
2. **What is *more* true?**
3. **What is *less* true?**
4. **What *else* could be true?**

While they appear relatively simple, the questions take a little bit of work and a lot of thought, which is why I'll ease you into the activity slowly. I will introduce some client examples that will illustrate how the process works before asking you to tackle all four yourself. But I know you're in this for the long haul—and you're willing to do the work, so let's begin to take an introductory look at the "truth" of your I.C. message.

In your journal or on a sheet of paper write down your predominant

I.C. message—the one that feels hottest and has the most energy for you *right now*.

Glance at what you wrote, and ask yourself: **Is it 100% true?**

Like most of my clients, you probably hesitated after reading the question, and have already started creating caveats and conditions and qualifications. "Well, but, see . . ." is how most people answer this question, at which point, I lovingly say, "Hold up! This is a binary question! There are only two possible answers: yes or no. That's it. You have 10 seconds to choose which one."

My client Anna's predominant Perfectionist I.C. message is, "I'm lazy." (When under attack, some variation of "I don't do enough," "I'm such a slacker," or, "I'm so lazy" echoes across the canyons of Anna's mind.) When I asked Anna her I.C. message was 100% true, she begrudgingly answered, "No," while giving me the stink eye (shows up as the glaring eyes or the dramatic eye-roll). Like she was upset that I took the wind out of her I.C. sails so quickly. Dang me!

I'm confident that by now you, too, will have answered no. And you're probably giving me the stink eye, too. Don't worry, there's more—let's proceed to the next question.

Given that your I.C. message is *not* one hundred percent true, what about it is *more* true—and what's *less* true? (It's generally easier to ask these two in tandem.)

Now this question duo is tough to do alone. It helps to talk it out with someone who can challenge your perspectives and thought processes. If you don't feel comfortable doing that, then let's go back to Anna's story so you have a picture of how your process should look.

I wanted Anna to figure out very specifically what was true about the statement, "I'm lazy." It was likely there *was* some kernel of truth in it, but that it would be a very specific kernel and *not* the all-life-consuming-label, "lazy." My goal was to help Anna pinpoint any specific truth hovering in and around the message so she could take action on it, or not. But at least it would be her choice and it would swing the balance of power back in her favor. Blanket statements are tools used by the critic to make you feel powerless; it's really difficult to take efficient, effective action on a sweeping statement. But you can take back your power by breaking the message down into the twin bite-size pieces: what's more true and what's less true.

To this end, I asked Anna to give me a specific example supporting what's *more* true about her message of being lazy. She told me that a few days prior, she'd had the choice to go to the gym (one of her coaching goals was to get more exercise) but she was too tired, so she took a nap instead. I asked Anna to give me more data about that day—why was she tired, why was it important to go to the gym, etc.? What she told me was a familiar story. After working all day (Anna has a demanding managerial-level job at a fast-paced company), she picked up the kids from school, fed them, drove to her parents' house to prepare dinner for them (her folks are aging and she's the primary caregiver), came home, caught up with her email, then found herself with a little free time wherein she could squeeze in a trip to the gym. But she chose not to because she was beat. Yeah, she's pretty lazy, huh?

In talking through the specifics of the situation, Anna also answered the question, what's *less* true about the statement, "I'm lazy?" Answer: She'd accomplished a *ton* that day!

When Anna shared the details and the specifics around the story of her day, her general I.C. message of being lazy just didn't hold up. It was perfectly reasonable that she would feel tired and want to take a nap, but Anna was disappointed in herself for not meeting her goal to exercise. So we also dug deeper into that goal (using the more true/less true questions) and uncovered a deeper want to feel healthier *in general*—which didn't equate to the number of times she hit the gym. After we shifted her goal to align with being healthier (versus exercising more), I asked Anna if taking a much-needed nap constituted a healthy choice. She hesitated, and with slightly less stink eye answered, "Yes, I guess it could."

Jason also struggled with the Truth Series questions. He worked in software development and had a raging Fraud Critic who told him, "You are *definitely* not technical enough to hang with this crowd! Just wait until they figure out how far behind you are in the latest stuff." It didn't help that Jason sat in the middle of a vast open office space, within arm's length, hearing range, and eyesight of at least ten brilliant coders. This set of circumstances prompted his I.C. to run amok.

Together, we went through the drill. "Is your I.C. message, 'I'm not technical enough,' one hundred percent true?" I asked Jason. "Well, look around, that guy knows everything about. . . ." I stopped Jason right there. "Yes or no?" I prompted him. Eventually, Jason begrudgingly admitted the message wasn't one hundred percent true.

Great. Now that I had Jason's incredibly smart brain on board, I continued. "What is *more* true about you not being technical enough? And what exactly do you mean by "technical enough"? Do you mean not technical enough for this particular team, this company, or this industry? Jason spoke about the warp speed of technology, the intricacies of coding languages, all the factors that had to be considered for platform, toolset, etc. Heck, I didn't understand half of what he said. It sounded like a foreign language to me! But Jason also shared that a couple of his colleagues had been deeply focused on one particular code and technology that he didn't know quite as well. "Why aren't you spending time on this with your colleagues?" I asked, looking to get as specific as possible. It turns out Jason had been assigned to a different research project at the request of their group V.P. "So, do your colleagues know as much as you do about this topic?" I asked Jason. "Well, no," he replied. "They have their own project focus." So why is it okay for them to have that one focus but you have to have both? Stink eye. We switched tacks by focusing on what was less true. Jason's V.P. had selected him because of his prior track record of learning quickly and finding innovative uses for new technologies. Because of his depth of knowledge, he was being asked to present training sessions to other developers. Jason found a number of examples that clearly refuted the *truth* that he wasn't technical enough.

ACTIVITY: Truth Series Deep Diving

Ok. Now that you're warmed up and you've seen how both Anna and Jason tackled the questions, you should be ready to tackle the Truth Series yourself in earnest. I've created a nice worksheet (included below) to make it as streamlined as possible. Ready? Ok, here we go.

1. Write your I.C. message at the top of the worksheet. You can use the same one as before or choose another one if something else has popped up that feels more charged.

2. Answer the question, "Is it 100% true?" by circling Yes or No. Don't skip this step; it's important! It will help fire up your brain to dig further by coaxing it into problem-solving mode.

3. In the column on the left, make a list with specific examples and data of the ways your message is *more* true.

4. In the column on the right, make a list of the ways it's *less* true. Get as specific as you can. I want details and examples. I want data and particulars (remember, I used to work in accounting and high-tech, so data is sweet goodness to me!). This exercise is about breaking down the message so you can gain a deeper insight and awareness into your own stories. There's no limit to how many answers you might have on each side. Write as many as you have energy for and just stop when you run out.

WORKSHEET: The Truth Series

My Inner Critic message:

_____

_____

Is it 100% true? [Circle] Yes No

What is more true about this statement?	**What is less true about this statement?**
_____	_____
_____	_____
_____	_____
_____	_____
_____	_____
_____	_____
_____	_____
_____	_____

What _else_ could be true?

Possible Truth/Reframe no. 1:_____.

Possible Truth/Reframe no. 2:_____.

Possible Truth/Reframe no. 3:_____.

Possible Truth/Reframe no. 4:_____.

Possible Truth/Reframe no. 5:_____.

Before you proceed to the fourth and final question—What *else* could be true?—I want to round out Anna's story. I asked her what else could be true about her Perfectionist Critic message, "I'm lazy." I had Anna explore this by writing down four other possible truths, or reframe statements.

Possible Truth/Reframe no. 1: "I aspire to live in a more healthy way."
Possible Truth/Reframe no. 2: "I want to feel energized by taking great care of myself."
Possible Truth/Reframe no. 3: "I want to make good choices about how I spend my time."

I interrupted Anna here to remind her of all she'd accomplished that fateful "lazy" day, and to reinforce her "healthy" choice to take a nap. Instead of using the aspirational verb "want," did Anna perhaps want to acknowledge and own that she had in fact achieved her goal that day? More stink-eye! Then Anna proceeded to write her final reframe.

Possible Truth/Reframe no. 4: "I am making good choices to be healthy and energized."

Bingo! In the process of reframing her message, Anna had completely reversed it! Her message evolved from a harsh criticism into an empowering and liberating series of alternate truths and, ultimately, into an energizing and affirming reframe statement. Man, I wish you could have seen the smile on her face and the surge of energy in her body (despite the well intentioned eye-rolls aimed towards me).

Do you see how this last question starts to open up other possible truths? It also serves to re-frame your Inner Critic messages in a way that's more supportive, less energy draining, and way more spacious in terms of your ability to take action.

Now let's return to your worksheet. Brainstorm three to five other possible truths about your I.C. message, like Anna's, above. Use all the data you've revealed around your critic message in this chapter to investigate new possibilities. Continue until your statements sing to you or just plain feel more spacious and energy lifting.

If you need further inspiration, read on to see how Jason reframed his message, "I'm not technical enough."

Possible Truth/Reframe no. 1: "I know a great deal about my area of focus. In fact, I'm considered the in-house expert."

Possible Truth/Reframe no. 2: "My current technical skills are strong in the area my boss wants me to focus on. In fact, he sent me to some pretty amazing conferences so I could learn more. I guess that means he trusts me."

Possible Truth/Reframe no. 3: "My boss has talked about upcoming projects I'll get to work on too; completely new stuff. I've always been quick to learn new technologies and codes. In fact, I totally geek out when I get to play with a new code language."

Possible Truth/Reframe no. 4: "I have massive respect for the guys working on the *other* project. I guess that's a cool thing. Although I get a little jealous, maybe it's good that I'm surrounded by smart people."

REFLECTION: What Have You Learned?

Do you see how some of the things you tell yourself aren't true? Can you come up with any specific actions you could take based on what you've learned? After completing his Truth Series, Jason realized how much he loves learning new things. He decided to take a class to learn the code his colleagues were using on their project—not to prove he was technical enough but because he knew it would be a blast.

What action can you take based on what you've just discovered in the data around your I.C. message? Perhaps there is no action to be taken. Great! Then take all that energy you've been devoting to your I.C. message and focus it somewhere else—where it can accomplish something useful and meaningful.

Do you see how many of the beliefs you hold aren't personal beliefs, but rather societal and/or cultural norms? This process demonstrates how oftentimes you're beholden to cultural or societal beliefs whereas I want you to be beholden to your *own*. It's a whole lot easier to hold fast to a set of beliefs in the face of external pressure (from society, your boss, your family, or your peers) if they're something you actually believe in. It's also a lot easier to change a personal belief than a societal or cultural mores. For example, Anna could try to change the way society perceives the link between sleep and health, or she could update her own belief about what it is to be healthy. Which one do you think is more feasible and within her control? **What have you learned about *your* beliefs? How might you change them?**

> **❝**Almost nothing that happens to you has just one cause. . . . There are multiple causes, so why latch onto the most insidious one? Ask yourself, is there any less destructive way to look at this? To dispute your own beliefs, scan for all possible contributing causes. Focus on those that are changeable (not enough time spent studying), specific (this particular exam was uncharacteristically hard), and non personal (the professor graded unfairly). —Martin Seligman, Authentic Happiness

ACTIVITY: Clarify Your Beliefs

In your journal, copy any statements from the above "What is more and less true" question that you feel require a little more excavation. For each statement, see if you can determine the primary source of the belief or judgment. Does it stem from any of the following:

- The societal beliefs that you live in (e.g., what media might show as a preferred way to look or act)?
- The culture you grew up in?
- The religion you grew up with or now practice?
- A set of family norms or how your family handled things when you were growing up?
- A part of what your company culture dictates or what your boss wants?

Of course there's an element of you in each statement you listed; the objective here is to figure out who else had a part in that story or statement. Once you begin to unravel these threads you have the opportunity to make a choice about what to keep as part of your personal beliefs, what to begin to let go of, and what you may just have to deal with as part—but only a part—of the reality of life. It doesn't necessarily reflect the totality of your reality. The goal here is that you take accountability for the beliefs you adopt as your own, as distinct from an external belief system that has influenced your beliefs in the past.

Jason learned that his belief around needing to know the language his colleagues were working with came mostly from himself, but that it also stemmed from a company culture that rewarded a wide range of technical skills. He was tempted to ascribe it to his boss as well, until I asked if Jason had ever verified the accuracy of that. "No," replied Jason. He'd never actually asked his boss directly. That's pretty typical. Most of us make up a set of assumptions based on what we perceive to be true, without actually verifying the accuracy of our assumptions. Jason decided to go talk with his boss and was surprised to learn that his boss valued the depth of experience and expertise Jason was building on the special project he'd been assigned to. He preferred that to developing a broader but shallower knowledge base. The conversation cleared up a great deal of Jason's assumptions—which resulted in a much humbler and quieter Comparer Critic. Bonus!

Check Your Assumptions

Like Jason, many of us base important decisions on what we *assume* to be true. Damon almost derailed his career trajectory because of a false assumption.

His boss was up for a big promotion and everyone assumed Damon would step into his boss's role. However, Damon's boss didn't get the job and Damon found himself in an awkward position. You see, one of Damon's personal rules is that loyalty trumps everything. Damon believed he had to remain loyal to his boss—even if it meant stifling his own success.

There was another position open elsewhere in the company for which Damon was perfect, but he'd decided not to put himself forward. In Damon's mind, putting his hat in the ring would constitute being disloyal to his boss. Damon was convinced that at best his boss wouldn't support it and at worst he would be hurt by it.

I challenged Damon to check his assumptions by actually having a conversation with his boss. He resisted, but I persisted. "Just have the conversation," I urged. One of the benefits of having a good friend (or a coach!) in your corner is they won't let you off the hook. They'll hold up a mirror that says, "Really? You're *so* not getting away with this!" It was really important that Damon challenge the assumption on which he was basing this crucial decision. He needed to get past the story in his head and realize that if he went after what he wanted and what was in his best interests, his relationship with his boss wouldn't crumble. And even if it did, it wouldn't be the end of the world.

Guess what? Just like Jason, Damon was shocked at the outcome of having a frank and open and admittedly slightly awkward conversation with his boss who, in reality, totally supported Damon and wanted him to succeed. In fact, he was mortified to learn that Damon had held back for fear of offending him!

Checking your assumptions by seeking other's feedback is essential if you're to operate with current, relevant, accurate information. When it comes to the Inner Critic, knowledge is the absolute power that liberates you from the tyranny of self-doubt and beating yourself up.

Create New Definitions of "Hot Words"

Words are incredibly powerful, and some are more powerful than others. I call these "Hot Words." Typically, they're terms you use all the time (usually, without having a clear and precise definition of what they actually mean). And they're almost always words our society makes even hotter. For example, take the word "power." What comes to mind when I say, "That man is powerful?" Now, let's tweak it a little bit. . . . What comes to mind when I say, "That woman is powerful?" Do you perceive them differently? When we combine the worlds "powerful" and "woman" in one sentence, it can have a very negative connotation. Oftentimes in culture, in media, and perhaps even in our own experiences, we've been exposed to a negative portrayal of a woman who wields a lot of power. We might have heard her described as a "bitch" or that she's too aggressive, that she's cold-hearted or mean-spirited, or that she's only in it for the money. This is how the word power is sometimes defined from a negative perspective. But what does the word mean to *you*? If you obliterated societal definitions, judgments and associations, how would you define it? What does power mean to you?

Your Inner Critic loves to use inappropriate definitions of Hot Words. As you've just discovered, it thrives on broad generalizations, so it's no surprise the critic adopts those definitions appropriated by society at large and mass media—without any consideration for what you as an individual believe the definition to be. For example, your I.C. might tell you that you're not smart enough, but have you ever actually considered what *your* definition of smart is? What does smart mean to you? How smart is smart enough? Are you using somebody else's definition of what constitutes being smart? This is yet another way to harness the laser-sharp focus of details, specifics and data, and to direct it towards the critic in order to reveal its flaws, follies, and fallacies.

I have my clients create definitions of their Hot Words. As we start to excavate their I.C. messages and dig into what is more and less true, I ask them to circle any words that have a lot of heat. I use "heat" to indicate a negative and higher intensity emotional response. These words can also set your thinking brain into more action with justifications, assumptions and perceptions. Another indicator of a word packed with extra "baggage" is if saying it aloud changes the tonality of your voice—an inflection that tends to indicates emphasis.

We spend some time talking about what the terms are taken to mean in their external environments. Then, I ask them to come up with their own personalized definitions. They key here is to be specific! One of my favorite Hot Words is success, because it has a ton of "stuff" hanging from it. I'll ask clients: what does success look like? Oftentimes I'll hear what I call "corporate speak" or "media babble," what a client thinks sounds good, or what a client thinks *I* want to hear. But my focus isn't on our culture, mass media, myself or anyone else—my focus is on *you*. What do *you* think success looks like? You get to define the word in any way you want. Does success look like a promotion, your kids getting great grades, being at a certain level of fitness, or having the respect of a certain group of people? If success is about having the respect of certain people, define who those people are. Who do you want to respect you? Everyone? One individual? A group of people? Who, specifically? What does that respect look like and how would you know it if you saw it?

ACTIVITY: Owning the Definition of Your Hot Words

Ok, let's figure out what your Hot Words are. Go back to your Truth Series worksheet and circle every word that has heat/energy for you. Select 3–5 words that are most potent. Stack rank those words according to their "heat index," starting with the most intense. Now, write that ordered list in the left-hand column of the worksheet.

WORKSHEET: Hot Words Defined

My Hot Words	Current Definition	My definition
_____	_____	_____
	_____	_____
_____	_____	_____
	_____	_____
_____	_____	_____
	_____	_____

Now let's start to delve into the meaning of your Hot Words. Pick one—the first or second, or any word you're curious about investigating—and ask yourself: how did I define it in the context of what I wrote in the Truth Series worksheet? In the column in the center, make a list of words or short phrases that reflect that definition.

When you're done, look at the words and phrases. Do any look like they're not yours? Do they belong to someone else? If so, to whom do you think they belong—your parents? Your spouse? Your culture? Your industry or company? Your religion? Put their name beneath the relevant words. For each one, ask yourself: does it also belong to me, and if so, do I want to keep it? This is where you get to decide exactly who gets to come behind the red velvet rope and walk into the club with you—and who gets denied. You'll want to make sure the words you're inviting inside are the words you *want* inside your club.

Continue this process for all your Hot Words. When you're done, scan the middle column and ask yourself: what definitions do I want to take on and take with me? Underline those you want to take on and "invite" them to the club—a.k.a. the column on the right—by drawing an arrow across. Now you'll polish your new, personalized definitions. Ask yourself: does this current definition work for me? What's missing? Is there anything I need to add? Anything I need to subtract? Amend each one accordingly by adding or subtracting words or phrases. Keep it loose. Your goal isn't to create a rigid, perfect (there it is!), or forever definition. I want you to create spaciousness—so the word can grow and change with you, and so you're always the root or the source of the definition. We all grow and change, so of course our words will need to be able to grow and change with us. Your vision of success five years ago is likely markedly different than it is today—so you wouldn't want to be pinned down to your old definition of success, would you? Of course not! Think powerful, possible and positive. You don't want the words to own you. You want to own the words.

Now that you have a whole new vocabulary defined by *you*, I encourage you to conduct a beta test. Write some of your Hot Words and their updated definitions on Post-it notes or index cards and carry them with you for a couple of weeks. If you have an I.C. moment related to those words ("success" being a prime example), see if you're in new definition mode or if you've swung back to ye olde definitions. Re-apply your new definition and see if it strips the critic of some of its power. Does the new lingo allow you a bit more space, more breathing room? At the end of the two-week beta period, update the definition if it needs some tweaking.

Rules In Play

The above exercise is just another tool for digging deeper and creating more breadth and depth in your I.C. story. The more specific and detailed you get, the more you will suck the power and punch out of the negative impact of the critic. We're going to continue adding tools like this to your tool kit, tool belt or tool handbag, including one of my favorites: "Rules in Play."

Whether you're aware of it or not, you're operating by your very own set of rules, such as, "If I start something, I have to finish it." But guess what? That actually isn't true—you don't have to finish everything you start. That's a rule you could pull off the field of play. "*What*? Really?" Yes. Really.

In the introduction, I described my shock when my coaching mentor, Mitch Loomis, suggested I "try" graduate school. Mitch reasoned that if I didn't like the course, I could just quit. And if I loved grad school, I could "try" another semester. Mitch's words sounded so foreign to me she could have been speaking Lebanese (which I am *not* fluent in)—I could not comprehend what she'd said. It was a Scooby-Doo moment, complete with the sideways head tilt of confusion.

"Huh?" I asked, baffled. "Quit? You can't start grad school and then quit."

"Why not?" asked perfectly reasonable Mitch.

"If I start grad school, I have to finish."

"No, you actually don't have to finish."

Mitch had just exposed the fallacy of one of my rules. It was like someone had just invented the light bulb: "Interesting, that's a good idea. Maybe we should invent electricity!" I lit up as I considered the idea of starting school and "seeing" if it worked out. I loved the idea that I could stop when I wanted and perhaps begin again later. The whole concept was a delicious shock to my system.

My buddy Jim exposed another of my Rules in Play about four months in to grad school. You'll remember in the introduction I shared the story of how miserable I was when Monday morning rolled around and I had to go back to work. While moaning and groaning over coffee one day, Jim suggested I quit my job.

"Huh?" Another Scooby-Doo moment. "I can't quit my job. I make six figures, nobody quits that."

"Don't you have any money in savings?" asked Jim. "Or stock options?"

"Well, yeah."

"Why don't you use that?"

"Huh?" Cue Scooby-Doo sound. "I can't use *that* money."

"Why not?"

"Because *that's* for retirement."

"Who says? You could think of it as an investment for retirement or an investment in your new career."

Jim told me he'd been working part time for the past five years—courtesy of stock options from his old job. I was in shock. I thought Jim was a responsible, upstanding citizen—when in fact he was a slacker! Of course, Jim isn't a slacker. That's just what my own programming said I would be if I worked part-time and lived off my savings. All of a sudden, I heard my dad's voice in my ear: "You don't spend your retirement money on anything but retirement." I didn't even know that code was written into my little video game of life, but evidently there was a rule in my system that said I don't spend any money that's gone into my savings or retirement accounts until the end of my life. And I realized the author of that code was my dad. It was a family rule. I didn't realize that I was playing by my dad's rules, not mine. Just like the Hot Words. Spot the trend?

OK, so how do you spot a Rule in Play? If you find yourself saying something hard and fast—like it's a truth with a capital T, that's a sign. If it's a totally rigid concept, and you've got the rigid body language to prove it, that's another indicator. Damon's rule about loyalty was pretty rigid until he added more space by checking his assumptions and talking to his boss. Also be on the lookout for those Scooby-Doo, head-tilting moments, and notice if you react swiftly and with "certainty" in the face of a well-meaning suggestion that you think about a situation differently.

Some Common Rules In Play

- You don't quit a perfectly good job just because you're unhappy.
- You can't make a living doing what you love.
- You can't say no to a perfectly reasonable request.
- If someone has more credentials, they're automatically better than me.
- If I don't have X number of Y experience, then I'm a Fraud.
- I have to make my boss happy, no matter what.
- As a leader, I have to treat everybody exactly the same.
- I have to climb the corporate ladder, even if I'm not interested in what's at the top.
- I need to have more time in my day before I can start exercising.
- If someone on my team screws up, it's my fault. The buck stops with me.
- If my boss is in a bad mood it means that I'm the cause.
- If I want it done right, I have to do it myself.

ACTIVITY: Be the Author of Your Rulebook

Take out your journal and write a list of three to five rules you think might be in play on your field. Now run them through the same drills you did with your Hot Words: what's more or less true about each rule? Where did it originate? Do you want to keep that rule and take full responsibility for it? Or is it time to delete it from your rulebook?

If you're unsure whether to keep or toss a rule, road test it. Write it on a Post-It note and keep it on your desk or in your car. Over the next two weeks, pay attention to how often it comes up and where and how it limits or prevents you from seeing other possibilities. The minute you bring your awareness to it, the answer tends to become pretty apparent.

If you're totally stumped as to your Rules in Play, I recommend two activities:

1. Go into researcher mode. Spend the next two weeks consciously trying to spot rules. Make a note of anything that comes up.

2. Ask those who know you best. I discovered my Rules in Play when talking with Mitch and Jim. It's often my closest friends who help me spot the rules I'm oblivious to.

You've gained new tools to make hot words your own and written your own rulebook to play by. You've used data and specifics for the superpowers of good. Now you'll move outward for more perspective on the critics and gather more range of motion.

5

Taking a Different Look

My dad taught me to play pool at the local tavern when I was a kid. (Ah, the beauty of growing up in a small town!) When it was my turn, I'd be chomping at the bit to jump in and take my shot—already eyeing that solid yellow ball sitting near the corner pocket. "Slow down, Stace," my dad would say, "make sure you walk all the way around the table and see every shot." At eight years of age, I didn't really want to slow down, I wanted to sink that yellow ball (No. 1, corner pocket!) But my dad patiently coached me to see the big picture of the game itself—versus zeroing in on the easiest shot to take next. He stressed the importance of looking at the whole table, making sure I'd viewed it from all perspectives, before choosing my move. Inevitably, my patience would yield a completely different shot I hadn't seen at first glance or a golden possibility masquerading as a seemingly impossible angle.

I've since adopted my dad's pool table wisdom as a philosophy I apply to all areas of my life, including my work around the Inner Critic. I still don't like to slow down but I do, because I've learned the value of seeing all the perspectives of the Inner Critic—every angle, all the possibilities—before reacting to an attack.

For the most part, your critic voice represents *a* perspective on what's happening in your life—one that you can rely on to be negative and limiting. By stepping outside that perspective and seeking out other viewpoints, you'll find that the data doesn't actually support the critic's one-sided stance. In this chapter, you'll learn to slow down, take a good look around and shift your perspective—from how the I.C. has hurt you—to all the possible ways it might actually have helped you. (Yes, really. You'll discover that there's actually a tiny hint of method in its lop-sided madness!) You'll investigate what other potentialities might lie hidden in the messages of the critic, you'll learn to navigate away from "all-or-nothing" thinking, and you'll take an exploratory step outside your own head to check out some fresh new viewpoints. You'll even explore the possibility of surrendering to the energy of the critic—instead of expending valuable energy resisting it.

How Has the I.C. Helped?

Yes, I did just ask how the Inner Critic has helped you! That's a radical new view, right? Believe it or not, the I.C.'s original purpose was to be of service to you. I know. I know it's a nasty little beast you've been battling for years and you certainly don't want me to take its side. Except that it's true. As I explained in chapter three, the critic's origins stem from when you were a small child and needed a set of rules in order to survive and thrive in your family, culture, ethnicity and religion of origin, your educational system and society at large. Whether it's a Perfectionist or a Pleaser, or both, the critic's intent is still to protect you. As difficult as that may be to accept, your inner critic has actually protected you in some ways. We're going to explore how.

Without delving too deeply into your past (as I said before, that kind of work is best supported in the context of one-on-one counseling with a therapist), we will identify some of the key sources of your Inner Critic messages and how they relate to your current situation.

The following pair of questions will help you explore whether or not your I.C. message has other possibilities you can utilize as fuel to grow stronger and more resilient.

How Has Your I.C. Benefitted You?

I know your I.C. is often a debilitating, energy-sucking pain in the backside, but is there another way to look at it? My Perfectionist proved a major asset when I was carving out a career in the software industry. Thanks to this critic, I always strove to exceed my boss's expectations. When my boss gave me an assignment, I always delivered over and above what was asked of me. For example, if my assignment was to identify the top five features customers wanted in the next software release, I'd do that. But I would also create a set of PowerPoint slides graphing the results against the size and status of each customer—and then the number of likely customers in each sales channel. *And* I'd include an appendix charting out the *next* five features clients wanted, too! I ended up working a lot of overtime, but my boss loved me. She found my work invaluable and ultimately promoted me to Director of Strategy. That's one way my Perfectionist has helped me.

What about your I.C.? Make a list of all the ways your critic has proven itself an unlikely asset.

What's Useful and What Isn't?

Looking back, it's clear that the useful aspect of my Perfectionist critic was anticipating and exceeding people's expectations—and this aspect is worth keeping. The less useful part I could have tossed overboard—being a workaholic who logged upwards of 80 hours a week. I can see that while my autopilot operational behavior serves me, it comes with a cost. When I raise my awareness to what's useful and what isn't, I can move from a reactionary stance (I *must* exceed expectations) to a more discerning stance where I have choices (I choose to work less than 40 hours a week). Now I decide *when* to exceed someone's expectations—and I step into that decision with my eyes wide open.

INNER CRITIC — INNER SUCCESS

What aspect of your I.C. has served you well? And what are you ready to toss? Is there a middle ground you can stand on—are there certain instances where you see value in engaging that aspect which has served you in the past?

Grey Matters—Embracing Both/And Thinking

I'm so excited to introduce this concept! It's created so much space and fluidity in my life and I know it's going to do the same for you! OK, let me explain. Most of us tend to view things in a binary way—either this is true *or* that is true. In the book, *Built to Last*, Jim Collins and Jerry Porras call this the "Tyranny of the OR"—the kind of thinking that pushes people to believe things must be either A OR B; they can never be both. For example, I often hear clients say, "I love the work I do now" OR, "I could become a manager," meaning they can either be an individual contributor doing the work they love OR they become a manager and therefore will have to forsake the tasks they formerly enjoyed. And while it's true that being promoted invariably means learning to delegate, I challenge my clients around their beliefs that they have to choose between one OR the other—I challenge them to open up to a BOTH/AND approach. Collins and Porras note that it is a habit of "highly visionary companies [to] embrace BOTH extremes AND a number of dimensions at the same time." I encourage you to adopt this invaluable philosophy. It may help you become a highly visionary individual *and* see beyond your critic messages.

Initially, my clients are resistant when I suggest they think outside the box. "Just for a second," I'll say, "let's dream that anything is possible. If anything is possible, and if you could do a little bit of hands on work AND be a manager, what would that look like?"

"But that's just the way it is," most clients will respond, resignedly. "You don't understand. If you understood, you'd see that there are no other options."

I get it. It can be hard to contemplate unlimited possibilities. It's oftentimes easier and more comfortable to fit things into nice, neat little boxes, particularly when you're talking about human behavior and human endeavor. We prefer solid, binary choices—black or white, this or that. But it's a very stifling way to approach life. Instead, why not try vetting out the grey matter between black and white or, better yet, all the colors in the spectrum of possibility?

Nitya's passion is giving back. But it was fixed in her mind that her boss would never allow her to expand the scope of her role to include creating community within her company. She couldn't even contemplate that it might be possible to fuse her passion and her job. "Did you ask him?" I said. She shook her head. "No, I didn't." Nitya's critic had stopped her. "Why bother?" it said. "You're never going to get the go ahead." Nitya needed to build her resilience around asking for what she wanted in order to explore the grey area that might exist between working at this large Fortune 100 company AND giving back. With a little prompting from me, we explored possible ways to combine her job and bring in some non-profit fund raising. By exploring the possibilities she found the courage to ask. Her boss loved her ideas and asked her to write up a proposal, which he subsequently green-lighted. Nitya created a wildly successful program built around her values of community and teamwork and fund-raising and giving back. It proved so effective that it's since been rolled out in other offices. And as a side bonus, she got to practice a whole new skill: asking for what she wants, especially when she explores ideas without limitations—which has become an important ongoing practice for Nitya. Sometimes she gets a no, but she gets yes often enough that she's becoming increasingly comfortable thinking outside the box and putting her requests out on the table—which allows her to live more and more in the grey area that exists between A AND B.

I see the "Tyranny of the OR" wreak havoc in all areas of clients' lives. A lot of guilt-ridden working moms tell me, "I can either be a working mom OR I can stay at home and take care of my kids"—as if those are the only two choices available to them. Yet, lots of mothers have figured out all sorts of ways to have successful, thriving, satisfying careers AND spend quality time with their kids. One client works from home two days a week. Another created a flexible schedule around a 2 pm–8 pm break for family time at home (she works from 8 am–2 pm, and then from 8 pm–10 pm). As long as she gets her job done, her boss is happy.

And don't believe for one second I don't also share this limiting way of viewing the world. My rational, logical brain (and my Inner Critic) would much rather there be One Right Answer. Remember my story about asking my muse and mentor, Mitch, how to become a coach? I was mired in the black, sticky mud of OR thinking: I could stay at my Microsoft job where I was less than happy OR I could go to grad school to pursue my dream career. When Mitch had the audacity to suggest that I keep working AND try grad school for a semester, it was a full-on mental pileup. My rational brain almost busted an axle trying to hold both possibilities at once! However, it proved a pivotal turning point—I embraced BOTH AND went for it.

BOTH/AND activities are extremely valuable tools for moving beyond limited thinking and into bigger possibilities, both on a personal and a group level. At a recent corporate leadership team workshop I facilitated, I sat down with the group to review one of their mission statements. It had supported their success—and unfortunately had created a widespread case of Imposter Syndrome throughout the company. The statement, "Never Settle," had created super high standards for their products and their people—so much so, many of them felt they could never be good enough.

I charged the team with taking that statement (along with some others) and finding completely different ways to view it and utilize it. At first the team resisted, arguing that it was a great guiding principle; why change it if it worked? I agreed: It had worked. *And* to stretch themselves even more, they could practice thinking of more possibilities! This team loves a challenge so, of course, they took the bait. And they rocked the assignment, finding completely new ways to stay true to their impeccable standards AND ensure their people knew when they were doing great work. Once they were willing to explore they realized it was less about the guiding principle needing to change than about a pattern of behavior. They had meetings where they pointed out every detail of what was wrong in a services plan, rendering the project manager of said plan feeling completely inadequate. That wasn't the team's intention. They wanted to ensure they never settled and covered every aspect of a plan. Now they still point out critical problems *and* they point out where the project manager is headed in the right direction. The team also expanded "Never Settle" to include employee engagement and motivation, raising their own standards of how they will lead people to do their best.

"There's no use trying," she said, "one can't believe impossible things."
"I daresay you haven't had much practice," said the Queen.
"When I was your age, I always did it for half-an-hour a day.
Why, sometimes I've believed as many as six impossible things before breakfast." —Lewis Carroll, Alice in Wonderland

ACTIVITY: Explore the Grey Area

Try it on for size: What area of your Inner Critic and Inner Success stories could use a trip down the rabbit hole by way of some deep "unlimited possibility" space exploration? What tales have you been telling yourself that have a distinct black/white, either/or feel? Use your favorite method of journaling now and write them down. Now, ask yourself how you can see things differently. Replace "or" with "both/and" and see what possibilities present themselves.

To get your possibility vibes flowing, I invite you to peruse some recent examples from my clients, each of which had stemmed initially from inner critic limiting narratives.

- I could become a Director OR I could maintain the great work/life balance I have now.

- *What does it look like to be a Director AND have a healthy life balance? How could my life balance look different AND be just as satisfying after putting myself forward for promotion?*
- I can stay at X company where I enjoy a good salary and great benefits OR I can try finding work I love but be broke.
  - *What salary RANGE would be enough to support my family AND is there work I'd enjoy doing in that range? On a scale of one to ten, how much do I need /want to love my job?*
- I could accept the challenge of managing people on a bigger project yet risk looking like a fool OR I could stay where I am, and stay abreast of emerging technologies so I maintain my technical chops.
  - *Who do I admire for their technical knowledge AND their people management skills? What can I learn from them? Let's imagine I'm doing an enormously successful job at leading people—how important would my technical skills be then? How could I realistically maintain my technical skill growth AND manage people? Would I be willing to try that for a year?*
- Either I change my work routine completely OR give up the idea that I can exercise regularly.
  - *Can I explore different ideas of "regular" exercise? If my work routine isn't structured enough to plan, can my exercise be unplanned? What would it take to be fifty percent more satisfied with the amount of exercise I'm getting AND not change my work schedule?*
- There's no way I can succeed in this division; it's a boy's club at the top. I have to be satisfied with what I've achieved thus far OR I have to leave and seek success elsewhere.
  - *How could I combine my own definition of success AND work within the company's definition? Are there any examples from the past where I've been successful in a difficult culture? How could I define success differently within this company AND within my work group?*

The Possibilities In Your Shadow

We're going to step back from the pool table to take yet another look at your Inner Critic—this time, as an aspect of your personality that you've kept hidden because you've deemed it unacceptable, undesirable or unbecoming. This neglected part of oneself is often referred to as a "shadow." Sometimes a shadow has echoes of the Inner Critic. But while a shadow sounds like a typical negative I.C. message, it could actually be something you *need* to pay attention to, something that wants and needs to see the light of day. I've one such critical voice that warns me, "Don't get too high on your horse, Stacey." I've discovered that rather than a regular critic, this voice is actually a shadow side of me that craves attention—it aches to play on a bigger stage and play a bigger game. This shadow represents an aspect of me that's longing to be heard, longing to be accepted and longing to become *part* of me. Only I've denied it because it runs contrary to one of my family's values—humility. I've denied it, negative-ized it and horrible-ized it, effectively turning it into an Inner Critic.

Debbie Ford describes shadow work brilliantly as a co-author of the book *The Shadow Effect: Illuminating the Hidden Power of Your True Self.* Her view of the shadow is similar to how I want you to think about your Inner Critic.

> I believe that the shadow is one of the greatest gifts available to us. Carl Jung called it a "sparring partner"; it is the opponent within us that exposes our flaws and sharpens our skills. It is the teacher, the trainer, and the guide that supports us in uncovering our true magnificence. The shadow is not a problem to be solved or an enemy to be conquered but a fertile field to be cultivated. When we dig our hands into its rich soil, we will discover the potent seeds of the people we most desire to be.

Maggie's shadow manifests as a critical voice that tells her, "You'd better not let them see your soft side; no one respects a Softie!" In Maggie's mind, soft is a negative characterization, because she believes that softness and business are mutually exclusive. In reality, Maggie's big heart is one of her greatest assets—she's emotional and she's intuitive, and these are two of her greatest gifts.

However, she's terrified to reveal that side of her at work. Instead, she hides behind her Professional persona, which is very rational, very rigid and very cold. Maggie believes that if she shows up as her complete self—equal parts aggressive and yielding, hard and soft—people won't take her seriously.

When we explored what was positive and possible in Maggie's I.C. message, we discovered that her passion, drive, creativity and integrity all come from her heart. What she negatively labels "soft" is actually integral to her success, but she keeps it in the shadows—afraid to let it be seen. As a result, Maggie's colleagues only see her mechanical, analytical side, which makes it very hard for them to relate to her, connect with her and, frankly, to like her. Another cost of keeping her emotions bottled up is that Maggie stifles her creativity, her energy and her joy. It's no surprise that work has become a serious drag.

Maggie's homework is to see the value of her "soft" side and draw it out from the shadows. She utilized several of the tools in this book, including the Truth Series questions (from chapter four) which she used to explore the statements, "They won't accept me if I show my heart," and, "They only want the rational, methodical me at work." I asked Maggie to explore possible and positive ways to reframe her critical statement by substituting "soft" with other words she was less hooked by (i.e., having a highly charged emotional response to the word, similar to a "Hot Word"), such as care, integrity and heart. My goal for Maggie is that she get very clear about the real and tangible costs of denying this shadow aspect of herself—so that ultimately her fear of those costs outweighs her fear of being judged a "Softie."

It's likely that you, too, have a hidden "shadow" aspect that's gasping for breath because it needs to emerge into the light of day.

Externalized Shadows

Sometimes the shadow shows up as an Outer Critic whereby you become hyper-critical of someone else because they represent who you *want* to be but won't allow yourself to be. If you find yourself saying, "I *hate* the way John does this," it's possible that John has that quality you wish to draw out in yourself.

I once worked with a guy who would utter these grand, sweeping statements with so much confidence and conviction, he would leave his audience in no doubt but that his words represented scientifical-ly-proven facts. It used to set me off like a rocket! I'd get triggered, agitated and emotional (chapter three, where are you when I need you?) and I complained about him relentlessly (which is a big clue there's a shadow in play). When I finally settled down and spent some time examining my over-the-top reaction, I realized this man had something that I, in fact, craved: Confidence. I wanted to be the kind of leader who's *that* confident, to say the things I hesitated to say, and then didn't, because they weren't scientifically proven facts. Instead, I'd cave to my Inner Critic, who constantly challenged my beliefs and questioned whether I *really* knew what I was talking about. The thing is, on some level I did know. And deep down in my gut I knew that if I could have the courage and the confidence just to say it, like my colleague did, I'd be a profoundly more influential, inspiring and insightful coach and facilitator and therefore could help people even more that I was doing.

Once I became aware of the heightened reactions and judgment, I could name it for what it was—my own shadow. I could remind myself that I was in fact envious of this person's confidence and conviction. And I made a mental note to find my own version of his confidence. Because the truth was that I do, in fact, know a great deal more than I give myself credit for. I just needed to own it *and* have the confidence to speak it.

" *You have only one self. It is the real you. It is beyond good and evil. —Debbie Ford,* The Shadow Effect: Illuminating the Hidden Power of Your True Self

Light Shadows

When I was in grad school, I was awed by one of my professors. She was intelligent, witty, wise, compassionate and had a wealth of experience under her belt. I respected and admired her deeply, I hung on every word she uttered—and I was totally intimidated by her.

One day, during a progress meeting, I began showering her with compliments that communicated that effect. She paused for a moment, then told me that while she appreciated my words, she felt a disconnect between us. "It's really hard to have an authentic relationship with you when you've got me on a pedestal," she told me. "I feel a lot of pressure to live up to this idealized image, Stacey. I'd really rather just be me." As someone who prides herself on authentic relationships, I was stunned.

She went on to suggest that I might be projecting some of my own strengths onto her, probably because I wasn't yet sure of my own skills. She asked me to take the tiara I'd placed on her head and instead make it my own—and wear it proudly. First, I had to get over the word tiara (I was a basketball player, not a dang prom queen). Then, being the Perfectionist I am, I took her advice way too literally. I went to a friend who handcrafts crowns for weddings and together we created the crown of all crowns, which represented my strengths and skills, newly acknowledged by me. I wore that crown to my next meeting with my professor and thanked her for helping me see myself, and for giving me the impetus and the courage to own my own greatness.

I call this distant cousin of an Externalized Shadow the Light or Positive side of your Shadow. It still trips me up. A couple of years ago, I fell into a state of deep admiration of Brené Brown and her work, to such an extent I began to question my own abilities. One day, a good friend of mine noted, "You know Stacey, the way you talk about Brené reminds me of how you used to talk about your professor. I wonder if you need a new crown?" It is so good to have smart friends but I was disappointed I'd done it again.

"Don't worry," my friend reassured me, "it happens to the best of us."

ACTIVITY: Explore Your Shadows

What aspects of yourself have you been suppressing or denying? Who do you publicly criticize (but privately envy)? Who have you placed on a pedestal? Who's wearing your crown? Use the following questions to explore what's lurking in your shadows:

- Is there a prominent part of your personality that you stifle because you believe it isn't "right" or acceptable—at work, at home, or among your friends? What is that trait? What might you or others be missing out on by keeping it in the shadow?

- Are there certain people and/or characteristics that consistently trigger you and bug the heck out of you in a way that seems disproportionate and/or more emotional than the situation warrants? These are either traits that truly go against your values and beliefs—or they're aspects of a shadow side of you that are begging to be claimed and brought into the light.

- Is there someone who makes you so star-struck you've become blind to your own greatness? Debbie Ford suggests making a list of the characteristics you admire in that person. Then do an honest assessment of whether or not you possess those qualities or strengths. You may discover you do possess them—but you don't let them out very often because of Inner Critic messages or Rules in Play that say they aren't appropriate or desirable or socially acceptable. Make a choice: do you want to leave them hidden, or practice bringing them out of the shadow and use them rather than admiring them from afar?

Getting Outside Your Own Head (a.k.a. Gathering Feedback)

You've been discovering different ways to look at the critic and gain a new perspective—which necessitated re-training yourself to not believe everything you think. However, to gain a truly panoramic view of your I.C. data, it's really helpful to hear what *others* think.

You've learned a lot about your I.C. story and the environment in which it thrives. You've seen how your own beliefs as well as the external beliefs of your family, culture, religion, ethnicity and society at large make up your mental model—the way you see the world and operate in it (chapter four). Now, if everybody on the planet has their own unique mental model, then it holds true that yours is but one of billions. So, a great way to not believe everything you think is to find out what *other* people think.

You do this by gathering information—other people's perspectives on topics related to your I.C. story. While some of you will relish this, I know it will intimidate the rest of you. Usually, it's a little bit of both (as in BOTH/AND thinking, cue drum roll). My best advice is to start with someone you trust—someone you absolutely know has your best interests at heart. You'll be asking him to share his perspective on your Inner Critic, which is something that already feels vulnerable and scary. So this is *not* the time to "push yourself" by choosing a person you might label as "direct." You're already hard enough on yourself, don't add to it. Your goal is to expand your self-awareness, not take an emotional beating! Choose someone you feel safe being vulnerable with.

Get Feedback to Challenge Your IC

Does the word "feedback" make your stomach churn? Yeah, me too. That's because in the business world feedback has become a hair shy of a four-letter word. In leadership and team development, it's one of the most informative and powerful processes a coach can use. However, far too often feedback is used as an opportunity to point out everything that's wrong with you, and all the ways you could and should do things better. (You're familiar with the political games I'm referring to, right?)

My workshops on effectively giving and receiving feedback take up a whole day, so it would take another entire book to share my tips here. However, I will share the most effective tips since the more you practice reaching out to others, the greater the impact this book will have on your life.

There are two components of feedback that, when combined, provide the most relevant and actionable value to the receiver. These are behavior and impact.

1. **Behavior** refers to indisputable factual data observed by the feedback giver. Think of it in terms of what a video camera would pick up, for example:

   a. "Rick walked into Thursday's strategy meeting 10 minutes late."

   b. "When we talked Friday about the project update, the volume of Ira's voice rose and he made dramatic, emphatic movements with his hands."

2. **Impact** refers to the effect the feedback receiver's behavior had on the giver—in other words, your thoughts and feelings around the indisputable facts. It's wildly important to remember to own this part of the feedback process by using "I" statements, because this represents what *you* thought and what *you* felt. What trips people up most often in sharing feedback—and the main reason people get defensive—is projecting our thoughts and feelings on to others. To illustrate what I mean, let me share some examples of "unhelpful" and "helpful" feedback statements.

   a. Unhelpful: "*You* don't care about my meetings."
   Helpful: "When you walked into the meeting 10 minutes late, it made *me* think you didn't care about *my* agenda and goals, and that bothers *me*. *I* feel disrespected."

   b. Unhelpful: "*You* were angry."
   Helpful: "When *I* hear your voice go up and see your arms flail around, *I* make the assumption that you're angry. *I'm* not sure what to do in those moments; *I* feel intimidated."

Carryn has a tough pair of Perfectionist and Pleaser Critics. Her main I.C. message is: "I'm not a good manager," and according to her I.C., she'll never be good enough. Whenever one of her employees does something wrong, Carryn blames herself. Her Pleaser drives her to make all of her employees happy, all the time and to take full responsibility for all of their actions. Her Perfectionist reminds her that she has to fulfill every management function perfectly—or all her efforts are futile.

Carryn desperately needed external feedback to broaden her view and lend much-needed balance and perspective. I ever so gently coaxed her into sitting down with a peer so she could see herself through someone else's eyes.

"Am I a good manager?" Carryn asked her colleague. "In what areas do you think I excel as a manager? And can you please share some specific examples."

"Yes, you're a good people manager," confirmed Carryn's coworker. "Your people feel like you really care about them."

"Really? How's that?"

"The other day I saw you talking with Jane in the hallway. You were leaning in and nodding hard—it was clear you were *really* listening. I knew you were talking about the late hours she'd have to put in to complete the project you guys are working on. And I know you were asking about the impact it would have on her family."

"Where do I have more to learn in order to be a better manager?" asked Carryn, looking a lot more relaxed. "Please give me some specific examples."

"I notice that sometimes it's hard for you to give constructive feedback. I think you need to make sure you have those tough conversations, whether they make you uncomfortable or not."

"Can you give me a specific example?" asked Carryn, looking a little less comfortable—but still receptive.

"Well, I know you're having issues with Ingrid about the delivery of her project. She's not meeting her deadlines, but instead of talking directly to her, I overheard you discussing it with Todd. You're afraid of putting too much pressure on Ingrid, but she needs to step up to the plate, and you need to remind her of that."

Note how Carryn kept prompting her coworker to get as specific as possible. "You care about your people," is just an opinion. Carryn kept going until she got concrete examples of *how* she demonstrates that she cares—and *how* she backs off having those uncomfortable conversations.

Broaden the View

Adding another's perspective to your own greatly enhances, deepens and widens your view. Adding multiple other perspectives creates a full-on surround-sound, panoramic experience. While it's totally fine to start off with one trusted friend, I encourage you to widen the net and gather feedback from a variety of sources.

To illustrate what I mean, let's revisit Phoebe's story from chapter three. Just to recap, Phoebe felt old, irrelevant and obsolete amongst her decades-younger colleagues at the game studio she'd recently joined. One of my favorite coaching tools is what I call a Stakeholder Review (a.k.a. 360 Review), so named because I select a panel of people who represent a spectrum of a client's managers, peers and direct reports, and interview them for the purpose of gathering feedback. In Phoebe's case, I selected eight people in her company and targeted our feedback-gathering process to focus on her incapacitating Comparer Critic. I posed the following questions to her colleagues in each interview:

- Phoebe has a lot of experience behind her. Of all the knowledge and expertise she brings to the table, what specifically do you value? How important is her experience to the work you guys are doing now? What impact does her experience have for you personally? Please include specific examples.
- When and where do you see Phoebe contributing, both in terms of projects and meetings? From your perspective, is her input sufficient? Would you like to see her give more input or less? Why? Please be specific.

- From your perspective, explain Phoebe's importance to this team and to this company? What specific skills and character traits does she bring to the table that result in concrete results? Please share some examples.

My goal was to understand the **impact** Phoebe had on her colleagues, both in terms of what they thought and how they felt about working with her. I also asked for **behavioral** data. Then, I summarized the major themes and relayed the results to Phoebe, without attributing comments to specific individuals. Phoebe was able to get outside her own head, move beyond her Inner Critic messages and hear what others had to say.

She was shocked to learn that her colleagues—especially her direct reports and peers (all younger!)—placed tremendous value on her 20 years of experience. In fact, each person I interviewed wanted Phoebe to speak up more in meetings and share more of the vast knowledge she'd gained from her prior experiences.

In your case, *you'll* be the one asking the questions. Know that few people have had the opportunity to be trained in healthy feedback-giving skills, so my advice is that you act like a good dance partner. If your interviewee isn't following the practices I've prescribed above, take the lead and help them. Ask for specific examples. Ask them to describe your **behavior** using irrefutable facts. Have them describe your **impact** by sharing how your actions made them *feel* and *think*.

Remember, their time (and yours!) is valuable—use it wisely. The following tips will make sure you don't get sidetracked:

- Ask questions related to the Inner Critic messages that have the strongest (i.e., most negative) impact.
- Focus on your blind spots. Avoid areas where you've already developed a lot of self-awareness and instead target areas where you're lacking the most clarity, data and perspective.
- Focus on your triggers. If your critic persistently challenges you in a particular topic area, ask for multiple specific examples to flesh out the one-dimensional view of your I.C.

- Give your feedback friend a heads up, let them know what you want and why it's important to you. This gives them time to be thoughtful and prepared.

Not all feedback is easy to hear. Sometimes you'll learn that there is some element of truth in your critic message (while you've already discovered this yourself in the Truth Series questions, it's hard to hear it from other people.) However, remind yourself that this knowledge is actually a gift—because you now have the choice to take action on it instead of ruminating on it and allowing it to run circles in your brain.

Phoebe learned that some colleagues wanted her to be more open to creative ideas in her brainstorm sessions—ideas that were off-the-wall and had never been done before. Hearing that hurt for a moment because it reinforced her fuddy-duddy self-image—but only for a moment. After letting it settle and mulling it over, she felt grateful for the specific suggestion because it was something she could act on.

Catching feedback as information

Let me also share another valuable saying: "Feedback is information, not definition." While there's no doubt getting input from others helps give you another viewpoint, you also need to be discerning. Treat the information you receive as data only—not as a definition of who you are. Imagine feedback as a softball that gets lobbed from one of your colleagues toward you. Picture the scene: you've got your baseball mitt on and you put both hands in front of your chest. You catch that ball and "Boom!" it thumps you right in the heart. Ouch! Hurts, right? That's what happens when you receive feedback as something that defines you. Instead, remind yourself that it's simply your colleague's perception of you, based on the information they have about you. This is analogous to catching that softball off to the side, and then taking off your mitt, turning the ball over in your hand and asking what you want to do with this piece of information. Do you want to take it in? Make some sort of change based on it? Or take it in and not make any change because it's not in your best interest to do so.

Finally, I want to cover perhaps the most *essential* feedback skill: to acknowledge and thank your dance partner for having the courage and the willingness to offer honest feedback. Put yourself in their shoes: how hard is it to give feedback, especially when it's not all positive? It's darn tough, right? Most of us hold back or hesitate to give feedback so when someone does accept your invitation to share—and help you win the war against your Inner Critic—**say thank you**. Tell them you appreciate their time and thoughts. Goodness knows we can all stand to hear Thank You more often.

ACTIVITY: Phone a Friend, for Feedback

OK, it's time to start flexing your feedback muscles. Remember, the goal of this exercise is to have your trusted person (and, eventually, people) lend their external perspective to your internal Critic message, allowing you to take a different look. Other people can often see our actions in a much clearer and cleaner way than we can—as long as we *believe* them! As I said, trust is key! Together you'll dig into the data and, from the vantage point of their fresh, unbiased view, they'll be able to point out the good in you—absent your self-critical lens. You'll want offer them some context, explaining some of the activities and results you've found, and that you are now seeking their perspective.

Map out at least an hour—you can do this over the phone, via Skype or, better yet, in person. At the appointed time, come armed with a notebook and pen and be prepared to brainstorm together on the key I.C. activities you've completed thus far, which include:

Chapter Two: Meet the Cast of Inner Critic Characters

• Briefly describe the six Classic Critics to your friend, which critic do they think bothers you most?

* If they could imagine your Inner Critic as a role or character, what would that be? Have them personify the critic for you.

Chapter Three: Know Thyself; Know Thy Critic

• If your friend could hear your Inner Critic, what do they imagine it tells you? (If they know you well enough, it's likely they're already very familiar with your I.C. message!)

• From your friend's perspective, what events, people and/or situations trigger you—to the extent that it provokes an Inner Critic attack?

• What kind of emotions do you typically display in these moments?

• What's your default coping mechanism?

Chapter Four: Show Me the Data!

• Share your most prominent I.C. message (choose the one that's most charged at that moment in time) and have your friend run through the Truth Series drill (i.e., Is it 100% true?) with your message. Remind them that it's a yes or no answer. Assuming their answer is no (which I'm fully sure it will be), ask what about the statement is more true? And what about it is less true. Ask them to give you specific examples.

• Ask them to share what Hot Words they think might trigger you.

• Have they ever noticed you playing by internal Rules in Play that they believe you could and should update?

Chapter Five: Take a Different Look

• Given what they already know about your Inner Critic and what they've just learned, ask if there are any ways in which they see how your I.C. might have helped you? Ask what's useful in your critic message (a keeper) and what isn't (toss it)?

• What characteristics, traits or strengths have they seen you stifle (that perhaps you shouldn't)?

- What's the greatest asset you possess, but rarely utilize?
- Do they see any similarities between you and people you admire?

As I mentioned in chapter one, I'm a huge proponent of sharing your story with others and capitalizing on your strongest, most enriching relationships to enhance and enrich the activities in this book. So, I'll be suggesting that you seek out others' perspectives again as we roll through the Inner Success side. Consider yourself warned!

A Provocative New Perspective

Congratulations! You've been both adventurous and brave in challenging your Inner Critic worldview, and in so doing you've had a radical shift in how you see yourself and your negative self-talk. Now, I'm about to ask you to shift perspectives yet again to take a very unorthodox and potentially challenging view. I want you to consider the idea that having inner doubts and fears is actually normal. Yes, I said it: normal.

Normalizing the Critic

The reality is, I've not yet met a human being who doesn't have an Inner Critic. Sure, the intensity varies from person to person—from barely there, to low burn, lukewarm, tepid-water-sitting-on-the-table, getting warmer, yep, it's hot now, ouch! From, it's white hot, to ouchie coal burn! But no one, and I mean no one, gets a free pass. In my book, that counts as normal. So if that's the case, can't we all just cut ourselves some slack and engage in a little bit of, dare I say it, *acceptance* of our Inner Critic?

The Cocktail-Free Mixer (a.k.a. Index Card Activity)

In chapter one, I shared the slightly unorthodox way I kick off my Inner Critic Inner Success workshops: the cocktail mixer with a twist (a.k.a. the Index Card Activity). To give you a quick recap: I give everyone a blank three-inch-by-five-inch index card on which to write their top two most frequently recurring I.C. messages—the ones that feel most alive or heated that week, that day, or at that moment. I then ask them to stand up, walk around the room, approach someone, introduce them-selves—and exchange cards. "Read their card," I instruct my horrified audience, "look them in the eye, show your appreciation for sharing with you, and then move on to the next person with their card in your hand—and yours in theirs."

Without fail, you can feel the room literally suck in its collective gut, as anywhere from 30 to 100 people give me the stink eye. I know what they're thinking:

- "Are you kidding me?"
- "You're *seriously* asking me to do this?"
- "*Whoa*! I didn't sign up for this!"
- "I wonder is anyone would notice if I slipped quietly outside. . . ."

You can feel the tension. "Did everyone feel that?" I'll ask, acknowl-edging the feeling in the room. "This is an E.I. moment—you're all acutely aware of your emotions right now. I know most of you are cring-ing, but I'm going to ask you to trust me on this one. And don't worry," I joke, "cocktails come later." That usually breaks the ice.

When I say, "Ready, set, go," people—including me—reluctantly stand up and start moving around, making introductions and exchang-ing cards. I have to share my own I.C. message or it wouldn't be fair (and to this day, I still get nervous!). The noise level in the room slowly amplifies as people start circulating. After about 10 minutes—enough time to mingle with five people—I call time.

Once everyone settles back in their seats, I ask how they felt as they stood up and started to circulate. Nervous, embarrassed, tense, mor-tified, exposed, terrified—this is the feedback I hear time and again. "What about *after*," I ask. "How did you feel *after* you'd read a couple of cards?" Without fail, I'll hear some variation on the following:

- "I was shocked. I thought, 'Wow! I'm not alone!'"

- "I felt sad as I wondered why we're all so hard on ourselves."
- "I felt disbelief. I had someone else's card in my hand, but it could have been mine—I wrote almost the *exact* same thing."
- "I feel a little better, strangely, because now I know I'm not alone."

The *raison d'être* for this activity is to normalize the I.C.—to show people that it's actually normal to have one. Everyone does. After my most recent workshop, Lydia shared that when she first sat down and looked around that morning, she'd spotted a woman sitting two rows up and a little to the left. She was well dressed, polished, pretty and confident as she sat and chatted easily with the person on her right. "Oh man," thought Lydia, "she has it made. She's sitting there, oozing self-confidence and smelling of success. God, I wish I was like her." Later, as Lydia stood reading this woman's card—on which she'd written, "I'm scared I'm not good enough at my job. I feel like I'm always watching my back."—Lydia realized that despite external appearances, *everyone* has worries, fears and doubts. You can make up any story you want about a person based on your first impression, but I guarantee you there's more going on beneath the surface than you can possibly know.

Sharing What Thrills and Terrifies You

Don't try this at home—unless you *do* provide cocktails! Just kidding, they're not a prerequisite to hosting your own version of my Mixer. However, I do strongly advise that you soften the exercise by including both ends of the spectrum—that is, what scares you *and* what thrills you? Or, what keeps you up at night worrying *and* what entices you out of bed in the morning?

I recently invited a group of team leaders at a large services organization to do this version of the Index Card Activity. The number two guy in the group, a man with a lot of power and rank, stood up and spoke about what gets him excited—his values, his leadership style, what motivates him. When I asked what keeps him up at night, there was a pause. You could tell it required a huge amount of courage to admit,

"I'm afraid of making a mistake." I asked if he could be more specific. "No," he replied. "I'm afraid of making *any* mistake."

Silence. You could have heard a pin drop. Everyone was thinking, "*Whoa!* He's the smartest guy in the room—and *he's* afraid of making a mistake?"

It took so much courage for this guy to share his biggest fear, but by admitting to it, he normalized it—and made it so much easier for the rest of his team to follow suit. Admitting to self-doubt is usually taboo in the business world, but there's so much of it in the workplace! The sooner we all start talking about doubts, the sooner we'll begin to trust each other more and the sooner we'll start to feel more connected. That's exactly what happened with this team: after spending a day learning more about each other—both the passion and the pain—they felt much tighter as a group. In fact, they decided to have all their teams do the same workshop because it had such a transformative effect on their ability to trust and connect with one another. Isn't that what we all crave?

Emotions Are Normal

Joy is normal. Happiness is normal. Excitement is normal. So too are fear, doubt and worry. You don't get to appreciate just how normal until you start to share—and normalize—your dreams *and* your fears. That's why telling your story is such a profound exercise. I want you to know that as you're sitting there reading this book, many others are reading it, too, because they also want to learn how to tame their Inner Critic. It's not just you, we all have I.C. moments. It's totally normal.

You may be wondering: if everyone has an I.C., and we can't get rid of it, then why did Stacey write this book? To prove to you that it's normal so you can let yourself off the hook. To teach you how to use some awesome tools so your critic doesn't pack nearly as much of a punch. And to show how your I.C. is intrinsically linked to some seriously valuable things you won't want to miss out on—which is a whole other perspective we'll get to in the next chapter.

6

Your Divine Flaw

All right, this is it—the money chapter. This is the big moment, the big transition, the big enchilada, so pay close attention. *This* is where I get most excited as a coach because it's such a leverage point for change. This is where the gold sits, awaiting discovery. This is where the mystery and the clarity co-exist. This is where an incoming storm meets blue sky and suddenly the horizon turns a stunningly beautiful blend of orange, purple, and gray. Okay, enough chatter. What's the money point?

Our Inner Critics, self-doubts and fears are part of a dynamic relationship with what's most important to us. They point us towards our greatest gifts, what really matters and what makes us super-successful. The two opposing forces—self-doubt on one end of the spectrum and success on the other—are *not* mutually exclusive. Rather, their co-existence can help reveal just how we can leverage our best selves to tame the critic. *This* is the dynamic relationship that I want you to explore.

I want you to get a ton out of this book. But of all the possibilities, perspectives and philosophies I'm asking you to explore, *this* is the one I want you to put all your money on—Texas Hold 'Em style. *This* is your Divine Flaw.

In literature, a "tragic flaw" is a personality trait that ultimately leads to the downfall of the central character. In this book, a "divine flaw" is that aspect of you that's unique and important—because it's integral to your life and who you are. It's also part of what gets you hooked up in the spiral of self-doubt and harsh Inner Critic attacks. It's responsible for your greatness *and* how hard you are on yourself.

Words have power to convey ideas, emotions and values. For instance, I use the word *success* because it has the power to grab our imaginations. And I use the word *divine* for the same reason: because it has power. I want to emphasize how important, integral and special these aspects of you are.

Discovering my Divine Flaw was a major turning point in my journey from Inner Critic to Inner Success. It was an "Aha!" moment when I realized that there's a very real and very illuminating relationship between my I.C. and that which I care most about—i.e., the essential ingredients required for a life that feels Success-full to *me*.

How I Learned about My Divine Flaw

When I was in graduate school, I took a course to learn how to design and facilitate group sessions. One week, we were given an assignment to design a session around the theme of diversity and to facilitate it in front of our faculty and peers. We could focus on any element of diversity— gender, ethnicity, religion, etc. "Fantastic!" I thought. "I'm passionate about diversity and inclusion. I'm gonna knock this assignment out of the ballpark!" I worked tirelessly as I created and recreated, shaped and reshaped, tweaked and refined my design, like, a thousand times.

And then I delivered. It went . . . okay. It was . . . fine. I received a passing grade, but my spirits were crushed. It didn't matter that I'd passed. It. What mattered was the impact wasn't what I'd hoped it would be. And, therefore, all the work I'd put in was in vain; my inner Perfectionist had been triggered, and she was *raging*. "You bombed!" she yelled at me. "You ruined it! Your presentation was a complete waste of everyone's time! How can these people *stand* you?" Ouch. It stung. I was miserable.

Knowing me and my self-critical tendencies only too well, my professor, Pam Johnson, pulled me aside. She asked a bunch of questions about how I'd approached my project and as I talked her through my process, it became clear to both of us that I'd fallen into my old pattern of over-working something to death in an attempt to make it *perfect*. As a result, it was too much—the design was too complicated, the expectations too unrealistic, the delivery too heavy-handed. I asked Pam how I could fix my problem, i.e., make my perfectionism disappear—forever.

Pam asked me *why* I'd tried so hard. I told her I'd wanted my training course to be the best it could possibly be because I care very deeply about helping people. Like *really* helping people—in a way that sticks. Pam explained to me that this is my "divine flaw." My "flaw" of perfectionism showed up because of my "divinity"—my deep-rooted value around helping people in a very meaningful way.

Pam told me I could probably get rid of my perfectionist tendency. I practically jumped into her lap asking how, how, how can I get rid of this horrible aspect of my character? She softly laughed the laugh of the wise and generous. "Stacey," she said, "to get rid of your obsession with perfection, and stop being so hard on yourself when you fall short, you merely have to give up caring so much about helping people." My body sagged. I'd been hoping for the elusive silver bullet—a simple answer to getting rid of my critic. But her solution wasn't going to work for me, because everything in me knew I couldn't make the trade. My passion for helping people was non-negotiable. In that moment, I had the realization that the most important matters in my life would come with difficulties I would have to manage—like trying to keep my perfectionism at bay while I lived out that divine aspect of me that was compelled to help others.

In that moment, I also saw very clearly that when my I.C. appears, it's because one of my core values is in play. Rather than allowing my critic to steamroll me—and allow my value to become a "tragic flaw" that leads to my downfall—Pam helped me see the critic message as a deep-rooted value. Seen in this way, it became something positive and powerful—my Divine Flaw.

Pam helped me define my own Divinity—those parts of me that are so vital and important, what I care about so deeply. Since then, I have adapted and built upon the term and it's become a cornerstone to my Inner Critic Inner Success work. On a personal level, it's one of my most used techniques for dealing with a critic attack. In this chapter, you'll learn how to recognize *your* Divine Flaw, so you can catch your critic early—and shift from negative message to positive value in a flash.

As I said earlier, this is the point in the book where we get to the cool stuff—the hidden treasures that make you worth your weight in gold!

"Divine Flaw *is a flow of energy and emotion around those things that are most meaningful, powerful and significant to us—and therefore where our Inner Critic is most likely to attack. When the critic strikes, it's a signal to shift our energy back to the positive end of the spiral by reminding ourselves of what really matters.*

The Infinity Spiral

This little symbol has proven invaluable in understanding the interconnectedness of all things—especially the Divine (Success) and the Flaw (Critic). The infinity spiral inspired the logo for my business, the graphic on the book cover, and the rubber band on the back cover. I even have it tattooed on my arm as a constant reminder that everything is connected in a universal way. In fact, I use the symbol so much, I'm proud to say that many of my clients have appropriated it for their own use!

One part of the spiral represents your Divinity and another, your Flaw. You might also use it to represent a strength on one side and a liability—a strength that's over-used—on the other. The important thing to remember is that the symbol represents a *flow* of energy that's in constant motion—sometimes fast and unsteadying; at other times slow and stabilizing. There are times when I'm in a smooth, healthy flow, minding my own business and staying close to the Divine side of the spiral when, suddenly and without warning, my energy scoots way back towards the Flaw as my Inner Critic gets triggered. However, as long as I remember it's just a flow of energy, and I focus my mental and emotional energy on my Divinity, I can shift the energy back, if not all the way to the Divine side, then at least to a healthy middle ground.

The significance of the spiral

The dual spiral is a symbol found on many artifacts dating back thousands of years, spanning many cultures and continents. Interestingly, it always represents a similar concept: the inter-connectedness of all things. In some cultures, it stood for the sun and moon—how they worked in concert to provide for the earth. Spirals have also appeared in mathematical fractals, like the Fibonacci Spiral, and in biological organisms, for example the Nautilus shell, one of the most basic building blocks found in nature. I chose this dual spiral as my logo because it reflects my belief that all things are inter-related. My philosophy is that growth and development work truly begins by connecting to the self: learning more about who you are, what you do and why. When you find the appropriate connection to work on, this positive, personal impact has a percussive, expansive effect on relationships and organizations reflecting multiple, growing connections.

Mining the Depths of the Flaw and the Divine

While it may seem counterintuitive, the best place to search for clues about your Divinity is in the derogatory words of your I.C. We're going to take a look at your I.C. message to see what it has to say about who you are, what you value the most, and what gifts you bring to the world. In other words, we're going to find the positivity in the critic's negativity. Yes! There is goodness buried beneath the bad and it awaits those brave enough to look. This is where the diamond is revealed amidst the dust, and it's MasterCard priceless!

While conducting my Inner Critic workshop at an event in Paris, France, Aliene volunteered to help me demonstrate the Mining the Depths exercise. Standing on a continuum line at one end of the room, I had her first look all the way to the left, which represented the "negative end," and then to the right (the "positive end"). We started out by exhausting the bad in the negative: I explained that I would ask a series of questions about Aliene's I.C. message, and each time she answered, we would each take one step towards the negative end of the line. Here's how our conversation played out.

"Aliene, what's your core I.C. message? By this I mean, what's the message you hear most often, or what's the one that feels hottest for you this minute?" [Standing at the center of the line]

"I'm not organized enough. I should be more organized." [We both step to the left]

"You're not organized enough. Ok. What's comes next, the next thing your I.C. tells you?"

"I'm cluttery and I'm messy." [We take another step to the left]

"You're not organized enough, you're cluttery and you're messy. What's the next thing you tell yourself?"

"My messiness and my cluttery-ness create a picture of who I am—I'm a messy and cluttery person." [We take another step]

"You're not organized enough, you're cluttery and you're messy, and that makes you feel like a messy and cluttery person. When you're thinking this, what comes next? Is there another negative message?"

"I'm messy and cluttery, and my husband doesn't like that." [Another step left]

"Oh, ok. You're not organized enough, you're cluttery and you're messy, and that makes you feel like a messy and cluttery person, and your husband doesn't like that. How's that make you feel, or what does it make you think of next?"

"My husband's totally organized; he's not messy or cluttery at

all, and we just don't fit together. I'm just not as good as him."
[Another step]

"Ok. You're not organized, you're cluttery and you're messy, and that makes you feel like a messy and cluttery person, and your husband doesn't like that. He's very organized, so you just don't fit together. And you're not as good as him. How's that make you feel?"

"I'm afraid he can't stand my messiness. I'm afraid he's going to leave me." [We take another step]

[I take a deep breath and look at Aliene because it's a big moment; I can see fear and uncertainty in her eyes.] "Wow. OK. You're afraid he's going to leave you."

By now, we're standing at end of the continuum line, all the way to the left. Together, we turn and look back toward the center of the room—which seems like a long way away.

"Aliene, you're scared your husband is going to leave you. . . . It feels pretty awful here, huh? Do you see when you mine the critic message you move all the way from that center point to here? From 'I'm not organized enough' to 'My husband's going to leave me?'"

"Do you see what happens when the critic goes off and is allowed run amok, totally unchecked? Do you see how quickly and easily your message can snowball into something out-of-control that's exponentially worse than the statement you started with?"

"Aliene, thank you for being so courageous in sharing this with us. Everyone here has had some version of this experience where we spiral pretty far out there. I ask you to do this because it's extremely important to explore the negative side of your I.C. message to find some important information about what matters to you. Now that we know that territory well, it's time to vet out the positive side. Let's walk back to the center, shall we? OK. Remind us again, what's your starting I.C. message?

"I'm not organized enough. I should be more organized."

"Why does that matter? Why is it important that you be organized?"

"I care about being organized because I don't want to be messy. I

want to have things together." [We take a step toward the posi-
tive end of the line, to the right.]

"You care about being organized because you want to have things together. Why is that important, why does having things together matter to you?"

"If I have things together, I'm getting a lot done in my life—I'm accomplishing a lot." [We taken another step to the right.]

"You care about being organized, because you want to have things together, because that makes you feel like you're accomplishing a lot. Any ideas around what kinds of things matter to you when you're accomplishing a lot?"

"It matters when I'm taking care of my family." [And another step.]

"Oh, OK. You're doing great. You care about being organized because you want to have things together because that makes you feel like you're taking care of your family. Is your family your husband? Do you have kids, too?"

"Yes, it's my husband. We don't have children." [And another.]

"You care about being organized, because you want to have things together, because that makes you feel like you're taking care of your husband. Why is it important that you take care of your husband?"

"Because . . ." [Long pause. She got stuck.]

"Don't make this more complicated than it is, Aliene. Why is it important to you that you take care of your husband?"

"Because I love him." [Another step to the right.]

"OK. You love him. Good. It's important for you to take care of your family because you love your husband?"

"Yeah, I really love my husband. He's so amazing."

By now, we're all the way to the right. Together we turn around and look back towards the center.

"Aliene, you started at, 'I should be more organized,' but beneath that I.C. message lies something that's positive and really, really important to you—your love for your husband. Do you see how both ends of the line directly relate to each other? On that end your husband leaves you and on this end you love him?"

"Wow. I had absolutely no idea these things would come out."

"Can you see that you care a great deal about accomplishing things that make your husband feel loved and cared for? Can you see how your love for your husband is related to your desire to be organized?"

"Yes. Wow. I just get stuck hammering on myself for being messy. I never realized what else was going on."

"Aliene, this is one of your Divine Flaws. You hammer on being messy, but next time that happens I want you to remember <u>why</u> you hammer: because you want to care for your husband. When you make that shift, it will be easier to take action—get organized, clean up your desk, or just be more relaxed about being messy."

"I feel so relieved right now."

At this point, everyone in the room clapped and whooped like crazy (in a totally chic French way), and several people reached out to Aliene as she walked back to her seat. I asked all of the people if the room to raise their hands if they could relate to Aliene's story in some way—almost everyone raised their hands. Yes, it's a human experience—we're not alone.

When you really get in there and start to dig and drill beneath your I.C. message, you'll be amazed at what you'll discover. In Aliene's case, it was her love for her husband that was the driving force behind wanting to be the most organized person she could be. While talking with her after the session, she shared her subsequent realization that she displayed the same pattern at work: she would berate herself for disappointing her team by not having it "all together" (Flaw). This related back to how important it was to Aliene that people feel cared for (Divine).

Before we move on to deconstruct *your* I.C. message, I'd like to share some more examples of what a Divine Flaw can look like. I want you to be clear on what you're looking for before beginning to dig for yours. Divine Flaws come in many variations. We're all unique in our humanity, after all. So there are a few ways you might discover your Divinity—which is the key that unlocks the door between how you can be hard on yourself and where you can make the biggest impact in the world. This is where both sides of this book come together—your Divine Flaw is the bridge between your Inner Critic and your Inner Success. So it's super-important that you get clear on how to use this priceless tool.

Christine's Divine Flaw: I Write in Service to Humanity

In addition to corporate leaders, I also get to work with some amazing entrepreneurs, visionaries and artists, like Christine. Christine's core I.C. message is, "I'm not a writer." This is an interesting message since she writes for some of the most read and recognized magazines in the country. However, Christine's got a merciless Fraud Critic who tells her it's only a matter of time until she's "found out." She's in the process of writing her first book and her I.C. has been harsh. Eventually, I just had to stage an intervention. I had Christine work through the Mining the Depths process. While exploring the negative side of her message, it snowballed. Here's the summary:

> "I'm not a writer because I'm a fraud and it's only a matter of time until I'm found out, and then I'll stop getting work, and I won't have any income, and I'll be poor, or worse, I won't be able to support myself at all. I'll feel helpless, and trapped, and stuck. And I'll have to give up on my dream to be an author and get a real job."

Haven't we all experienced these cycles of doubt that plummet us to the bottom of a big black hole?

Next, we explored what might be possible and positive about Christine's I.C. message, moving another step towards her Divinity each time we focused on what mattered. Once again, here's the summary:

> "I'm not a writer, because I'm not good enough to be a writer.
> It's important to be a good enough writer, because if I am, then
> I can connect with people on a very deep level through my work.

136

It's important to connect with people, especially in this book about my sister's death and its impact on my family, because if I can do that, then I can help others who've had to go through something similar. When they read my stories, they'll see if I can get through this, then they can, too. It's important to be able to help people through my writing because it's integral to my spirituality and purpose. I really believe that God wants me to tell my story and help others, it's my way of being in service [to other people and to God]. It's why I'm here.

I had Christine take a deep breath and let that one sink in. It was a huge revelation for her. Once she realized *why* writing—and specifically writing this book—was so important to her, it allowed her to channel something infinitely more powerful than her fear: her dedication to living out her life purpose of writing in service to humanity and ultimately, to God.

The I.C. message that had been hanging over her like a sinister, dark cloud all of a sudden became a portal to a part of her that's light and spacious and divine. Not only is she about half-way through her book, she's totally reorganized her work portfolio to include only those projects that are in alignment with her core values. She's happier, more creative and more inspired, and she has freed up valuable time for her passion.

Divine: I write in service to God, to help people heal.

Flaw: I'm not a writer.

This is another truth I've found in the course of developing my Inner Critic work: the more important something is to you, the more likely it is the critic will not only show up, but potentially do the worst damage of all—by keeping you from doing the most important work of your life. In *Now, Discover Your Strengths*, Marcus Buckingham writes:

> All failures are not created equal. Some are fairly easy to digest, usually those where we can explain away the failure without tarnishing our self-image. . . . When the cause of the failure seems to have nothing to do with who we really are, we can accept it. But some failures stick in our throat and lodge there.

It is on this fear that the Inner Critic feeds. It is when the stakes are highest of all that our Inner Saboteur seeks to stage the mother-of-all-interventions. And when it does, remember that you only get this one life. Ask yourself: am I going to let my Inner Critic, or a moment of failure for that matter, keep me from doing the very thing that matters most of all?

In Christine's case, the answer was definitely not. Whenever her Fraud comes knocking, which of course it still does because it's such an important book, Christine has the ability to zoom her energy back across the infinity spiral. She simply asks herself: why is it that I care so much about being a good writer? Answer: Oh, I know, because that's why God put me here—to use my talent and my compassion and my hard-won wisdom to write stories that bring healing and hope to those who are suffering.

Heath's Divine Flaw: I Encourage Others to Step into Their Greatness

Heath has a relentless voice that drops such delights as, "I can't believe they made you a manager. Don't they realize how often you screw things up?" The source of these negative messages is a massive, World Wrestling Federation-size Fraud that sets his anxiety off like July 4th fireworks. Heath questions every move he makes, worries about how his team shows up in meetings, hates having to give difficult feedback to employees, incessantly tries to analyze what he should have done better.

To learn more about why Heath holds himself accountable to such impossible standards, we mined his Inner Critic message. And beneath the mud and crud, we uncovered Heath's core value around making sure everyone feels included, gets to have a voice, and is acknowledged for their contributions. Heath believes people operate at their best when they feel valued. This is the Divinity in his human nature—he's a believer in lifting others up and encouraging them to step into their greatness. It's exactly why people are so attracted to him and clamor to be on his team. Unlike Heath, they can see his Divine value.

The challenge for Heath, like many of us, is to see his I.C. Flaw as merely a signal that he's rubbing up against something profoundly important to him. Now, when the negative fireworks go off (as they still do and probably always will), Heath quickly reminds himself of the connection between his Flaw and the very best part of him—his Divinity—and shifts his energy to the powerhouse of his value of encouragement and inclusion.

Divine: I believe people should feel encouraged and included.

Flaw: I'm a screw up as a manager.

Even though Christine's exploration revealed a very big life purpose, and Heath's a major life philosophy, please don't become married to the idea that your Divine Flaw should be profound. And whatever you do, don't expect to find The Answer to The Question: what's it all about? It's unrealistic to expect that identifying your Divine Flaw means you'll have solved the ultimate puzzle. That's just harkening back to Perfectionism and Either/Or thinking—which isn't how life works. You have more than one Divine Flaw, just as you have more than one Inner Critic and more than one Success story. And with time, practice and attention, you'll begin to uncover them all.

To give you as broad a frame of reference as possible, below are some additional, abbreviated examples of less lofty, but important, Divine Flaws:

- Jessie's Inner Critic gets fired up when she feels like she's not delivering in an effective and efficient way. Why? Because respect for people's time is part of what really matters to her (Divinity).
- Brett's Divine Flaw is nurturing creativity and contribution—which is why his Inner Critic acts out when someone disrespects him—or, worse yet, one of his employees—in a meeting by not paying attention to what's being said.
- One of my Divine Flaws is empathy, which is why I beat myself for being a "bad" friend, boss, sister or daughter.

ACTIVITY: Mine Your Message

OK, it's your turn! You're going to walk the steps Aliene took and flesh out your own I.C. story. You may not be standing in a large space right now, but we're going to pretend you are! It's super-helpful to physically perform this activity, so imagine yourself standing in the middle of a long line that extends to the left and right—better yet, put masking tape on the floor and stand in the middle. To your left is the negative side; to your right is the positive. As you answer each question, take a step in the appropriate direction. If you are working on your negative I.C. message you step to the left. When you are mining for the positive aspects of the I.C. message you step to the right.

Pick your core I.C. message. If you're unsure which one to choose, pick one that's alive and has energy for you *right now*. Choose something juicy, not trite, something that when you think about it, your stomach involuntarily twists into a tight knot. Or maybe you noticed while reading the last sentence that a message came up and you immediately swatted it away because it's the one thing you *don't* want to talk about? If so, that's *exactly* what you want to explore right now. It doesn't have to be as dramatic as Aliene's story, nor as epic as Christine's. We're not trying to shoot for ultimate gloom here, nor ultimate glory; we're just trying to explore all that comes with your I.C. message. Our goal is to mine the negativity so we can see what we're really dealing with.

State your I.C. message. Begin by exploring the negative (left) side. Ask yourself a series of probing questions to clarify what you mean and mine for information. Repeat back to yourself everything you've cumulatively revealed in your answers—just like I did with Aliene. The object here is to really explore. Imagine you're talking to a total stranger whose "story" you're unfamiliar with. You've no idea where they're coming from, what their background is, or what their thought process is. Your job is to gain as much understanding as you can by asking as many questions as it takes to explore the depths of their I.C. statement. Remember to take a step to the left each time you answer a question. One step per answer, one answer per question. Don't get ahead of yourself! I know you're all a bunch of over-achievers, but remember this isn't a race. Slow and steady wins this awareness game.

If you get stuck, dip into the following pool of questions to prompt you and keep you moving.

- When you hear [insert I.C. message], what's the next thought that comes into your mind?
- Is there another thought that seems naturally to follow that one?
- Where does your mind go next when you think of that message (e.g., being disorganized)?
- What happens after that—i.e., if you're (disorganized), then what happens?
- What then—is there another I.C. message that comes up as a result of that last piece?

You've reached the end of the negativity side of this spectrum when you feel like you've hit the spot. It doesn't have to be the "perfect" spot, or a big "aha" like Aliene had, but it should feel like all of a sudden something's sunk from your head to your heart to your belly and you think, "Oh, that's it!" Feel it? Good.

Look back to the center to get a clear visual on how far you've traveled.

Then walk back to the middle. Remind yourself of the negative I.C. message you started with. Now, your intention is to explore what might be possible and positive about that I.C. message.

State your I.C. message. Then start exploring the positive (right) side by asking yourself a series of probing questions. Again, if it helps, imagine you're talking to a total stranger and you're trying to gain a deeper understanding of their story. Don't forget to take a step to the right each time you answer a question.

If you get stuck, use the following questions to prompt you.

- Why does that critic message dig at you?
- Why is that important to you?
- What aspect of you is the critic calling into question?
- What feels at stake? What's on the line here?
- What is it that you care so much about, that is related to this?
- Why does that matter to you, what's at the heart of it? (Feel free to repeat this question as often as is necessary.)

Now that you've explored this side, what ideas do you have about your Divinity?

Whatever you've written is the jewel that's been hidden beneath your I.C. all this time. It's something that's super-important to you because it's part of the core of who you are—it's a statement around how you want to lead your life. In other words, it's your Divine Flaw. Congratulations! You just found a diamond!

How do you feel? Right about now most of my clients tell me they feel like a heavy weight that they didn't even realize was pressing down on their chests has been lifted and a huge space has opened up inside them, right beneath their rib cages. You've just experienced a giant shift in awareness as your perspective opened up to a whole new possibility and meaning around your I.C. message. It actually has value to you now. It's no longer a dark and shadowy monster you run from.

You've seen all the way across from one end—the dark, heavy, limiting and negative side of your I.C. statement (I'm disorganized, I'm a failure, I'm a fraud, I'm obsolete, What's the point?)—to the other end; the bright, light, spacious and positive side of your Divinity (I love my husband, I love helping people, I want to create meaningful change, I work to serve God, I'm loyal to those I love, I care so much). Do you see that *everything* on that axis is you? Do you see that the entire line represents *all* of you? It's really important that you see all of it—take it all in and own the entire axis that runs from the negative all the way to the positive.

Do you see now that without the heavy, dark, "I've-totally-spiraled-out-of-control" end, and the gnarly I.C. statement, you wouldn't have the distance and the perspective and the contrast required for your Divine Flaw to glisten like a trophy?

Let me now offer you the same deal Pam offered me: If I told you right now that I can get rid of your Inner Critic, that you'd never again have to hear that critical, doubt-filled message, would you want that? Now, before you jump up and down screaming, "Yes! Absolutely!" let me add a caveat: in order to get rid of your Critic, I'd have to also get rid of your Divine aspect as well. Is *that* OK? Do we still have a deal?

I didn't think so.

Now, does saying yes to your I.C. message mean you have to say yes to the cruddy, dark part lurking at the far left negative end of this line? No. Can you guess why? You just lightened it the up significantly by bringing your awareness to it and exposing the bright, shiny truth at the other end that is its natural counterpoint. All you're saying yes to is that you know it's there and you now know what drives it, but you don't have to experience the depth or darkness of it. This isn't some sort of Law of Attraction deal—acknowledging it does *not* mean you'll attract it. Quite the opposite! Now that you know what's on the other side, you can say, "I know it's hard, but I also know it's important—because it's attached to what's important to me." And you can quickly move on over to the other end of the axis by reminding yourself of the magnificent, meaningful, magical parts of you.

Understanding on a deep level how one extreme of the I.C. message relates to the other gives you a choice—a powerful choice—over how much of your energy is spent at any place along the axis. Next time you experience an I.C. attack, you'll have the ability to zip-line your energy back across to the positive side simply by asking yourself: Why is that I care so much about that?

I've practiced this so many times, it's become second nature to me. The I.C. will quickly insinuate its negativity into my brain—such as, "They'll never hire you for another project there, you haven't made nearly enough of an impact"—and I can grab that energy right back by reminding myself that I care about every person I work with, and I give every job one hundred and ten percent. I tip my hat to the I.C., thanking it for reminding me that my work is so important that I will always push myself to do my absolute best. Then, I do my little sideways smile and just keep on truckin'.

ACTIVITY: Create Your Own Infinity Symbol

I strongly encourage you to create your own personal rendering of the Infinity Symbol to represent your Divine Flaw. It's a powerful visual aid to see the relationship between your critic and what really matters (your divine aspects). You don't need to be a Picasso nor have an easel to do it! All you need is a pen and a Post-it note (I should buy shares in the company!) or an index card.

Ready? OK. Draw the symbol or use the one here in the book. On the left, write your Inner Critic character name and message. On the right, you're going to write what's most powerful, meaningful and amazing about you—your Divine aspects. This is the beginning of creating your authentic statement of Inner Success, which you'll explore in great detail in later chapters. For now, brainstorm some ideas of what you think it might be, based on what you know about your Inner Critic and what you've learned about your Divine Flaw. Which idea resonates most deeply? What feels like it has a ring of truth? Which one feels like it captures that dynamic relationship and flow of energy between Inner Critic and Divine Flaw?

Carry your symbol with you for a week. Next time you experience an Inner Critic attack, pull this powerful visual cue out and see if you can zip-line yourself back to that positive Divine energy. After practicing this several times, I guarantee you it will begin to offer relief, reduce the negative impact of the Critic and free you up to move forward.

Below is Phoebe's Infinity Spiral. On one end her Comparer Critic and its message that she can't compete with her younger colleagues represents her fear of being irrelevant. The other end represents her Divine aspects. The bridge connecting the two, and maintaining the flow, is her Divine Flaw: "I am hungry to explore, experience, and learn." Phoebe has been committed to learning all her life. She's worked long and hard in her career to constantly improve her professional skills. On a personal level, she's undertaken adventures on boats, bikes, buses and on foot—literally hiking across continents—in order to expand her knowledge of different peoples and philosophies. This constant striving to educate herself—so she can share her knowledge with others—is Phoebe's Divine Flaw.

Divine: I am hungry to explore, experience, and learn.

Flaw: I have nothing to offer, I'm irrelevant.

Now, you don't have to go out and get a tattoo of the Infinity Spiral like I did, but I do suggest you tattoo it into your brain! As we progress through this chapter, and throughout the book, I encourage you to use this powerful, ages-old symbol as a visual aid to engrain in your mind the interconnectedness between your Divinity and your Flaw; that is, your Inner Success and your Inner Critic. Hold it close to your heart. After all, it's *you*!

Divine Intervention: Acceptance

In chapter five I presented a provocative perspective on the Inner Critic: that it's actually just normal. Now, I'm about to hit you with another radical view inspired by my client, Gordon.

We were working on the Truth Series questions around Gordon's Perfectionist Critic message of "I'm not good enough." When I asked if that statement was one hundred percent true, Gordon paused, took a deep breath, and out rushed, "You know what? Right now, yes, it feels one hundred percent true."

It was the first and only time anyone has ever responded to that question in the affirmative. I looked at Gordon and could instantly see it was a truly painful moment. He was in the grip of an Amygdala Hijack, in full I.C. attack mode, and in that moment it did feel one hundred percent true to Gordon that he wasn't good enough.

I wanted to respect and acknowledge where Gordon was at mentally and emotionally. I encourage clients to sit in difficult emotions, and he was showing enormous courage. But I wanted to make a finer distinction so he didn't stay there. So I shifted a little on the questions, asking if it was it one hundred percent true *all* of the time?

"No," Gordon replied, "not all the time." "So it's a part of you right now," I continued. "But it's not *all* of you right now?" "That's true," he nodded. "It's not all of me."

I stopped there. There was no point in doing the rest of the activity while Gordon was in the midst of a hijack. Instead, we shifted to acknowledgment and acceptance that in that moment there was a part of him that just didn't feel good enough. Sometimes the I.C. is a little version of ourselves that just wants some attention—a little Mini Me jumping up and down, yelling, "Just admit I'm here!" And when they get that focus, the emotional intensity instantly abates. Just like a little kid who stops crying as soon as they get a little attention.

Magically, right around the same time, I experienced my own moment of acceptance. I had a call with my own coach, Kavita, because I was so frustrated about my own feelings of unworthiness—particularly around finding love. I've often struggled with an Inner Critic that tells me I'm not enough, there's something wrong with me, I've got to do and be more in order to be worthy. I knew it was getting in my way with dating and relationships, and I just wanted to figure out how to *Fix It* (yes, I coach on this and yes, I'm human, just like you). Kavita's response was, "What if you just accepted that it's true? What if you just stopped fighting it, because the reality is *what you resist persists*." She was right. The harder I worked to disprove my I.C.—struggling and striving exhaustedly to prove myself worthy, the more I proved I was lacking. I kept taking on all these self-help projects to make myself better—thereby reinforcing the idea that I was broken and needed to be "fixed."

We can hear a message a million times but we only really hear it when we're ready. In that moment, I heard it from my soul to the tips of my fabulous shoes. Yes, there's a part of me that doesn't feel worthy and I'm probably always going to struggle with it and that's just part of who I am. Instead of working on feeling worthy, which paradoxically proves I'm not, I decided to accept and acknowledge that it's something I'll have to deal with occasionally. As I date and hopefully find love, that man will be happy with me as is—not expecting a perfect package. There are certain things we'd rather not deal with—like cleaning behind the refrigerator—but we have to. It's just the way life is.

This revelation blew me away and, like a true external thinker, I called my friend Jim to share it with him. "I'm coming out," I told Jim. "I'm coming out as a flawed human being who doesn't feel good enough. I'm not good enough. I'm not worthy. And I'm no longer going to hide it, try to fix it or struggle with it."

I thought for sure Jim would understand. He came out as a gay man at the age of 35, and he'd told me amazing he felt to finally accept and acknowledge all of his identity. "This is so hard," groaned Jim. "I want to push back and say, 'No Stacey, you *are* good enough, you *are* worthy. But it'd be like someone telling me, 'No Jim, you're not gay.'" (I realize I don't actually have to encounter "coming out" in the same way that phrase is used for gay and lesbian people, so please know my intention was to use it respectfully.)

The cumulative effect of speaking with Gordon, Kavita and Jim really served to ground for me on a much deeper level the realization that within my identity there's a part of me that sometimes doesn't feel good enough. And I'm going to accept that about myself; I'm no longer going to fight it. It felt simultaneously big and profound and small and subtle. It also felt like a deep sigh of relief—the good kind where your body finally releases long-held tension.

As I continued to let this digest over the next few days, another facet of my Divine Flaw clicked into place: This disowned aspect of my identity, not being worthy, is part of the reason I wrote this book—so others will realize *they* are worthy. This dang critic is part of why I became an applied behavioral scientist—to learn how better to deal with it. It's why I'm fascinated by human behavior. It's maybe even a teeny bit responsible for why I found the work love of my life. So, I gave myself the stink eye and acknowledged that this critic is also part of my Divinity.

However, being a coach, I also decided to have some strategies at hand so when my I.C. shows up at my door, like wacky Aunt Betty, I know how to dance with it rather than fight with it. I decided that instead of turning Aunt Betty away, I'm going to let her come in. I know she won't stay long, and I can deal with her for a little while. I've taken all that energy that used to be spent pushing Aunt Betty away and freed it up for other, more productive uses. Sometimes, I even enjoy having Aunt Betty stop by. Hey, she's just a branch of the family that makes us all more *interesting*!

I also gained a whole new perspective on the Infinity Symbol. Instead of focusing all my energy on shifting to the positive side, I realized that it actually doesn't matter where I am—as long as I'm conscious and in flow—instead of blind and stuck. My Inner Critic doesn't define me or have the whole say. For that matter, neither do the Divine parts of me. You and I both know that real life has both good times and bad. Like a diamond, we have facets and flaws, we incur cuts and we gain clarity. Hey sugar, we're complex creatures. We are, after all, human beings. The wisdom is in knowing and accepting that reality, not in fighting it.

ACTIVITY: Accept Yourself

Practice some deep belly breathing to ground yourself, then reflect on the following questions.

- What do you work so hard to disprove, that you actually prove it exists?
- How could you "come out" as more of yourself?
- How much energy could you save by accepting some of the flaws in your facets?

Now, "try on" a little self-acceptance by sizing up your Mini Me compared with your Whole Self. If it were a part of your body, what might it be? Your elbow? A rib? The tip of your thumb? Now, imagine you're the Colorado Rocky Mountain range and your self-doubt is just one peak. Sure, it's hard to see anything when you're hanging in a tree at the base of mount I.C. But if you take a helicopter ride above the mountains you will get a panoramic view. How big is that peak now? Not nearly so big and scary, right?

Infinitely Divine

As I explained at the beginning of this chapter, your Divine Flaw is the bridge that links both sides of the Infinity Spiral. Up till now, we've focused our exploration on the Inner Critic. Over the course of the next six chapters, we'll delve deeply into Inner Success. As you discover how to amplify and live your strengths, you'll gain more insight into how the flow of energy plays out. And you'll discover how to boost the weight and depth and robustness of your Success side so it becomes as familiar to you as your Critic—which will permanently tip the scales in your favor.

7

Work Your Core

In the last chapter, you discovered your Divine Flaw, which is the golden bridge connecting your Inner Critic to what really matters—your unique, authentic definition of Inner Success. You learned that on the other side of fear, doubt and self-criticism are those things you hold near and dear—contained in the mirror side of the spiral. In this chapter, we start to move to the other side. The journey begins with your Core Values, Identities and Emotions.

A healthy *physical* core is essential to a healthy body. Your torso (specifically, the muscles of the abdomen, obliques, back and pelvis) is the link between your upper and lower body. A healthy core ensures you can move effectively and powerfully, with the greatest ease and flexibility. The stronger your physical core, the stronger your body, with greatest ability to withstand injury.

So it is with your *interior* core. The more robust this core is—your values, your identity and the feelings you want to populate your life experience—the more robust your ability to navigate between self-doubt and success. Attending to your interior core with awareness, understanding and respect will allow you to be effective, powerful and flexible. Like your body's physical core muscles, this interior core is the link between the lower body (your heart) and your upper body (your brain). In fact, it is precisely these interior core elements that drive most of your decisions, behaviors and actions (or inactions). Understanding your core is fundamental to understanding what moves you. When you make choices that are congruent with your interior core, you will live a happier, more satisfied and more successful life.

As you learned in the last chapter, what you care most about proves to be the ripest territory for fear and doubt, because your Inner Critic steps in to "protect" you from what it deems too big a risk—the risk of failing at that which most matters. These are the areas we'll be exploring in this chapter, because awareness is kryptonite to your Critic—awareness is the secret sauce to your Success. When the negative tape starts to play, you'll know which part of your interior core is involved—and shift your attention and energy to that solid understanding of yourself, instead of being deceived by that nasty I.C. message playing in the background.

Take a deep breath as we prepare to dive into yet another inner landscape—that of your inner guidance system—your core. We are continuing on your journey towards defining success on your terms. This is a journey I want you to enjoy! Over these next several chapters, we'll bring our focus back from what anyone else thinks to what *you* think. These next chapters are all about *you*!

Core Values

"What really matters?" is not only a very good question, it's also the tagline for my business and a mantra for my life. To me, "what really matters" is both a question and a statement. When I help my clients gain clarity around what really matters to them and why, and when I anchor it to their deepest values, they do the work, period. No exceptions. Exploring Core Values means connecting the dots so you know what really matters to *you*.

Every action you take, or don't take, is as a result of living out your values. Often, however, many of us haven't taken the time to know what those values are. We operate based on those values, even if we can't articulate them in clear words or statements. The clearer you are about what specifically you value, and the greater awareness you have of yourself and why you do the things you do, the better choices you can make about how you spend your time and who you spend it with. In addition to gaining the clarity to guide your choices, values also help you see where and why the Inner Critic attacks.

As human beings, the motivation to do things differently must be greater than our natural resistance to change, and that motivation must stem from within. When I begin coaching with clients, we start by identifying goals for change and what success will look like. (You learned about this in the Coaching 101 section of chapter one.) Clients usually start rattling off reasons for a goal or change because it matters to their boss, their company, their family, or their culture—which are external motivators. That's fine but people do the work of accomplishing goals much more effectively when they are internally motivated—which is done by aligning goals to your values. This is why the second of my Three Key coaching questions is: "Why does that matter to *you*?" The intention is to uncover the client's own, personal, values-related reasons for the goal (which we can partner with the external motivation). Core values bring greater clarity and effectiveness when trying to reach a goal.

Shala was a wife and mother of two young kids, with an MBA, a high-powered job, and a secret dream to quit and become a stay-at-home mom. When I started working with her, Shala couldn't move past the terror of her Inner Saboteur, who told her that quitting her job would create a big black hole in her résumé she'd never be able to climb back out of—until I had her get explicit on her values, which include:

- Being a loving mother.
- Taking an active role in my children's education.
- Pace and peacefulness—allowing my kids to move and create at their own pace, versus being rushed around according to my hectic schedule.

- Service, community, volunteering and participating in Meals on Wheels with my kids after school.
- Injecting more creativity and play into my day.

It was only when she got clear about her values that Shala was able to let go of the debilitating fear stirred up by her Inner Critic. When she shifted her energy and focus to her values, and really grounded herself deeply in them, she realized they were much more important than her fear of being judged. Shala found the courage to take the plunge and quit. She's never looked back!

In Ethan's case, gaining clarity on his values allowed him to rediscover his passion for his job. Six months earlier, he'd been moved to a different team and his role was re-tasked. Ethan wasn't enjoying his new position and he found himself beginning to procrastinate. Because he wasn't as productive as usual, his energy and enthusiasm were super-low. For of all these reasons, Ethan felt he didn't deserve to have "Integrity" on his list of values. I reminded him that values aren't about how we behave one hundred percent of the time; they're about what's important to us and how we *want* to behave—even though we sometimes miss the mark. "I know that Integrity matters to you Ethan, or you wouldn't be giving yourself such a hard time about how you're showing up at work," I told him. "You hired me to help you get back to that productive, efficient, high-quality, energized person you want to be. You *want* to be in Integrity." That's all Ethan needed to hear. He was ready to sit down and start mapping out ways he could change his attitude about his new job so he would be acting in integrity—instead of beating himself up about not being in integrity.

What Exactly Are Values?

Values are principles that are so personal and so important that you're either living your life in alignment with them—or you're aspiring toward that. Therefore, gaining clarity on your values greatly enhances the quality of your decision-making around where and how you spend your time, talents and resources. If you're giving yourself a hard time, critics saying mean things, I'd bet it's related to an area where you're not living according to your values.

Values are not so much something to be achieved (like goals) as they are a way to live. This is an important distinction! There will be days you don't do such a great job at living a value—respect, for example—but that doesn't mean you failed in your value of respect. It doesn't mean you cross it off your list of values, it just means you had a rough day (or a rough couple of months, as in Ethan's case.)

Values are unique to each individual. When I do a Values Clarification activity with clients, "integrity" often shows up. However, if I were to ask five different people to describe what integrity means to them, I'd get five different descriptions. Sure, there'll be some similarities, but the word "integrity" doesn't mean the same thing to all people, because all people are not the same. The key question here is: what does the value word "integrity" mean to *you*? What does it represent in *your* life and how do you define it in the context of *your* personal experience? Conversely, it's amazing how often people will use different terms to describe the same value. For example, I have one client whose number one value is "family," another "relationship," another "belonging," and yet another "teamwork." Yet, when asked to explain what the "value word" means to them, all four will share similar descriptions.

Your values language changes over time. For example, I always used to list "faith" as my number one value, and then one day I switched it to "trust." Did that mean that all of a sudden faith was no longer important to me? No, it absolutely didn't mean that—just that the way I thought about faith and how it was showing up in my life was now better represented by the word trust. At that moment in time, trust for me represented not only trust in my chosen higher power but also trust in myself and in others. And if I could trust in all those things, I was practicing and living my faith.

Values evolve over time, typically as a result of major life events. For example, one client never considered "health" a value until he had a health scare that radically changed how he operates and behaves—and what he values most.

Values can be overlooked. The value that's most integral to you could be something that seems as natural as breathing—so much so, you don't even think of it as a value. I have one client to whom the practice of "compassion" comes so naturally that she didn't consider it a value until she saw the word on my Values worksheet. "Love" and "kindness" are other examples of values that people are often oblivious to, that they discount or dismiss because these values are such an "easy," organic part of their lives.

Values are oftentimes counterintuitive. Sheryl had a hard time accepting that "family" wasn't one of her top values, because she thought it *should* be. In fact, her Inner Pleaser Critic went on a rampage, telling her she was a terrible mom! (See the box below for how Sheryl used the three E.I. Builder questions to move from emotional paralysis to intentional action.) I asked Sheryl if there was any relationship between "family" and her other top two values of "integrity" and "achievement." After some reflection, Sheryl told me she wanted her children to be proud of her career and to realize they could do and be anything they wanted. She was also the primary breadwinner so her husband could work part-time and be with the kids after school. Seeing the relationship between her values had the effect of quieting Sheryl's I.C. and allowing her to be more realistic in the story of her values—and to be kinder to herself as a result. There is almost always more to the story than the Critic would have you believe.

E.I. builder moment

Remember those three E.I. Builder questions from chapters one and three? Let's use my conversation with Sheryl as an example of how to integrate them when you're in the grip of an emotional hijack.

"Sheryl, what are you feeling right now?"

"I feel really guilty, almost angry at myself."

"OK, yep clear on feelings. What are you thinking?"

My family should be in my top three values. And they're not. That makes me a terrible mom."

"What's your physical reaction? What's happening in your body right now?"

"I'm fidgeting and shifting around in my chair, and I just let out a big sigh.

Remember, self-management is the ability to use self-awareness—of your feelings, thoughts and body responses—to make intentional choices around what to do with the information. When Sheryl slowed down to answer these questions, the emotional intensity began to calm down. She could then move on to seeing the relationships across all her values.

ACTIVITY: Values Clarification

OK, are you ready to explore your values? Great! Let's get started.

Step 1: Take out your journal. Quickly and intuitively jot down a list of five words or short phrases that describe what you know, in this moment, about your top values. (Don't go into Perfectionist mode, it's just a starting point!)

Now, you're going to clarify them. Please follow these steps sequentially, without jumping ahead. I hope you'll trust me when I tell you it's the best way to do this process.

Step 2: You've got two minutes to complete this step; set a timer to start *now*! Take a look at the value words chart. Once again acting quickly and intuitively—draw a line through all words that represent values that are *less* important to you, which leaves the values that are *more* important to you. (Of course they're all important. You're eliminating the ones that carry *less* weight for you.) Stop when the timer goes off.

WORKSHEET: Values Words

Accomplishment	Diversity	Intention	Relationship
Acceptance	Duty	Involvement	Reputation
Accountability	Effectiveness	Knowledge	Respect
Achievement	Equality	Learning	Responsibility
Advancement	Excitement	Leisure	Results
Adventure	Fairness	Loyalty	Risk
Altruism	Faith	Mastery	Security
Autonomy	Family	Openness	Self-improvement
Belonging	Freedom	Order	Self-realization
Challenge	Fun	Originality	Simplicity
Collaboration	Goodness	Patience	Spirituality
Communication	Growth	Passion	Spontaneity
Compassion	Health	Play	Structure
Commitment	Helping Others	Pleasure	Teamwork
Community	Honesty	Power	Tradition
Competition	Humor	Practicality	Tranquility
Connection	Independence	Prestige	Trust
Control	Inner Peace	Productivity	Variety
Cooperation	Innovation	Quality	Wealth
Creativity	Integrity	Realism	Wisdom
Curiosity	Intelligence	Recognition	

Values not on the list _____ _____ _____

Step 3: Repeat step 2 with the remaining words. Glance at the unmarked words (the ones that don't have a line through them). Set a timer for one minute—trust me, the brevity will help you stay intuitive versus over-thinking it—and draw an "X" through all value words that are *less* important. Again, it's all relative; some have *more* meaning to you which will remain on the list. Put an "X" through the others that are *less* important. Bear with me—we're going through an intentional process of narrowing it down.

Pause: Right about now, you're likely asking one of the following questions:

• Should my values pertain to my work life or my home life? Completely up to you.

- Should they be values I'm currently living—or values I aspire to? Great question! Up to you.
- How many values should I end up with? You'll see. Don't look ahead! Trust the process.

Step 4: Of the words that remain on the chart, choose six—and only six—value words that are the most important to you. Circle them.

Step 5: Write your six value words in your journal. List them in descending order of importance (first most important value, second most important, third . . . and so on).

Take a deep breath.

Thank you. I know that exercise took patience, focus and trust. I also know that it required you to dig deep into your emotional core, an uncomfortable experience for many people. We usually value, or aspire to value, lots of different things but it's important to become aware of what you value *the most*.

Bring Your Values to Life

Sharing your values is a fantastic means of animating and cementing them. It's also a wonderful relationship builder. When I work with teams, I have each person share the results of this Values Clarification exercise, along with some stories and examples that bring the words to life. This sharing has a powerful effect on teams. They come away with more understanding, trust and respect for one another. Many of my coaching clients find it so valuable that they introduce it to their own teams. Some even bring it home to their spouses or partners. Sharing your values with the people you live and work with helps them gain a much deeper understanding of who you are and why you do the things you do.

If you're unsure how to communicate your values and share them with others, here are some suggestions for conversation starters that I use in workshops:

- Share a story that illustrates how you lived, operated from or made a decision based on one or more of your Core Values.

- Share a story of how this value came to be in your top six—did you learn it from a family member or mentor? Was it forged by a significant event in your life?
- Share a story about a time when your values were challenged. Describe what that was like for you.

The Clarification exercise provides a list of words for your values, but the power of the words is in the stories you tell and how they show up as you live your life. In fact, it can be very useful to translate your six words into six statements. This makes your values more active and dynamic, transforming them into a set of Operating Values, or Guiding Principles, you can use as your own guidance system.

Use Values to Get Unstuck

Whenever I feel stuck on a decision I'm struggling to make or I'm being pushed around by negative Critic messages, I'll pull out my top six value cards and arrange them on my desk in order of how I'm *actually* operating in the moment. (I have a deck of value cards I use in workshops; I highly recommend you improvise by writing yours on those trusty Post-Its or index cards.)

Below is how my values usually rank:
1. Trust
2. Relationship
3. Helping Others
4. Growth
5. Humor
6. Security

What I've discovered is that when I'm feeling stuck, inevitably security (number six) has taken over first place from trust—and trust has dropped off the list completely! The practice has not only made me aware that these two values sometimes compete against one another, but the very act of pulling out the cards and arranging them on the table slows me down enough to center myself and make a choice about what's most important *in that moment*. Sometimes, it turns out security *is* important, but mostly it serves as a reminder to trust people—especially myself.

This play between security and trust comes up a lot whenever I'm facilitating (which basically means I'm coaching a room full of people, rather than working with an individual) and arrive at a point when I'm unsure what to do next. I want to feel the security of knowing I'm doing the right thing by following my design plan—versus trusting myself and my clients that the right outcome will occur organically by following my intuition (the body's brain). Trust *always* yields great results—whether it's the outcome I planned for or not—but with more risk and less certainty than I have with a rigid design (security). Yet there are times when I'm hired to deliver a very specific outcome in a workshop. Even if the energy of the people in the room aren't moving in that direction, in this case I need to drive the conversation towards the requested outcome. In those cases, I utilize my security value to get us there.

My point in sharing this story is to illustrate that the choice is not always black and white. Sometimes we just have to make a choice in a moment *in time*, but these are exceptions to the rule and not how you operate *over time*. Be kind to yourself. Don't label yourself a bad person just because every once in a while you put security or achievement first.

ACTIVITY: Consult the Cards

In those moments when you're feeling under I.C. attack, or you're feeling challenged or stuck, pull out your list of top six values (or values "index" cards, if you've written them out) and rank them based on how you're operating in the moment. Now, compare this to your actual values ranking and ask yourself a few questions:

- Are there are any insights to be gained by comparing your "current" list with your "usual" list?

- Do you see any way to look at the situation differently?
- Do you see how you might change your behavior so your values are ranked in the order you'd *prefer*?
- Or can you gain an understanding of *why* your values are showing up in the way they are right now—so you can let yourself off the hook?

Core Identity

What would you say if someone were to ask, "What is your identity?" It's most likely your answer would include some or all of the following: name, age, nationality, ethnicity, gender, sexual orientation, marital status, parental status, religion, socio-economic status, education, possibly even your dietary preferences. These are explicit labels to which we align ourselves, that usually either serve to help us fit in or to set us apart. There is, however, a whole other set of implicit labels that reflect your Core Identity. Much like your values, these identities reflect your childhood, your family dynamics and your key experiences in life. And, similar to values, many people operate based on the identities they are attached to without a conscious awareness of them. Gaining clarity on these identities allow us to make more intentional choices.

Think about it as the answer to the question—who are you?—after having stripped away anything with an external label or anything that can be purchased with money. When a client is being challenged by their Inner Critic or having difficulty in defining meaningful Inner Success I will often pose the question, "What's on the line here?" to zero in what aspect of their Core Identity is involved.

In their book *Difficult Conversations: How to Discuss What Matters Most*, Douglas Stone, Bruce Patton, and Sheila Heen refer to moments when our Core Identities are challenged as "Identity Quakes." According to the authors, "You can't 'quake-proof' your sense of self. Grappling with identity issues is what life and growth are all about, and no amount of love or accomplishment or skill can insulate you from these challenges." What you can do is stay grounded in what really matters when challenges arise—which is exactly what you're learning to do in this book. Once again, the keys to staying grounded are self-awareness and self-knowledge. "Thinking clearly and honestly about who you are can help reduce your anxiety level," write Stone, Patton and Heen. In this next section, we're going to build your awareness and knowledge around "who you are," and "what's on the line."

Aleeca was feeling deeply hurt and disappointed because she wasn't included in some social activities at work. Her home office was hosting a visiting team from a satellite office and Aleeca's inner critic would have her believe she was being excluded from some of the welcome mixers, callously telling her, "They don't want you around." Though she's communicative and articulate, Aleeca struggled to talk about it. Sensing a raw nerve, namely an infringement on Aleeca's Core Identity, I asked her what was on the line? (With the exception of your Divine Flaw, Core Identity is probably the Inner Critic's next most favored point of attack.) Aleeca told me that during previous visits, *she* had arranged and hosted several functions so guests would feel welcome and comfortable, so they would be able to mingle and get to know people—because it was important to her that the visiting team felt included. Aleeca discovered she had two Core Identities at play—that of Mother and Connector. And these two identities were at the heart of her disproportionate emotional charge. Not being included hurt and quaked two of her Core Identities, which kicked her I.C. into over-drive.

One of the things I find so fascinating about Core Identity is that what we're attached to on the inside is not always obvious from the outside. Conversely, what we see on the outside isn't always a match to the identities we're attached to inside. (Yes, I did say fascinating, which I realize makes me a behavioral science nerd!) This is most evident when we meet someone new and automatically assign identities based on external, contextual factors.

At a conference I attended, we were asked to participate in an identity exercise. We were instructed to choose the top three labels we use to identify ourselves, and share them with the person sitting to our right.

My partner was a woman, who displayed her Indian ethnicity proudly in her clothing, and worked for a large software company. I made the assumption that these three external factors would comprise the three requested identity labels. However, none of them made her list. The terms she did use to describe her identity were Mother, Chef and Artist. I actually enjoyed being so far off the mark—it triggered my curiosity and we dove into a wonderful conversation. I hope this story illustrates how little bearing external factors often have on your Core Identity.

Carl is a great example of this. He worked for a defense contractor and his boss called me up out of desperation. He was on the verge of firing Carl because their relationship had become strained to the breaking point. Coaching was a last resort. When I walked into his office, I could see why Carl's boss was having troubling getting through to him. Carl sported tattoos, a long beard, a flannel shirt, a defensive air, unfriendly manner, and body language that said, "Don't mess with me. I'm the tough guy."

Carl had been with the company for fifteen years. He'd experienced a lot and had seen a lot of people come and go, and he felt angry to have this "skinny young pimple-faced guy" waltz in and take over as his boss. He was rebelling.

However, it turned out that beneath Carl's Tough Guy persona was a huge fear—that if he "gave in" to his boss, and to Corporate America, he would have to cut ties with his family. It turns out Carl was from a small, working class town. He was the first person in his entire family to go to college—ever. Carl had a raging Fraud Critic (with a side of Saboteur and a dash of Comparer) that jammed him with messages like, "Look at all these young guys with their MBAs; you'll never be good enough. You'll never measure up to them. And if you are good enough to hang with the likes of them, then you don't belong in your family anymore."

Carl was clinging to his Tough Guy image because he believed he wouldn't have anything in common with—and therefore no connection with—his family without it. In other words, he had a huge identity crisis. In order to reconcile Carl to the idea that he could live according to his Core Identity *and* retain a connection to his family, I challenged him to check his assumptions: What specifically tells you that your family doesn't accept you? What data do you have to back that up? Using the Truth Series and the Rules in Play activities from chapter four, I helped Carl see the truth in the data of his story and come to a realization that he had to make a choice. He could either continue to live this Tough Guy image that no longer made sense for him (not only had it scared off his boss, it was also affecting his relationship with clients)—or live according to who he is, i.e., explore his Core Identity.

It was only by excavating his internal Core Identity and grounding deeply in who he is that Carl was able to let go of the external identity he'd been clinging to. Ironically, the more Carl started to let go of his Tough Guy façade, the more he was able to step into his confidence. He trimmed his beard and he shed the crippling self-doubt and fear that had kept him stuck in no man's land. Next time he went home, he got some teasing for his "preppy" new look—but the world didn't end. Carl's family didn't cut him off and he didn't get fired. In fact, Carl and his boss had a much better relationship and he even got the chance to lead a big, high-profile project!

ACTIVITY: Update Your Identity

Carl had built his identity around an old story that needed to be updated. That's true for many of us. Be on the lookout for "Identity Quakes"—emotional reactions that are disproportionate to the situation at hand. Ask yourself: what's on the line here? See what identities bubble to the surface, then ask yourself: do I want to retain my attachment to this identity—or is it time to update and choose my Core Identity?

Scan the worksheet to begin to explore which identities fit you most authentically. You may or may not choose an Identity related to the explicit identity labels. They are listed only to prompt your awareness and choices, you do not need to fill any out that don't fit your exploration of Core Identity. The implicit identity words are not meant to be exhaustive, merely to prompt ideas for what choices you may make for your identities. Then, use the following questions to bring clarity and awareness to your Core Identity and to update it, if necessary:

WORKSHEET: Identity Words

EXPLICIT IDENTITIES

Family role _____
Gender _____
Race _____
Ethnicity _____
Nationality _____
Age/Generation _____
Religion _____
Orientation _____
Education _____
Social class _____
Partner status _____
Economic group _____
Eating style _____

Identities not on the list

_____   _____

IMPLICIT IDENTITY WORDS

Boss	Artist
Individual	Contributor
Musician	Coworker
Singer	Team member
Painter	Leader
Writer	Follower
Philosopher	Strategizer
Introvert	Organizer
Extrovert	Idea generator
Optimist	Harmonizer
Pessimist	Peace maker
Adventurer	Bridger
Homebody	Connector
Suburban	Challenger
City	Intellectual
Rural	Learner
Rational	Activist
Emotional	Pacifist
Physical	

_____   _____

- What are your Top Three Identities? Make one list for Work and another for Home. How do both lists compare? Is there any overlap? Are they totally different? Are they the same? Is that okay with you?
- What do each of these Identities mean to you? Why are they important? How do they relate to what Success means to you?

- Which Identities do you want to have most awareness of, because it's *essential* to who you are and how you want to live?
- Are any of your Identities attached to outdated stories that are no longer in alignment with your Core Values and what Success means to you *now*?
- Can you think of a time when one of these Identities felt challenged? How did you respond? (E.I. Builder time!)
- Does your Inner Critic use any of these Identities as an attack point? What's the typical message?

When Core Identity meets Branding

You may not have been aware of it, but it's likely you've experienced and possibly even explored Core Identity work in a business setting. Leadership Branding (a.k.a. Identity) empowers a leader to define who they are and what they stand for, so they can communicate what is most important to others. Team Identity enables a group of people to have a clear sense of what they stand for, how they operate and what they want to be known for. Great leaders know that when a team has a strong Identity, the group tends to build solid, loyal, trusted relationships, and are not easily thrown off by change. Great leaders also know who they are and have intentionally defined how they want to be identified.

Identity work also extends to branding for businesses and products. As the CEO of Connect Growth and Development, I've been through two full-blown rounds of defining our brand as we've grown. Both times it proved incredibly useful—for us as a company, and for me as a leader—in gaining clarity about what we stand for and how we want to be known through our work with clients. In the most recent re-branding process our partner, Braid Creative, had us do an exercise called the Dinner Party. It proved so useful—both personally and professionally—that I asked Kathleen and Tara, the founders, if I could share it in this chapter and they very generously said yes.

You've probably heard this variation of it before: "You're having a dinner party, and you get to invite six guests—it can be anyone, famous or not, alive or deceased. Who do you invite?" Kathleen and Tara take it further by putting a unique spin on it: "Imagine *yourself* as four dinner guests. They can be real people, fictional characters, or your own made-up personifications. Who are they?" Their Dinner Guest activity card explains the intention, "Your company brand is a reflection of your personality, but no one is one-dimensional. So let's get to know the different outward representations of you."

I brainstormed my own four different personalities (dinner guests) , and then exercised the "Get Outside Your Head" practices in chapter five by running my list by three trusted confidants. "Did I capture my most vital Identities, based on what you know about me?" I asked. "What else might you add? What did I miss? Does anyone else (famous, fictional, or real) come to mind when you think of me?"

Boy, did I miss some things—namely, the two bookends of the spectrum that are me. This is why I so emphatically recommend that you do many of these activities in tandem with other people. So, if I haven't said it enough, whenever possible go *talk to others*!

I ended up with six (yes, I did more than four!) important personalities that are part of my company, leadership and work: Business Mogul (which was so obvious that I'd missed it), Geek Scientist, Creative Rocker, Witness, Preacher and Tender Soul (which I also missed because it's a shadow side of me I don't often reveal). As for the famous names I associate with these labels? Sorry, I'm holding out—you'll have to guess who they are!

ACTIVITY: Create Your Dinner Party Guest List

I strongly recommend you bolster the findings of the Update Your Identity activity by brainstorming on your "Dinner Party" guests. It provides further insight into why each identity may be important to you and what intentional choices you'll want to make about the space and energy it gets:

- Imagine *yourself* as four dinner guests. They can be real people, fictional characters, or your own made-up personifications. Who are they?
- If each identity had an area of expertise, what would it be?
- What are three core values of each identity?
- What is the favorite topic of conversation for each identity?

Now, let's take Kathleen's and Tara's exercise one step further by adding an I.C./I.S. layer. For each guest (Identity), ask yourself:

- Which of the Six Classic Critics might trip it up?
- How would it most likely be triggered and what would the I.C. message likely be?
- What's on the line for this particular identity, what really matters to it?

WORKSHEET: My Dinner Guest Identities

	Guest 1	Guest 2	Guest 3	Guest 4
Guest names/labels	_____	_____	_____	_____
Area of expertise	_____	_____	_____	_____
Core values	_____	_____	_____	_____
Favorite conversation	_____	_____	_____	_____
Likely Classic Critic	_____	_____	_____	_____
Critic trigger and message	_____	_____	_____	_____
What's on the line	_____	_____	_____	_____

Keep your dinner guests in mind. The next few chapters will take you down the road of defining your Inner Success, and your Core Identities will prove vital fuel for your journey.

❝ *When you make the finding yourself—even if you're the last person on Earth to see the light—you'll never forget it.*
—Carl Sagan

Core Emotions

While Values and Identity originate primarily in the thinking part of your Whole-Person Intelligence, I also want you to learn to attend to your Core through the feeling part of yourself.

We may be told to "check our emotions at the door," but we don't. Our emotions are what make us passionate about the work we do and they're the reason *why* we care so much about doing a great job. Our emotions are at the center of our love for our families and they explain *why* we care so much about being a great parent, partner, brother, daughter, or friend. Emotions are incredibly important fuel for our lives, and yet the goals, aspirations and choices we make rarely spring from this fertile ground with any intention.

In this section, I challenge you to take a radically different view of Success: describing it as a feeling. (Yes, a feeling.) We usually set goals to define Success, but what we're really after is the *feeling* associated with achieving that goal. So the crazy, new, hyper-efficient practice I want you to develop is to explore which *feelings* you want as part of your Core—those that you want to experience more of.

In her book *The Fire Starter Sessions*, entrepreneurial oracle Danielle LaPorte devoted an entire chapter to what she calls "the strategy of desire." It received so much feedback, LaPorte was compelled to take it even further with "The Desire Map," a multimedia guide that helps people clarify what it is they desire and how they want to feel. "Knowing how you actually want to feel is the most potent form of clarity that you can have," writes LaPorte. "When you're clear on how you want to feel, your decision making gets to the heart of the matter."

As you continue to move towards creating your own definition of

Inner Success, I want you to combine all the important data that will lead to a definition that's true for you and that's in alignment with what really matters to you with *what makes you feel totally fantastic.* Instead of goal-making and list-building, I want you to consider what emotions you want to feel as you ride the journey of your success. Yes, I said during the ride—not after you arrive.

ACTIVITY: Explore Your Emotional Core

To get you started, Ms. LaPorte has kindly given me permission to repurpose her Core Desired Feelings activity in the following exercise that will shine valuable light on the kinds of feelings you want to experience.

Step 1: Grab a journal (or those insanely useful Post-It notes!) and brainstorm on the following question: "How do you want to *feel* in your life?" Remember, brainstorming means no-holds-barred! Include any words, images, ideas or references that surface.

Step 2: Glance back at what you've written and see if you notice any patterns. If you had to sort all your feelings into buckets, describe three to four themes or patterns that stand out.

Step 3: Choose three to four key feelings that represent the main patterns or themes from Step Two and dig underneath them in order to get to their essence. For example, I dug beneath "strong" by asking myself: "What does 'strong' feel like?" I continued to journal on the question until I felt complete in my exploration. I ended up with the word "vibrant," which feels oh-so-right to me. As I work towards my Inner Success, I know I want to feel vibrant. Explore each of your key feelings by asking yourself: "What does [blank] feel like?"

Step 4: Now glance back at everything you've written so far— all the feeling words that have come up—and narrow your Core Emotions down to six to ten words. Write them out and keep them with you. Check in with them occasionally and make changes as needed. See if you can further edit the list to six words that are right for you, right now. We're going to use these again when we get to chapter ten.

Living from Your Core

Exploring your core requires reflective, thoughtful work, and I admit it isn't always easy. A yoga instructor once told me that our core muscles don't actually *want* to do any work. They can be pretty lazy—they'd prefer our legs, arms and shoulders do the heavy lifting. But that leads to injury. To build strong physical core muscles, you have to do exercises that specifically target and engage the core—which takes focus. The same is true for your mental and emotional core: you need to target and engage it with specific activities that make you challenge your brain and churn your emotions. You have to get specific, to be intentional and make choices that aren't always easy to turn into habits. If you do these activities, you will find that the results will absolutely be beneficial. With practice, your interior core will be that strong center that kicks into action when you need it most, without much thought. It will become second nature.

I have a Comparer Critic that loves to point out any woman who's thinner and in better shape than me. It reflects a Core Identity I've always had about being the "fat, out of shape gal." In Pilates, I finally found an activity I enjoyed enough to stick with. After a couple months of private sessions, my instructor, Jenn, suggested I come to a group class so I could see some of the other women. Jenn suspected it was time to update the story of my Identity and she was right. I realized that I was actually much stronger and more flexible than many of my classmates—including the lithe, lean ladies. I needed to update my Identity that having extra weight meant I was out of shape and weak because, clearly, I was far from it.

This is similar to the Core work you've done in this chapter, and which you'll continue to build on as we near the end of this book. From the outside, others may not be able to see how strong your interior core is—but you'll have the confidence that comes with greater strength, the knowledge that you can handle life's challenges and difficulties, and the awareness that you can adapt and move quickly without injury—because of your worthy investment in working your Core.

ACTIVITY: Work It!

Before we wrap up, ponder the following questions. They will prove to be invaluable aids as you continue to engage and flex those muscles you've worked so hard to isolate, tone and strengthen.

1. Of all the Identities you've unearthed this chapter, which ones do you *want* to be attached to? Which ones are worth fighting for? For example, if challenged—either by an Inner or an Outer Critic—what can you let slide and what's non-negotiable?
2. What values, identities and feeling do you relate specifically to Success? Are any of these an "I should" or are they an "I desire?" In other words, are they intentional choices?
3. When at your best, what are your Core Values, Identities and Feelings?
4. Be your own coach: How will you keep your interior Core strong and flexible? What specific activities and exercises do you need to do to stay engaged with your Core?

Keep these core elements in mind as we explore the next two chapters. You'll likely begin to see patterns and themes show up as we continue to dig into your Inner Success, which is perfect (but not Perfectionist)!

8

Know Thy Success; Know Thyself

Having coached thousands of clients who operate at all levels of business, one thing I know for sure is that most of us are intimately aware of our shortcomings and our Critic stories. What we're unfamiliar with and unpracticed in acknowledging are our achievements and our Success stories. We take up most of our energy and time talking about what we did wrong, what we could have done better, what we need to fix and where we need to improve. We're accustomed to talking about all of the above to our coworkers, our partners, and our friends. We rarely, if ever, talk about what we've done right, what we're great at, what we're proud of, what we've overcome and what we've achieved. My hypothesis is that it's essential to be able to talk about our Inner Success stories just as easily and readily as we do our Inner Critic stories.

Picture an empty canoe adrift in the middle of a lake. Imagine that a speedboat passes close by and creates waves. Because it's empty, the canoe is rocked quite violently, right? Now, imagine that same canoe weighted with a few bags of sand that act as ballast. When the speedboat rushes past, the waves come again; however, this time the canoe merely rocks gently before quickly resettling.

I'm sure you got the analogy right off the bat: you are the canoe. The waves represent change, stress or transition. The weight acting as ballast is the self-awareness and self-management you're learning in this book:

- Naming and claiming your Inner Critic
- Learning how to diffuse the Critic with data
- Seeing the Critic with new perspective
- Discovering your Divine Flaw
- Strengthening your Core

These (and a few more in the next chapters) are the ballast that will hold you steady and keep you safe when the storm clouds gather and the water gets choppy. These are the elements that will add just enough weight that the vessel feels stable and balanced but not so much that it sinks. Your goal is not to become heavy and rigid in your definition of who you are because, as you've learned, you are constantly evolving as life unfolds in its mysterious, unpredictable way. Your goal is to know yourself as you are now, with the spaciousness, flexibility and adaptability that will allow your knowledge to grow with you.

"_A ship is safe in harbor, but that's not what ships are for._
—_William G.T. Shedd_

Practicing Success Stories

How much time have you spent worrying about, thinking about and talking about your Critics? I'm guessing it's a cumulative total of weeks, right? How much time have you devoted to celebrating, acknowledging and sharing your Successes? I'm guessing it probably adds up to less than twenty-four hours. It's time to redress the balance. I want you to become as intimately familiar with your strengths as your weaknesses, your heroism as your fear and your triumphs as your failures. There are four enormous benefits to be gained by digging into the details of these moments of glory.

1. Exploring your past successes acts as a reminder that you've done amazing things and won significant victories. This is important,

especially in I.C. moments. As you begin to separate out the details in these success stories, you'll discover tools, strategies and solutions to current problems. In *Lean In: Women, Work, and the Will to Lead*, Sheryl Sandberg shares how she used reminders of past achievements to diffuse the power of the Critic:

> I learned over time that while it was hard to shake feelings of self-doubt, I could understand that there was a distortion. I could challenge the notion that I was constantly headed for failure. When I felt like I was not capable of doing something, I'd remind myself that I did not fail all of my exams in college. Or even one. I learned to undistort the distortion.

2. Mining past memories activates the neural pathways in your brain, lighting up all those areas in which memories are stored. As a result, they are restored to areas of more conscious and present thinking. This is a really good thing because it's the successful moments you want to award more prominence—not your failures!

3. Unpacking the details in these stories often yields the supporting "proof" of your interior Core elements. You'll gain fresh insights into your energizing strengths (which you'll learn about in the next chapter). New data, nuance, breadth and depth will help you to overcome blind spots and distortions, while living a life that embodies more of the essence of success.

4. Lastly, it just plain feels good to remind yourself how awesome you are! Sure, it may feel a little strange and uncomfortable at first (more on that in a moment), but in the end you'll find it's just great juju! And good energy is like high-octane fuel: we accomplish more when we feel good.

Remember Alex from chapter one? When we started working together, he was a nervous wreck. He had a million things on his To Do list (Driver Inner Critic alert), he was falling behind and felt overwhelmed. I asked Alex if time management had often been a challenge?

He laughed and said, "Oh yeah, this is *always* on my list of areas I need to improve. I always feel underwater." I had Alex do an E.I. Builder check-in on this topic. What came out was like an MTV Mash-Up with two critics (The Driver and The Fraud) crunched together, and smacking on him big time:

- "You're so not good enough to be a manager here."
- "You're not getting enough done."
- "They'll find out eventually and kick your butt to the curb."
- "You're not contributing anything of value.
- "You have to be in every meeting or they'll realize you've got nothing to offer."

Alex felt worried, anxious, even panicky at times—and it all lived in the pit of his stomach. His auto-pilot response was to become frenetic, flipping from one topic to another. I could see it in his body language—eyes darting around, toes tapping on the floor, fingers drumming on the desk.

I used the Truth Series questions to un-scramble Alex's mash-up. When exploring what was less true in his I.C. messages, it emerged that Alex had a vast and impressive series of Successes under his belt. I had him watch Shawn Achor's TED talk on "The Happy Secret to Better Work" (which I recommend that you watch, too). The main point to hit home for Alex was that he would continually "push the goal post out." Each time he reached a goal, he moved it, so he never let himself feel the satisfaction of achievement. He never marked or even acknowledged his Successes.

Alex's coaching homework was to practice recognizing at least one Success every day. Yes, he rolled his eyes at me. Yes, he was uncomfortable with it. "I get it, Sugar," I laughed with him (Alex didn't mind, he's a good sport). "But let's just call it an experiment and see what happens." Like the champ he is, Alex tried it. It worked. His confidence level shot up, he finally saw the value he added to the company, he was finally able to focus, prioritize his tasks, manage his time and, eventually, feel on top of things. Best of all, he was a much happier person.

I offer all my clients the following deal: I'll help you mine your I.C. story, but in return you owe me the time and energy to develop and practice your I.S. story. Now I'm going to offer you the same deal: We've spent a lot of time and energy exploring your I.C. Are you ready and willing to become equally acquainted with your I.S. story? You'd better be, because grand and glorious information about your future definition of success can lie within the stories of your past achievements. You'd think it would be a cinch to talk about success stories, but actually it's very difficult. Before we start to talk about yours, I want to make you aware of the following pitfalls:

You may get emotional or stuck. Almost every time I ask someone to write or talk about their Successes, they have a sudden, strong reaction. If that happens, stop and bring your awareness to what's happening. By that I mean ask yourself the three E.I. Builder Questions:

- What are you feeling: mad, sad, glad or afraid? Name the feeling. Remember, you've got to name it to claim it.
- What are you thinking? Notice any thoughts, stories, assumptions, and/or judgments.
- What's happening in your body? Did your stomach do a little lurch? Did your shoulders hunch up? Have you stopped breathing? Did you jump out of your seat and start pacing the room? Did you close the book and say, "time for a coffee break"? Don't worry. This is perfectly normal.

Most people are reluctant to talk about themselves in a positive, glowing light. No one wants to be seen as arrogant, bragging, or "that guy." I'm not asking you to become the Miles Davis of the office—tooting your own horn. But I do want you to practice what it feels like to talk about your Successes—and to stay present when the discomfort arises. Remember, emotional awareness and self-management is a cornerstone practice for increasing your Emotional Intelligence!

You'll probably try to share the credit with someone else. You'd be amazed how often a client starts telling a Success story when, all of a sudden, it becomes all about someone else. Sorry, that won't cut it in this exercise - I don't want to hear about your team, your boss, or your kids—I'm sure they're all just lovely, but right now I want to hear about you, you, you! I also don't want to hear about a time when someone else recognized you as being successful. That only counts if you truly believe it to be one of your all-time most successful moments.

You'll probably get a little judge-y. Clients oftentimes start to drift off, ever so gently, into what was wrong or not entirely perfect about the situation . . . and I will ever so gently remind them to stay focused on the positive side of their story. During a workshop, I was listening to Lisbeth describe one of her successes: getting the nod to run a big team in an engineering organization. Midway through her story, Lisbeth started the drift: "I realize they didn't have many other options, I mean there weren't many other suitable candidates." (Yup, Lisbeth has that dang Fraud Critic.) I leaned over to Lisbeth and encouraged her to stay on the strong side of the story and she drifted back. Afterwards, the whole group talked about how difficult it was to stick to the success, the positive, the upside. Yup, it's true and it's fairly normal, but it's also a discipline. And a good number of my clients tell me they want to become more disciplined at focusing on the positive because it's much more motivating and engaging.

ACTIVITY: Spotlight Your Successes

Cast your mind back to two occasions when you've felt unbelievably successful. Open your journal and write three to five sentences that describe each one. When you've finished briefly describing these, answer the following five questions for both success stories.

WORKSHEET: My Successes

Success #1— Brief Description:

_____

_____

_____

_____

_____

Success #2—Brief Description:

_____

_____

_____

_____

_____

What characteristics were true of you in each of these moments?

_____

_____

_____

How do these stories illustrate the Core Values, Identities and Feelings you uncovered in Chapter Seven? Have they highlighted any Core elements you might have missed—or been blind to?

_____

_____

_____

What were you feeling in each Success situation?

_____

_____

_____

What were you thinking?

_____

_____

_____

What was your physical reaction—what specifically was energizing about this experience?

_____

_____

_____

Take Pride In Your Prouds

Prouds—your proudest moments—bring things much closer to home, because they're less about what your culture, your parents, your peers, or your friends deem "successful" and more concerned with how you have experienced success in your life. Prouds reflect you at your essence. We're never compelled to feel "proud" of something based on what society at large dictates; we either feel proud or we don't, there's no cloud of expectation hanging over it.

Charley described one of her Prouds: the day she presented a session at the National Sales Conference and hers was rated the second most valuable talk of the entire event. This was a huge leap for Charley. She's an introvert—she's quiet, soft-spoken, and abhors being in the limelight. So standing up on stage in front of all her peers with a mic in hand was *way* outside her comfort zone. Charley told me how she was almost overcome by terror as she stood in front of the packed room and realized she was about to expose herself to judgment, criticism and possibly even ridicule. She felt incredibly vulnerable. However, much to Charley's shock, pride and joy, instead of judging her negatively, her peers *loved* what she had to say. She got a standing ovation.

Remember Nitya from chapter five, whose passion include creating community and giving back (i.e., Core Values)? When she finally had the courage to lay out what gave her energy and what she was interested in, and ask for what she wanted, her boss was super-supportive. She coordinated with colleagues in other offices to create a 24-hour run-a-thon that raised awareness and money for one of her favorite causes. It was incredibly successful and it brought Nitya to the attention of some very important people within her company. She was asked to consult on different ways of modeling what she had created in other areas throughout the organization. Nitya ended up carving out a role for herself with a scope of creating community on a global level. When I first met Nitya she was on the verge of quitting her job. But because she gave herself permission and summoned the courage to go after what she wanted, Nitya was able to create her dream job—and by far one of her most Proud moments.

ACTIVITY: Explore Your Prouds

Think about two occasions when you felt really proud of yourself. Take out your journal and write three to five sentences to describe both Proud moments. Again, if you're an extrovert, you might want to write down some quick thoughts now and chew on them later with a friend. Introverts will likely be happy to explore their thoughts solo. When you're done describing your two most Proud moments, answer the following five questions for both.

WORKSHEET: My Prouds

Proud Moment #1—Brief Description:

_____

_____

_____

_____

_____

Proud Moment #2—Brief Description:

_____

_____

_____

_____

_____

1. What characteristics were true of you in each of these moments?

_____

_____

_____

2. How do these stories illustrate the Core Values, Identities and Feelings you uncovered in Chapter Seven? Have they highlighted any Core elements you might have missed—or been blind to?

_____

_____

_____

3. What were you feeling in each Success situation?

_____

_____

_____

4. What were you thinking?

_____

_____

_____

5. What was your physical reaction—what specifically was energizing about this experience?

_____

_____

_____

You've been following Phoebe's story throughout the book. She experienced a seismic shift while exploring her Prouds. After initially stumbling and faltering, Phoebe finally opened up—and she blew me away when she began telling a fantastic set of stories. Phoebe had hiked and cycled her way across a continent with her partner. She told of their wild escapades, having no plan and very little structure, yet finding the most wonderful locations and meeting the most amazing and generous people. With my encouragement, Phoebe shared about all the trips she'd taken over the years. The moments she was most proud of occurred when she was exploring new cultures and countries, and soaking it all up like a sponge.

Phoebe answered the above questions without hesitation. She listed off her characteristics of courage, adventure and spontaneity, her traits of being adaptable and flexible, her Identity as a Learner and Explorer, and her Core Value of sharing the knowledge she'd acquired on her adventures. She told me she'd felt vibrant, excited, challenged and peaceful in these special moments. Her physical reaction was impossible to miss: Phoebe lit up like a Roman Candle!

In reliving these amazing tales, Phoebe connected with the strongest fibers of her Divinity and realized that she has, in fact, an *enormous* amount to offer to her young colleagues at work!

Like Phoebe, I know you probably found it uncomfortable to talk yourself up to such an extent, but I'll bet it also had the effect of reminding you about all the great stuff you've done. At a workshop I once facilitated, I had people pair up to do these exercises. I vividly recall Ellen putting her hand up afterwards because she had something she wanted to share with the group. "You know, I set such a high bar for myself and I work in such a competitive culture that I've forgotten all the really cool things I've done in my career," said Ellen. "It feels *great* to remember that and to reconnect with it. Even though it was hard to talk about, I feel better than I have in years." I asked her partner in the exercise, Grant, to stand up. "Grant, did it sound like Ellen was bragging or being arrogant?" I asked. "Not at all!" said Grant. "In fact, it was so cool to hear her talk about all these rad things she's done. I had no idea she'd accomplished so much in life!"

That's how I want you to feel after reading this chapter. The fact that you're reading this book tells me you're probably very hard on yourself—but you've also probably had way more Successes than you give yourself credit for. The discipline is in reminding yourself of your accomplishments and your achievements, your Successes and your Prouds. That's a practice in itself.

ACTIVITY: Meditate on This!

I want you to work a short meditation into your schedule every day for one week. This doesn't mean you have to sit cross-legged on a cushion and chant, "Om" for hours (unless you want to). This meditation activity is really very easy. Every night, while brushing your teeth, I want you to remind yourself of your Successes and Prouds from that day. If you had one of "those" days where you can't think of any—first, try a bit harder. If you're still stuck, go back to yesterday or the day before and find a new moment to bring to your attention. Just focus on your Successes and Prouds. That's it. Just bring your awareness to these precious moments and feel them seep into your bones.

Don't worry, this practice will not change you into "that guy." If you weren't an arrogant, egocentric jerk last week you won't become one this week. And you've probably got a good set of friends to call you out on it if you do.

The purpose of this exercise is to remind you of how great you are, and to help instill the practice of speaking to your Successes because that in itself has a way of making you feel more powerful —as it did for Alex. It's also a great way to take inventory on your assets—your talents, strengths and resources.

The reason I had you thoroughly explore your Successes and Prouds in this chapter is so you can look back into your history and remind yourself that you've already enjoyed huge success. You have done countless things you're proud of, displayed epic acts of heroism and have stepped into the best version of you. In undergoing this process, you've gained a huge amount of self-awareness and I hope you've also seen where and how you can intentionally take those assets that worked wonders for you in the past and add them to your present experience. My goal is that you learn to practice possibility and Success with *more* measure than you've practiced doubt and failure.

Share Your Energy

I want to emphasize once again the benefit of doing these activities in tandem with others. Sharing our stories helps us feel connected, seen, known and understood. An added bonus is that other people mirror back to us the parts of ourselves we're unable to see (remember, we're not the best observers of ourselves). Whenever I work with teams or large groups of people, I always ask what it was like to hear other people share their stories. The feedback unequivocally tells me that when we share our truths we feel more bonded, we learn so much more about each other, and we gain wisdom by learning of other people's experiences.

And when we practice sharing our Successes and Proud Moments, we open up space for others to share, too. Our society (and sometimes our own internal Rules In Play) shuns the sharing of these highlights. It's much more accepted to be disparaging of ourselves and others—you certainly don't have to search hard in today's media for sensational headlines that hint at lurid tales of wrong-doing, tragic loss and epic failures. We may not be able to change the world, but we can change ourselves—we can all practice opening up a little space for sharing examples of our best moments.

My dear friend and colleague Jan Gelman and I have been practicing this for a few years now. We'll call each other up and say, "Can I tell you something amazing that just happened?" When we started, our tendency was to preface our reveals with caveats—I'm especially guilty of this because of my Critic's "Don't get too big for your britches" mantra. I'd say, "Now, I don't want to brag . . . but I'm kinda excited . . . do you mind terribly if I share this?" Or, I'd share and then start to drift negative. One day however, we both agreed to practice what we preach: give up the caveats, focus on the positive, and enjoy the great energy of sharing a Success.

This is a great place to pause and remind ourselves of the brilliant quote by Marianne Williamson, used by former South African President Nelson Mandela in his inaugural speech on May 9th, 1994, in Cape Town:

> Our deepest fear is not that we are inadequate. Our deepest
> fear is that we are powerful beyond measure. It is our light, not
> our darkness that most frightens us. We ask ourselves, Who
> am I to be brilliant, gorgeous, talented, fabulous? Actually,
> who are you not to be? You are a child of God. Your playing
> small does not serve the world. There is nothing enlight-
> ened about shrinking so that other people won't feel insecure
> around you. We are all meant to shine, as children do. We were
> born to make manifest the glory of God that is within us. It's
> not just in some of us; it's in everyone. And as we let our own
> light shine, we unconsciously give other people permission.

Share your Success stories. See if it doesn't feel good (after you get past the discomfort).

I told you earlier in this chapter that Alex transformed his sensation of overwhelm by acknowledging his Successes, but I didn't tell you what took the practice to another level for him. It's a rather wonderful story. Alex enlisted his wife's help in holding him accountable to do his homework. She thought it was such a great idea that she introduced it as a nightly dinnertime practice wherein all five of them (they have three young children) would share something that happened that day that made them feel successful or proud. One night Alex's youngest son, Nicholas, shared that he'd crushed a spider in the yard and he wasn't one bit scared. It suddenly sunk in for Alex: he needed to stop and savor *all* the moments, big and small. The image of his small son being so proud of having the courage to face his fear of spiders filled Alex with pride and cemented for him the understanding that by constantly shifting the goal posts, he was cheating himself of a life of joy and innocence and fun. What an incredible impact for an entire family! Oh, and did I mention how much I love my work?

9

Rocking Your Strengths PLUS

Many books have been written in support of the theory that it's far more powerful and efficient to focus on our Strengths and what we enjoy doing, than to try and shore up our weaknesses. In studies of over 80,000 managers across hundreds of organizations, the Gallup Organization found that the world's best managers operate by an underlying principle that "each person's greatest room for growth is in the areas of his or her greatest strengths." As a coach, I'm a firm believer in this theory. It is much more energy efficient to utilize our Strengths to amplify our success and to compensate for our lesser developed skills.

The objective of this chapter is to take advantage of and put into practice these extensively tested theories by helping you identify your Strengths, Superpowers and moments of Flow. I want you to get very clear on the skills and activities that energize you. Countless studies have shown that the more we infuse our day-to-day lives with the activities we're energized by, the more we increase our overall sense of meaning, satisfaction and contentedness, which has everything to do with our Inner Success—and our Outer Success, for that matter. The other important benefit of increased satisfaction is that it leaves the Inner Critic with fewer opportunities to prey on and gnaw at us. My goal is that you become intimate with your Strengths and use them intentionally, finding ways to employ them in *more* areas of your life.

> **"**Casting a critical eye on our weaknesses and working hard to manage them, while sometimes necessary, will only help us prevent failure. It will not help us reach excellence . . . you will reach excellence only by understanding and cultivating your strengths. —Marcus Buckingham & Donald O. Clifton, Now, Discover Your Strengths

Expanding your energy, and your capacity for energy, is an important part of leading a fuel-efficient life. You want to go green? Figuring out your core elements—like Values—then aligning these with your Flow moments and energizing Strengths is the most fuel-efficient you can get—that's you at your most environmentally-friendly (if it's good for the Earth, it can be good for self!). Focusing on these three elements will make for a happier and more satisfied life than anything else you can do . . . except for maybe living in service to the poor of India like Mother Teresa did. But we can't all be Mother Teresa . . . although I would venture to guess that she was in Flow while serving the poor (which would make it essentially energizing for her). Most of us, on the other hand, can't imagine living that way because that's not *our* recipe for Flow. So, let's figure out what yours is, shall we?

Finding Your Own Flow

The first tool in gaining awareness and clarity, and for rockin' your Strengths, is to understand the concept of Flow. In his book *Flow: The Psychology of Optimal Experience*, Mihaly Csíkszentmihályi proposes that people are most happy when they're in "flow"—a state of such complete absorption with the activity at hand that they lose track of time. Do you recall a situation when you were so at-one with what you were doing, you lost all sense of space and time and felt totally energized afterwards? It might not necessarily have happened at work, it could have happened when you were running, rowing, taking a yoga class, painting, reading, writing, giving a talk, golfing, or goofing around with your children. It can happen in lots of different contexts. Clients often use phrases like these to describe such moments: "in the zone," "wired in," "on fire," "blissed out," "Zen present," "got game," "slammin & poppin." Okay, maybe not the last one, I got a little carried away. But you get the idea, right? All these phrases are infused with emotion and energy, great indicators of Flow moments.

When I think of Flow, I think of Neo in the movie *The Matrix*. Do you recall how, when all of the made-up Matrix stuff disappears, Neo becomes completely attuned to the present moment? So much so, he's able to dodge bullets so easily it feels like everything's happening in slow motion. And we all dig it when he does that back-bend!

I remember one of my Neo-like, back-bend Flow moments. Momma, I had game! It was my second "What Really Matters" event. (W.R.M. is a workshop I created to bring people together to get clear on what really matters, and to map out steps to implement it.) I'd decided to do this event all by myself (previously, I'd had other facilitators handle portions of the day). I had a couple colleagues in the room to support me, but I and I alone had the microphone *all* day. I'd never done it before and didn't know I had it in me. (My I.C. always told me I wasn't good enough to hold a room for that long: "Who'd want to listen to *you* all day?") But, contrary to my I.C. message, not only could I hold the room, I owned the room! I was on fire! I didn't do any back bends, though, because that would've hurt.

I met all of the qualifications Csíkszentmihályi describes as Flow:

1. *Intense and focused concentration* on the present moment.
2. *A merging of action and awareness.*
3. A *loss of reflective self-consciousness.*
4. A sense of personal *control* or agency over the situation or activity.
5. A *distortion of temporal experience*; one's subjective experience of time is altered.
6. Experience of the activity as *intrinsically rewarding (also* referred to as *autotelic experience).*

The time flew by. I felt completely energized throughout the day and I left the event feeling *even more* energized. I'd been on my feet for 10 hours, talking through a good portion of that time, working the room, getting other people engaged and joining in the conversation—yet, I arrived home feeling fresh, invigorated and thrilled. As if that wasn't astonishing enough, I continued to feel insanely good for two whole days after the workshop. My brain and all my neurons were firing at peak performance. My neocortex was in its supremeness. I was coming up with new ideas that stunned even me; I had to carry around Post-it notes to capture my thoughts, they were coming so fast. I called it the "after burn" effect. I also noticed that I felt more loving, compassionate and generous in the days that followed. In fact, I was a bit sappy. A bright sunny day went way beyond enjoyable; it was a masterpiece. I was feeling in tune with God and the universe. Don't get me wrong; I also experienced my usual post-workshop I.C. onslaughts. But magically, as soon as the I.C. message popped into my head I'd swiftly and easily toss it aside, knowing it was completely invalid.

I've never taken a drug like heroin or bungee jumped from a towering bridge but I wondered if the high I was feeling was similar to those activities. I felt spectacular, nothing else came close, and I knew I wanted to recreate the conditions that would allow me to experience this high again—as often as possible. So I sat down and made a list of the conditions and qualities that added up to my own personal "got game" moment, a.k.a. Flow (Bonus: it's much better than taking drugs or risking my life!). I want you to make your own customized Flow list too, in just a moment!

One of the elements of Flow theory I find particularly fascinating and useful in my coaching practice is that the degree of challenge in the Flow activity must match a person's degree of skill. If the degree of challenge is low and our skill level high, we become bored. If the degree of challenge is greater than our skills, we become worried and anxious. Marcus Buckingham writes about this concept in *Now, Discover Your Strengths*: "When we asked [excellent performers] what aspect of work they enjoyed most, we heard a common refrain: Almost all of them liked their job when they met a challenge and then overcame it."

It makes sense that we're at our best when we're challenged to use our unique Strengths in service to an endeavor that we consider important. Therefore, when searching for your Flow moments, recall times when you've felt the most challenged *and* the most energized according to Csíkszentmihályi's list of Flow qualifications, which I've tweaked a little so it's more user- friendly:

1. Time goes by so fast, you may lose all track of it.
2. You have a high degree of concentration and focus.
3. You're fully immersed and engaged in the activity at hand; you don't get distracted.
4. You're energized throughout the activity. In fact, you may have even more juice afterwards.
5. You feel great—meaning, you're thoroughly enjoying yourself— both during and after.
6. You're using everything you've got in service of this moment: your thoughts, your emotions, and your body.

ACTIVITY: Capture Your Flow

Think of a moment in your life when you lost all track of time because you were enjoying yourself *that* much. Don't self-edit! Go with whatever comes up instinctively and intuitively. Maybe it was one of your Success or Proud moments from the last chapter? If nothing comes up, then think about a time when you had more energy after finishing the task at hand than when you started. It might have felt like you were giddily dancing around or bouncing up and down or perhaps, like me, you felt like your brain was firing on all neurons.

Ask yourself the following questions:

• What was I doing?
• What were the conditions and qualities of the activity?
• What characteristic and skills was I employing?

Make a list in your journal of the specific conditions and qualities that were present—both in the situation and in yourself, putting particular focus on anything relating specifically to *your* involvement and contribution. Start now to develop the habit of noticing Flow moments occurring in your life and continue to track the condition and qualities inherent in them.

Energy Drainers

Conversely, it's helpful to know what activities deplete your energy and are oh-so *not* fuel efficient—like a 1975 Cadillac V8. You know, the clunker that does eight miles per gallon? Obviously these are the situations you want to avoid or minimize whenever possible. If it's not possible, please schedule a nice game of golf or a bath and bonbons to follow those energy-sucking tasks. This is where your body awareness will play a crucial role: you'll be able to sense your energy levels rising and falling by tuning in to your body's voice, what your body is saying to you.

Cara was working on a branding project for a department store, creating content for their website. Each day a group of five designers was featured in a series of banners. Her job included writing the short blurbs to go with them. It became a task she dreaded. The designers were on rotation, which meant that they were repeated about every two to three weeks. Cara had to write a new blurb each time, basically regurgitating the same information—yet endeavoring to make it sound fun, fresh, engaging and enticing. It was repetitive and it didn't call to Cara's greatness: her creativity. Worse, it was draining her creative abilities. The task failed to challenge Cara's cognitive skills (she has a big, beautiful, problem-solving, branding-genius brain that was being under-utilized). It also failed to satisfy her Core Feelings of fulfilled and challenged, her Value of truth, and her Identity of helper. Bottom line: it was both an energy and an emotions vampire and it was sucking her dry. Just thinking about the project was enough to make Cara feel sick to her stomach.

ACTIVITY: Track Your Energy Vampires

Think of a time when you were engaged in an activity that left you feeling more exhausted than usual, or than you thought you should feel. I'm not talking about a new activity—learning something new drains your energy faster than performing a task you already know how to do. This isn't what I mean by energy drainer. I'm talking about being engaged in doing something you've done before. You know the activity, you have experience performing the activity . . . nevertheless . . . time . . . just . . . crawls.

Ask yourself the following questions:

- What was I doing?
- What were the conditions and qualities of the activity?
- What characteristic and skills was I employing?

In your journal, make a list of the specific conditions and qualities that were present—both in the situation and in yourself, putting particular focus on anything relating specifically to *your* involvement/contribution. From here forward, start to notice energy-draining moments and continue to track the condition and qualities inherent in them.

> **"***My recipe for more flow is as follows: Identify your signature strengths. Choose work that lets you use them every day. Recraft your present work to use your signature strengths more. If you are the employer, choose employees whose signature strengths mesh with the work they will do. If you are a manager, make room to allow employees to recraft the work within the bounds of your goals. —Martin Seligman,* Authentic Happiness

Thanks for playing the environmentally friendly, go-green-with-your-bad-self game. Now, I want you researching your day-to-day world for opportunities to implement your new Green Me awareness. You can't be in "got game" moments constantly, but you can use the power of your awareness to create as many opportunities as possible to add Energizing Flow moments and to subtract Energy Drainers. When you put together both of these elements, you'll be richly rewarded with greater Inner—and Outer—Success.

Strengths PLUS

Like Working Your Core (Values, Identities and Feelings) and Knowing Thyself via your Successes & Prouds, it's important to gain clarity around your key Strengths. Just as with your Critic stories and your Successes stories, it's likely you're way more familiar with your weaknesses than your Strengths. If you're looking to create opportunities to utilize your Strengths and Flow moments, then you must know these Strengths intimately—not just as a passing flirtation! There's far more to this than just a Strengths assessment (Gallup has a great one), which is why I added "PLUS," so stay with me.

ACTIVITY: Clarify Your Strengths

There are three steps in this Clarify Your Strengths activity. Let's start with the first one, shall we?

Step 1: On the worksheet, circle *all* the Strengths you believe you can be counted on to deliver consistently and reliably. If it's something you do only once in a while, it doesn't count. It's only a Strength if you consistently bring it to the table. Clients usually ask if I'm talking about "work" Strengths (i.e., skills they utilize in the workplace). The answer is No—it's a great idea to inventory *all* your Strengths, regardless of where and when they show up.

The Strengths list presented is by no means inclusive of every conceivable Strength that exists—but it should provide enough examples to trigger your brain to come up with as many consistent Strengths as possible. You'll notice there are several blank spaces;

if any of your consistently delivered Strengths aren't listed here, write them in these spaces.

Go with your gut—don't try to limit or narrow or question what you circle. Some people will see a word like "gentle" and their first thought will be, "Well, I *am* gentle but I've never thought of that as a Strength." We're not always good judges of our own skills; in fact, sometimes we see our own Strengths as limitations.

This came up with my client, Chris. He was diligently going through the list, circling like crazy when all of a sudden he stopped. "Reserved?" questioned Chris, with a perplexed look on his face. "Why's that on the list? I consider myself reserved but I've always thought of it as a weakness." I asked Chris to think of someone he knows who's reserved. "My mother," he replied with a frown. That explained it. If there's anything on this list you see in a negative light, and it's a trait displayed by someone important in your life, trust that it's a Strength—it's just laden with judgment, and you don't have a fair or unbiased view of it. Guess why I personally don't like "authoritative?" But I could totally see Chris' "reserved" strength as a skill. People who have that trait—and put it to good use—are wonderful listeners and observers, they catch and pick up on way more than other people. However, it's also true that if Chris is reserved too much of the time, it can work against him.

What I asked him to do is be aware that he has this Strength, and apply it when it will prove most useful and effective—instead of simply allowing him to stay in his comfort zone. Don't strike a skill just because of its affiliation to someone in your life—you're not that person. But you need to be intentional in the use of that Strength.

WORKSHEET: Strength words

Adaptable
Adventurous
Affectionate
Ambitious
Analytical
Appreciative
Approachable
Authoritative
Broad-minded
Caring
Challenging
Clear
Communicative
Compassionate
Competent
Competitive
Connected
Consistent
Contextual
Cooperative
Courageous

Creative
Decisive
Dependable
Determined
Direct
Disciplined
Driven
Easygoing
Empathetic
Energetic
Enterprising
Fair-minded
Focused
Forward-looking
Gentle
Harmonious
Honest
Idealistic
Imaginative
Inclusive
Independent

Influential
Innovative
Inspiring
Intelligent
Loyal
Mature
Observant
Open
Organized
Original
Participative
Patient
Persuasive
Playful
Positive
Powerful
Practical
Precise
Protective
Purposeful
Quick

Realistic
Receptive
Reserved
Resourceful
Responsible
Restorative
Self-Assured
Self-controlled
Sensible
Spontaneous
Strategic
Supportive
Sympathetic
Systematic
Task-focused
Theoretical
Thorough
Tough-minded
Traditional
Visionary

Strengths not on the list _____ _____

_____ _____ _____ _____

Step 2: This is where the PLUS bonus comes into play in this strengths activity! I want you to determine what happens to your *energy* when you're employing these Strengths. I often describe this to my clients using the acronym LOL that is part of texting lexicon. LOL in this case indicates your energy being Lighter, feeling more Open, and Lifted (and in texting LOL is Lots Of Laughs, which I think is energizing too!).

Review the Strengths you've circled as those you deliver consistently. Now add a PLUS sign (+) next to anything that's energizing to you (hereafter referred to as an LOL). Put a minus sign (-) beside anything that's does the opposite to your energy (heavy, limiting, draining). The energizing effect of a Strength may very well be situational, you can leave those free of a + or − sign as neutral or variable. However, many of our Strengths have a strong tendency to be an energy lifter or an energy drainer—so indicate which happens most often.

Sure, we have lots of Strengths and capabilities, but that doesn't mean we actually *enjoy* using them all. One of my Strengths is organization, it would be circled. I used to work in accounting and I'm hell on wheels good with a spreadsheet. I'm good at organizing, but I don't enjoy it—it doesn't energize me so it would get a minus sign. Our goal is to narrow our focus to only the activities/endeavors/traits/strengths you *enjoy* utilizing.

John has many years of business experience and is blessed with numerous talents. In his current role, he most often utilizes his Strength of project management. He's very good at his job, but it doesn't make him happy—it doesn't *feel* satisfying, so John doesn't *feel* successful. He was really puzzled by this. As John and I reviewed his Strengths, I asked him to categorize them according to the energizing LOL factors he experienced when employing them. There were two glaring gaps creating a giant black hole that was sucking John in. First, the Strengths that served him well in his project manager role—organization, resourcefulness, and communication—were low on his LOL index. At the same time, we discovered that John enjoyed himself enormously when engaging a different set of skills—creativity, learning, and systems flow—on a side project where he was building an online learning tool. These Flow moments literally caused him to vibrate with energy, light up with enthusiasm and lose all track of time! However, John didn't perceive these skills as Strengths, so he'd discounted them.

I explained to John that being great at something you don't *feel* satisfied doing can suck you into a day filled with tasks that dampen your spirit and color your world a dull shade of gray. Trying something new, on the other hand, is risky. It requires that you defy your

Inner Critic and it takes commitment and dedication, but the pay-off—work that's satisfying, joyful and colorful—is totally worth it.

> **"**There are clear benefits to choosing the win-win option by using signature strengths to better advantage. This approach makes work more fun, transforms the job or the career into a calling, increases flow, builds loyalty, and it is decidedly more profitable. Moreover, by filling work with gratification, it is a long stride on the road to the good life. —Martin Seligman, Authentic Happiness

Step 3: It's time for the Clarity Dance. Look back to your Flow moments and see what Strengths you were employing. If any of these have not yet been circled, do it now. Or, if they're not on the list, write them in one of the available blank spaces. Put a PLUS beside them because they're clearly LOL's!

Step 4: Okay, I lied, there's actually another step! It's not so much a step as a time to reflect and plan for some *action*. I want you to review all the Strengths you've circled *and* marked as LOLs, then choose your Top Six. These are the Strengths that 1) you deliver consistently, 2) boost your energy, and 3) you really *enjoy* using. Yes, I said Top Six and No, you can't have more, and No, you can't have less. Just listen to your friendly coach and pick six! For each Strength, journal on the following four questions:

1. When do you find yourself using this Strength the most (think about situations in both your work and home life)?
2. When do you use it the least?
3. When do you never utilize it? Do those moments align to times when you have less energy versus when you have more gas in your tank? Are you beginning to see a pattern?
4. When and how could you start infusing more of this Strength into your life? Identify one concrete area where you can do it

immediately. This is what I call "coaching-to-action" or "putting your new insights to use"!

I was recently helping a group of leaders tackle this Strengths Clarity activity. They were very clear about Step One—easy peasy, done it a hundred times, what are my Strengths. But when I asked them to highlight the energizing (LOL) ones, they had to pause. This was clearly a totally foreign concept. Then I really had them when I asked that they select the Strengths they wanted to bring into their lives more frequently. Here each member of the group really had to slow down and get intentional: What do I really want to do more of? What do I want to create? At work we often go on auto-pilot and do the task that makes sense for the project or program. However, you can also be more intentional and think about who's energized by a task instead. Yes, we have to do some work that doesn't energize us—let's just not go that route if there's an alternative that works. That's the kicker—a Strengths inventory is fine, but I want you to go much further by:

1. Raising your awareness level around those moments that bring you to life and fill you up.
2. Knowing what Strengths you're engaging in these moments.
3. Taking action and **intentionally creating more of these moments**.

The result? More enjoyment, energy, happiness and satisfaction. Added bonus: The Inner Critic has a really hard time gaining any traction when you're happy!

Like most reflections and activities in this book, you'll want to keep track of this. Your Strengths are not static and they're not something to be carved in stone. As you continue to learn and grow, your Strengths PLUS will naturally shift over time. I want you to stay aware of the ones that play the biggest role in your *current* iteration of Inner Success—always being careful to use them intentionally and thoughtfully.

Use Your Superpowers

A Superpower is a Strength or skill you *really* enjoy using. You're very, very good at it. You've been identifying energizing strengths above, but here's the difference with a Superpower—it's so effortless and ease-filled for you, you may not even think of it as a skill. It's second nature. You assume that everyone can do it, but they can't—not like you can, because it's your Superpower. Your friends and colleagues are more likely to spot it than you are. Buckingham illustrates this succinctly in *Now, Discover Your Strengths* when he tells the story of Bruce, who won a prestigious teaching award. One of Bruce's Strengths is Empathy—he can really tune into students' feelings, which makes them feel heard and understood. When Buckingham was interviewing him, Bruce asked, "Doesn't everybody do that?" Many of us don't realize how incredible our Superpowers are. We assume they aren't that big of a deal, but they are. Our Superpowers are what distinguish us from everyone else.

What makes Superpowers so fantastic is that being second nature to you, they consume almost zero energy. They may well be the most fuel-efficient Strength you could ever have. Imagine a car that ran on air—with no need for gas or electric power? Wouldn't you want to buy hyper-energy-efficient car? In the same vein, wouldn't you want to know about and intentionally use a Superpower? I started learning about this in grad school. I was coming up with a list of my Strengths and one of my classmates, Susanne—who had by now become a good friend—suggested I include "humor." I mockingly scoffed, "Humor? That's not a Strength. That's just something I do." Susanne said, "Yes, but your humor is really effective and useful and valuable when facilitating. You might think about using it more intentionally." (Total Disclaimer: not everybody thinks I'm funny. This is what Susanne said. I'm not making any claims on the title, "Queen of Comedy!")

It's quite extraordinary how often we discount our Superpowers. A good friend of mine, Rose, once helped me pull together an event. I was organizing a women's conference and I desperately needed assistance because planning events (and anticipating the myriad issues that arise) is not my *forte*. Rose was happy to volunteer her services. "Oh, that's so easy!" she said, batting away my profuse thank yous. After a stunningly successful event, I once again attempted to thank Rose . . . and once again she deflected: "Ugh! It was *nothing*! Anybody can do *that*!" This told me right away that event planning is one of Rose's Superpowers because, as many of you know, pulling off an event is *not* easy. And if it came *that* easy to her, then *you know* she's good! That's the paradox of the Superpower: we don't often give ourselves credit for it because we don't even see it as a Strength.

ACTIVITY: Unlock Your Superpowers

One of the best ways to figure out your Superpowers is to ask other people what your Strengths are, then be on high alert for anything they bring up that you reject. (Again, choose someone whose opinion and integrity you trust.) If you find yourself saying, "Oh *that's* not a Strength," you've hit the jackpot.

Ask your friend: "How do you see that as a Strength? Do you have any ideas about how I could see that more intentionally as a Strength in my life?" It's amazing how we'll see something through a radically new lens when another person mirrors it back to us.

Once you've identified two or three Superpowers, keep them close to your chest like valuable poker cards—so you can play them at the right moment.

I want you to start to use those Superpowers intentionally and I also want you to give yourself credit for having them. Because claiming and owning the things about you that are great will fuel you to live a more gratifying life. Only, we're not accustomed to giving ourselves credit for something that's not hard. That's just ridonkulously insane-making logic. Feel free to give yourself credit for your Superpower, something that's totally easy for you.

Now, this advice confused the heck out of my "reserved" client Chris. "Hold up," he said. "I don't get it. I take my Superpower for granted. It's so natural to me, I'm not even aware I'm using it . . . so how do I use it *intentionally*?" I gave Chris the following exercise:

1. Articulate the value of your Superpower by writing a list of all of its positive attributes.

2. Reflect on times when *you've* been the beneficiary of that Superpower. How did it feel? In Chris's case, he asked himself: How did it feel when someone else demonstrated reserve? Do you see how what you've just described is how you enrich the lives of others when you share your Superpower?

3. To cement the value of your Superpower, ask a friend what value it holds for him. Perhaps he might share a story of how it impacted his life.

Another of Chris' Superpowers is compassion. His friend Holly shared a story about how Chris had once shown incredible compassion that touched her very deeply. He'd been helping Holly on a project. It was a very big deal as she was putting a lot on the line, and there were some very real risks associated with the project. One day, Holly was almost paralyzed by fear. Chris told her that he would hold space for her project, that he had utmost faith and confidence in her ability to pull it off. "Don't worry," he told her, "I've got your back. I've got this for you." Chris had totally forgotten about it but Holly hadn't. "She told me she'd felt cared for and loved," Chris told me afterwards. "How'd you feel when she told you this?" I asked. Chris was blown away. Compassion is so second nature to him that he thinks absolutely nothing of it. "I sense a need for it and I provide it," said Chris, matter-of-factly. I asked how he would have felt if he'd been *aware* of the value Holly received and spent some time reflecting on it later that night? "I would have felt like I'd accomplished something *huge* that day. I would have felt like I was living in line with my Values of nurturing and helping other people," Chris told me. "I would have felt

spacious inside and felt a sense of honoring and reverence—for myself."
Oh yeah sugar, that's what I'm talkin' about!

It was only through the eyes of his friend that Chris could see the
very real benefits of his Superpower. He's become much more aware of
his gift and what he contributes to the world as a result of using it. You
will, too. You'll feel better about yourself, more confident, more self-assured. "Wow, look what I can do!" you'll say. "I've got that big meeting
tomorrow but, wow, I got some good stuff to take in with me."

ACTIVITY: Nurture Your Superpowers

The whole point of the Superpower exercise is to allow you to love
a little more and hurt a little less—by recognizing how incredibly
awesome you are. Over the course of the next week, ask yourself
at the end of each day:

- Where did I use my Superpower today?
- To whom did it provide value?
- How did it provide value?
- Where might it be needed *tomorrow*?

You've seen how a good deed has a ripple effect, right? In other
words, when you do something good for someone they, in turn,
are inspired to do something good for someone else, and so on,
until all of that goodness is spreading out like ripples on the surface of a pond, with you at the center. Think of this activity as
dropping a stone in the water of your own soul—and creating an
amazingly powerful ripple effect inside *you*.

The Stretch Assignment

Okay, do you want to take it a step further? Do you want to really dig
in here? I knew it! Here is an activity we do in workshops that makes
everyone feel totally itchy and uncomfortable. And, in the end, they're
usually very appreciative that I made them take that stretch.

Once you have more clarity on your Strengths, Superpowers and Flow—stand up and claim it. Yes, I do mean literally. We have people get in small groups of three to five. Each person has to stand up and state their Strengths out loud. Yes . . . I . . . Mean . . . It. What often happens when I ask people to do this is they read straight off their worksheet—no eye contact, super-fast, and somewhat muffled. Their discomfort inevitably turns into nervous laughter. In a recent session, Tonya did just that. "I'm, uh, pretty good at analysis, thinking strategically, and um, getting people to work across yadda, yadda, yadda . . ." Tonya was mumbling so fast, she might as well have been speed speaking. I asked her to try again, go slower, articulate, enunciate, make eye contact. . . . I'm pretty sure if she'd had a weapon, I would've been on the way to the E.R. But Tonya hung in there and tried again. This time she even shared an example. I asked her group to describe the difference in Tonya's delivery. "I believed you the second time," one person shared, "I felt much more interested and connected." Another added, "In the first round, you didn't seem to consider what you do important, so I kind of assumed that, too. Second time, you owned it. And I totally bought it."

As I described in chapter eight, people get squeamish when I ask them to focus on their Successes, Strengths and Superpowers. No one wants to be seen as "that guy"—the one we all know who toots their own horn way too much, and who thinks they're all that and a bag of chips but doesn't have the goods to back it up. I get it. None of us wants to come off as an egomaniac, or even mildly arrogant; but we do ourselves a disservice by being self-deprecating, thereby giving the Inner Critic *carte blanche* to bash us. I like the way Buckingham puts it. "Building your strengths isn't about ego," he writes. "It is about responsibility . . . to avoid your strengths and focus on weaknesses isn't a sign of diligent humility. It is almost irresponsible."

There are two other good reasons for having people stand to do this exercise (besides being a wee bit sadistic):

First, it's good practice for expanding your emotional intelligence.

Be aware of what it feels like when you're standing and sharing your Strengths. Uncomfortable? Fine. Anxious? Okay. Shaky? No worries. It's perfectly fine to have these feelings. I just don't want them to get in the way of you owning and using your Strengths—especially in those vital moments when you need to do it in the real world. The first step is to be aware of the feeling and realize it's fine to feel that way. The second step is to *take action* even when the feeling exists. (This is much like learning to stay in the game during the anxiety of an Inner Critic attack—same principle). It gets easier with practice. You may not ever feel completely comfortable, but it *will* get easier.

The second good reason to do this stretch assignment is that the body remembers. When we practice the feelings, the thoughts *and* the physical actions, our body has this amazing ability to remember. That's why we practice presentations and role-play interviews ahead of time— It helps us prepare, it helps the body remember. When you go in to that meeting and you need to articulate what value you can bring to the table, your body will remember what you've practiced and raised your awareness to.

Start to Build Your Inner Success Story

Way back in chapter five, I had you gather feedback in order to benefit from the fresh, clear perspective other people can offer, which served to challenge the different aspects of your Inner Critic story. We're going to do that same thing again, only now the intention is to gather feedback to help build and deepen your understanding on the Success side. Flip back to chapter five to re-familiarize yourself with the great basics of feedback and who to reach out to.

ACTIVITY: Phone a Friend, for Feedback, Again

Now, it's not always easy for people to think off the tops of their heads. You might need to approach your conversation from a different angle. I want you to think of this as brainstorming with your friends—make it a conversation, not a questionnaire. If you need any prompting, I've included a bunch of suggested questions below to help explore your Inner Success story and to move the conversation along. Feel free to totally ad-lib your own questions.

Chapter Seven: Work Your Core

• What do you believe I Value most?

• If you could choose three ways to Identify me, what would those three be and why?

• What are the Feelings or emotions I express most clearly?

Chapter Eight: Know Thyself, Know Thy Success

• Tell me about two occasions when I've been really successful—in any context you want. (Don't specify work or life for them if you can, see where their instincts lead them).

  • What characteristics did I demonstrate? How did I seem to be feeling?

• Tell me about two times you've seen me feeling really proud of myself—in any context you want. (Again, don't specify work or life if you can avoid it.)

  • What characteristics did I demonstrate? How did I seem to be feeling?

• How do these examples reflect my Values, as you understand them?

Chapter Nine: Rocking Your Strengths PLUS

Flow:

• Have you ever seen me in a situation where I was on fire—I was so enjoying what I was doing that I lost track of time and was totally energized afterwards? What characteristics and or traits was I engaging in this moment?

• Have you ever thought, "Wow! He's got game?" What was I doing at the time? What skills did I employ in this moment?

Strengths PLUS:

- In your opinion, what are my greatest Strengths—activities I'm not only good at, but that actually energize me? Can you describe any specific occasions when you've seen me utilize these Strengths?
- When was the last time you saw me do something brilliant, skillful or really awesome? In those moments, what was I doing? What Strength was I engaging?
- Help me figure out what my top skills and traits are—and how I can use them more intentionally and more effectively.

Superpowers:

- Do I have any Strengths you think I'm completely oblivious to? Let's call it a Superpower—something I'm so good at that I make it look effortless. Can you give me any specific examples of when you've seen me use this Superpower?
- What about me is cool even though I'm not aware of it?
- What about me is great that I don't give myself credit for?

REFLECTION: What Have You Learned?

I'm sure you've learned a ton of new and valuable information because the people we live with and work with often have much greater perspective on just how awesome we really are. I bet you're feeling really good about yourself right now. Good. Mission accomplished.

Great, fantastic, persevering, tenacious work, my friend! It is *not* easy to plumb the depths of our best selves, getting specific about it, making choices, looking underneath and then ask others to do the same! I appreciate what you've done. Now we're ready to pull all of that together with the intention of helping you live a daily experience of Success, meaning and joy—a life that's robust and Super-powered enough to squash those critics, fears and doubts like tiny ants.

10

Your Definition of Success

We live in a super-competitive, fast-paced, self-critical world. For many of us, life in the twenty-first century feels edgy. And I don't mean that in a cool, hipster kind of way. I mean we're literally on edge. Many of us are in a near constant state of stress and anxiety as we attempt to anticipate and deflect what we fear might be coming at us next. Sometimes, it feels like we're dodging actual bullets, a la Neo, minus his incredible back-bending skills.

How do you stay true to yourself and to what's important to you *while* navigating fear and doubt *as* you move towards Success? By integrating all aspects of yourself—the deepest, darkest depths of your Inner Critic *and* the most authentic truth of your Inner Success—and by creating a solid container to hold both as you take the heart-pounding ride that is life. Now's the time. You've done the work. You have everything you need. You've learned a ton of priceless, practical, practicable information about your Inner Critic. Now, it's time to balance that by painting an equally provoking, memorable and moving picture of Inner Success. It's time to write your Success story, speak it aloud, let it settle into your bones and your memory banks, share it with others—then go live it.

Conventional wisdom takes a very narrow view of what constitutes

Success. Usually, it's a goal to strive for—for example, a sales target, a bonus, a promotion—beyond which happiness lies. The problem with this goal-oriented version of Success becomes obvious when you reach that goal. What comes next? There's another one. Meet your sales target? Great. Now the bar is set higher for next time. Get a promotion? Great. Set your sights on the next rung of the corporate ladder? Result? Instead of "achieving" happiness, it's moved again. It was within your grasp, but just as you stepped up, it shifted. It's as if someone or something else is moving your goal posts.

The reality is, Success isn't about achieving the goal—Success is about how you *feel* about achieving the goal. Most of us are chasing after a Success recipe that doesn't actually make us *feel* good because it's not *our* definition of success. Why do you think so many people suffer from Sunday Night Blues? Because it doesn't *feel* good to live someone else's idea of what our lives should look like.

“ *We need a third metric, based on our well-being, our health, our ability to unplug and recharge and renew ourselves, and to find joy in both our job and the rest of our life. Ultimately, success is not about money or position, but about living the life you want, not just the life you settle for.*
—Arianna Huffington

Instead of chasing something that's ever-elusive and "out there," I want you to embody Success as something tangible that resides deep inside *you*. I challenge you to dig deep and ask: What vision of Success looks *and* feels good to *me*? Whether it's to become C.E.O., start your own business, launch that blog, write that book, become a stay-at-home parent, go back to school, create that non-profit, or travel the world. Whatever your vision may be I want you to define Success in *your* own words and on *your* own terms.

It's also important to allow room for this definition to live, breath and evolve as you grow and experience life. Just as you're constantly changing, so your definition of Success should change, too. I'm not saying you should be a "flip-flopper" or that you should change your Success statement as often as you change your sheets, but I am saying that it should be neither rigid nor static; your definition of Success should be as alive and adaptable as you are.

I asked Aasim to write his Success statement from the perspective of his future self, and then to share it with me. "I have a legacy of leadership that has been impactful to both people and the business," began Aasim. "I helped our team create customer satisfaction while building an agile and growing business." Aasim had lost me by the time he got to the words, "customer satisfaction." His statement sounded lifeless. Even Aasim sounded bored—he might as well have been reading me the directions on how to patch a rubber raft. To help him get specific about what his statement actually meant—and what he envisaged for his future self—I had Aasim answer a bunch of questions, including:

- What does "legacy" mean to you?
- What specifically did *you* do that helped your team create customer satisfaction?
- Can you give me an example of what "agile" means to you, and why do you like that word?
- Tell me about the best, most thrilling team you've ever led.

While answering the last question, Aasim's energy did a one-eighty as he described being captain of his amateur soccer team. "I loved that experience," he shared. Aasim was on the edge of his seat, his hands gesturing wildly and his eyes ablaze. "When you're captain, you're the leader on the field. I got to anticipate the flow of the game and, knowing the skills and strengths of each player, I got to put my team in exactly the right positions." He was electrified. "So Aasim," I said, "What I hear is that you feel alive when you get to make the decisions. You want to *run* the show. Is that right?" Aasim looked down, paused and with a shy, quiet tone said, "Yeah, I do."

Bingo! This was Aasim's genuine Success statement: "I run the show." It was short, it didn't say much—but Aasim knew exactly what it meant, both tactically and emotionally. It defined Success for him in a way that encompassed energy, attachment, satisfaction, meaning and joy.

Shift Your View of Success

My graduate school buddy, colleague and friend Matt Walker helps people climb mountains in search of Success. His company, Inner Passage, creates rock-climbing trips for business leaders, teams and individuals. I've shared that I have a Critic who taunts me with negative, critical body image stories so, being the good friend that he is, Matt pushed my buttons by challenging me to come on one of his trips, in this case to California's Joshua Tree National Park. Since achievement is both one of my Strengths *and* Values, I ended up taking on Matt's challenge.

First day, first rock, first pang of fear that I'm going to look like a fool... I'm one of four: an avid outdoor climber with five years under her belt, an indoor climber with three years' experience, a sometime climber who's joined some of Matt's expeditions in the past and a novice who's never climbed anything but a ladder (yup, that's me). Matt gathers us together, takes out a whiteboard on which he draws a simple peak and asks the seemingly innocuous question, "Where's the top?" We all give different answers because we all have different expectations of the day, of ourselves, and of the rock. My version of "the top" wasn't the top of the peak that day, it was to just to get up on the rock each time it was my turn. I achieved it that day and much more than I expected!

What I learned from this very simple exercise is that in any given moment, each one of us gets to define where the top is. In other words, not only do I get to define my authentic and alive meaning of Success for my *life*—I get to do it within any given *moment*. It was the first of many lessons I learned on the trip. In his book, *Adventure in Everything: How the Five Elements of Adventure Create a Life of Authenticity, Purpose, and Inspiration*, Matt shares some of his clients' most inspiring stories. He recently told me about Robert.

Prior to signing up for one of Matt's trips, Robert had experienced Success in the universally accepted cultural context of making money, amassing power and running a big business. While climbing a major peak in Tibet, however, Robert was unable to achieve his version of Success: to summit. He was in spectacular physical shape, he had all the best gear, he'd trained hard but as he faced the challenges of the climb, Robert's stamina lagged. He would tell himself to buck up, push harder, dig deeper, but the more Robert punished himself for his perceived failure, the more steadily his stamina, spirit and physical health weakened. His usual go-to "push" method didn't work on the mountain. In fact, it made things worse.

One day, forced to admit defeat, Robert slumped down on the side of a trail, exhausted. As he sat there, he watched the porters as they nimbly negotiated the steep uphill trail weighed down by the huge backpacks they were carrying on their backs, all the while singing or laughing or both! Robert had a life-changing realization: there's a whole spectrum of people and personalities, lives and lifestyles, and therefore successes and failures. Robert had always measured success in terms of money and power; he had plenty of both. However, these porters had nothing—they were dirt poor, they had no fancy climbing equipment and they wore flimsy tennis shoes in place of high-tech mountain boots—but they were unbelievably rich in spirit. For the first time in his life, Robert found himself questioning wealth and power as markers of success.

The experience shook him to the core, and caused him to radically rethink his vision of a Success-full life. Chances are you, too, may have been telling the same old tried and tested story for years. Isn't it time for a new story—something that fits who you are *now*? As we walk through this chapter, allow yourself to be open to new possibilities of what Success might mean, how it might look and how it might feel.

Taking Inventory

You've been gathering a ton of data as you've worked your way through this book. Now, like any good analyst, you're going to sift through the information and look for consistent patterns and trends. Do you see any commonalities across all of the activities, reflections, feedback-gatherings and story-sharings you've done in the previous chapters? If you're the analytical type, you might want to search for commonalities across the data columns and rows. If you're not that kind of analyst, just look for recurring patterns and trends across the whole field of information. It could be as simple as searching for one common thread. In chapter eight, you read about Charley. She discovered that having a voice and being acknowledged was a thread that ran throughout most of her stories.

What do you notice as you review *your* stories? What can you learn about yourself as you revisit your Successes and Proud moments? What attributes or aspects of yourself consistently show up? You might be surprised by the themes that emerge. Charley was unnerved to discover that terror was a common theme for her. In almost every story, she was terrified to speak up. She also noticed that in almost every case, the stakes were high: she ran a huge risk of ridicule, rejection or criticism. However, also in almost every case, things turned out far better than she'd feared. (Therefore, the stories showed up in her Successes and Prouds.)

What Charley realized is that staying true to herself, speaking her truth and being authentic are all essential ingredients in living a fuel-efficient, "LOL" life—not *despite* the terrifying conditions, but *in the presence of* the terrifying conditions. In fact, her best moments consistently occurred *during* these terror-inducing situations. Charley learned that she feels most energized and transcendent when she's able to speak her truth and be authentic *in the presence of near-debilitating fear.*

Looking back at the lists you created in chapter seven—that is, your Core Values, Identity and Feelings—do you notice any commonalities or consistencies between those lists and what you've learned about your Successes and Prouds in chapter eight and your Strengths, Superpowers and Flow in chapter nine? Have you since discovered anything new that needs to be added to these lists? In Charley's case, she discovered that in many of her stories she consistently displayed the Strengths of courage, compassion, integrity, truth, and honesty.

It's quite common to uncover new data about yourself at this stage of the process because, rather than picking from a list (as you did in chapter seven), you're now looking at information gathered from your own experiences. It's likely you'll spot some major trends as key pieces of information rise to the top of your attention and awareness.

> **"**When well-being comes from engaging our strengths and virtues, our lives are imbued with authenticity. —Martin Seligman, Authentic Happiness: Using the New Positive Psychology to Realize Your Potential for Lasting Fulfillment

Taking Stock of Your Stock

Leading a life that feels successful, satisfying, and meaningful requires that we have clarity and awareness of our Values and Strengths. It also requires that we intentionally align our actions and behaviors to those Values and Strengths. When we're doing that, we feel the most successful. (Many people find the term "successful" jarring as they begin to unburden themselves of a Success story that's been thrust on them by society. If you are one of those people, please feel free to substitute another word that resonates, such as "happy," "satisfied," "joyful," or "meaningful.")

As you move toward Success, I want you to use the information you've gathered about your Values, Strengths and energizing LOL's (lightening, opening, lifting) to your maximum advantage. I urge you to spend time strategizing on how to call on these powerful allies. What stories do you need to remind yourself of when the Inner Critic comes to call? How can you call forth your Divine Flaw? What relationship exists between your Values, Strengths and your Inner Critic?

Remember, our I.C. attacks with the most ferocity and frequency that which we prize most—our Core Values, Identities and Feelings. Therefore, the Critic enables us to trace the path of an attack back to what matters most.

Charley was initially confused about this; she didn't see a connection.

In fact, she saw a glaring disparity between her Values and her Inner Critic. "My I.C. muzzles me," said Charley, looking perplexed. "She tells me I'm no good, that no one wants to hear what I have to say, and that I don't have the talent to say it anyway. It seems at odds with what I've just learned: that I need to speak my truth and be authentic. It seems to me that my I.C. doesn't reflect my Core Values at all. Quite the opposite: it tries to *stop* me doing what I most *need* to do."

Charley was right. Her I.C. does *not* act in her best interests—but it's *related to* what's most important to her, speaking her truth. Think of it in terms of the infinity symbol. Speaking one's truth sits on one side of the spiral (Inner Success) and feeling muzzled sits on the other (Inner Critic). While the I.C. is directly related to what Charley values most, it doesn't necessarily act in service to it. Your Critic may even appear to sabotage it. That's because fundamentally, the I.C. seeks to deter you from the very thing you most want and need to do—because it's trying to protect you from what it considers might be an epic failure.

In Charley's case, her I.C. tries to protect her from ridicule by telling her she has nothing important to say, and that therefore she shouldn't say anything at all. Charley's learning in this process that she absolutely has something important to say. In fact, she feels most alive and energized when she faces the challenge of speaking up—despite her terror. Charley has dug into the Critic side and shone a light in the dark corners; she's dug into her Success stories and found a recipe for what makes her most happy and fulfilled. Because of this, she's now aware of the relationship between her greatness and her greatest fear, which has opened up a whole new level of choices for her.

Charley began leaning toward her fear, and the more she trusted herself and her voice, the more confidant she became in using it. Now, when her I.C. shows up, Charley knows it's actually an indicator that she's being challenged to live close to her Values. So she intentionally uses this information to plan for her future and embody her definition of Success: My truth is my strength, my strength is my words, my words are my gift.

This statement has fueled and fortified Charley to pursue her dream to be a motivational speaker. Her greatest fear has indeed become her greatest gift.

Charley found the recipe for her special Success sauce. Here's a recipe for finding yours—as with any good recipe, alter to your taste:

Start with the Data

Gather together all the data you've compiled to date about your Core (Values, Identities and Feelings), Divine Flaw, Flow moments, Successes and Prouds, Strengths and Superpowers. Review all that priceless information, then take a pen and paper (or a keyboard) and write up a short statement or paragraph that loosely defines what Success looks like to you.

Look at what you've written and ask yourself, does this feel true and does it resonate with me? Does it inspire me? Is it an energy LOL (lightening, opening, lifting)? Does it feel spacious and flexible? Will it allow me to adapt as I continue to evolve and grow? Is it holistic? Does it reflect my life as a whole?

Success doesn't usually stem from only one source; it's often a summation of the compound joys you derive from many facets of your life. Mike used to beat himself up about his lack of ambition at work—until he wrote his Success statement and realized that his definition includes *all* of the following:

- Having a job that meets two basic needs: a minimum financial threshold (which meets his Core Identity of breadwinner) and a good relationship with his manager (which meets his Values of integrity and relationship).
- Having a solid and satisfying marriage (reflecting his Strength PLUS of communication and empathy).
- High quality time spent enjoying his kids (a nod to his Core Identity as a father).
- Getting to play golf as least twice a week (that's when Mike is in Flow).

For Mike, living a joyous life isn't just about work—it's a package deal that, when added together, represents a Success-filled life.

What about you—are you deriving all your satisfaction from work? Is that *really* your definition of Success? Continue playing with your definition until you start to feel electrified. You may need to create several versions until you come up with a draft that feels good. But don't go all Perfectionist on me here! We're not at the final step. Your goal right now is not to create a perfect, final Success statement to be carved in stone for posterity. Your definition of Success is designed to be a living, breathing, expansive, ever-evolving entity.

Add Some I.C. Know-How

Review your success statement draft and ask yourself: What Inner Critic(s) is most likely to show up as I move towards this vision of Inner Success? What message will it try to use against me? What's likely to trigger me?

When I realized it was time to add "author" to my Success story, I knew my Inner Perfectionist would go crazy. Sure enough, it did start jumping up and down, screaming, "Who do you think you are? What makes you think you're good enough to write a book? That's a terrible idea! You're not an author!"

What's your I.C. going to try and tell *you*? What have you learned in chapters two through five about your own version of the I.C.? Jot down some notes about what comes up.

Add a Dash of Strategy

Based on the above, and everything you've learned about how to manage an I.C. attack, what key strategies will you employ to shift your energy from negative to knowledgeable?

Remember Janine from chapter two, who named her Critic Betina? Her key strategy is simply to salute Betina. That's it. Janine will say, "Oh hi Betina, thanks for that input, you can leave now." Acknowledging her Critic by name allows Janine to externalize it, recognize why it's shown up, and empower her to push it off to the side and out of harm's way.

My colleague Jan's favorite strategy is to use The Truth Series questions from chapter four to figure out what's more and less true.

One of my personal favorites is to recall my Divine Flaw. When I'm being super hard on myself, this serves to remind me *why* I care so much about whatever I'm ragging on—or raging about—which sucks the energy right out of the negative Critic and channels it into the parts of me that are powerful, strong and pretty darn amazing.

My client Mason incorporated imperfection into his statement of Success. His daughter was his inspiration. While teaching her how to snowboard, Mason realized that the more his daughter fell, the faster she accelerated her learning. As he helped her navigate the slopes he also encouraged her to not fear falling, "that's how you learn what you're doing right and what to try next time." Mason decided that instead of allowing his own Perfectionist Critic to beat him up for not always being flawless, he would reframe "success" as "learning" and give himself the same graciousness he gave his daughter. Now, rather than stunting himself by striving for a day free of errors, Mason gives himself the width and breadth it takes to learn. His mantra is: "I will make mistakes, but I will make them less often. I will recognize them sooner and I will know how to repair them." Explained Mason, "Reminding myself of this allows me to be way more creative and intuitive, because I'm no longer holding back and restraining myself for fear of making a mistake."

Your strategies can be those that help you tame the critics and fears combined with those that navigate you back to the elements of your success. Combining these remind me of that cartoon where the superhero twins are stronger together and say "Wonder twin powers . . . activate!"

Shake, Stir and Pour
Update your draft with any key strategies around heading off—or defusing—a Critic attack. When you're done, write or print out an updated version of your Success statement and put it somewhere prominent (for example, on your computer screen, fridge, bathroom mirror, phone screen saver or social media status) and let it simmer

for a bit. Each time you read it, pay attention to what feelings and thoughts arise (E.I. Builder!).

After a couple good days of stewing and reducing, check in. Ask yourself: do I need to update anything? Add anything? Subtract anything? If, like me, you're an extravert, you'll want to run your success definition by your closest confidantes. Ask them if the statement rings true, based on what they know about you? (We'll be going into more detail on the value of those confidantes in chapter eleven.) Pay attention to any words that pop.

Go back to your draft and see if you can distill your statement down to one or two sentences, or perhaps, a single word. My colleague Jan developed a sentence to describe how she wants to live her life but she often just uses one word to summarize it: Joy. It encapsulates everything she has learned around her Core, her Successes and Prouds, her Strengths and Superpowers, and her Inner Critic and how it attacks. It acts as a trigger that moves her down the path of remembering her Values and grounding in her Divine Flaw. She's shared it with me and with her closest friends so that we might remind her of it in times of need: while discussing work, life, or relationship issues, when she's grappling with a major life decision, or while she's in the grips of a powerful I.C. attack. In these moments, the word Joy brings Jan peace as she's reminded of what's absolutely most important to her.

Katie's Success statement is a poetic paragraph. She had spent a full day at one of our workshops, quietly following along. At the end of the day, when I asked for someone to share their statement, she bounded up. When Katie read her Success statement, I knew that every word counted and that it represented the core of her absolute truth. I could see it in her body language, read it in her energy, and hear it in her voice. Here's what Katie shared:

I will lead a full and authentic life that captures my creativity
and nurtures my passions. I will let myself share all of myself,
even though it scares the heck out of me. And it will be hard;
I'm not perfect, and my work's not perfect. But I will take solace
in the fact that I'm not alone. I'm going to freak out about

this along the way. I'm going to move kicking and screaming towards an authentic life that includes sadness, anger, fear, and imperfection. But I have to remember that I will bounce back. I am a wicked analyst of my own thoughts, and I will always be able to pull myself back to positivity. Have faith.

I was delighted to hear Katie's definition of success—it had everything, inspiration, aspiration, strengths, emotion, realistic expectations, knowledge and possibility. Sweet sounds of success!

Being the Critic/Success Relationship Master that I am, I use three statements, interchangeably:

"What really matters?" As I explained in chapter seven, this phrase is the tagline for my business, a question I ask myself in the moment of an I.C. attack to remind me of my Divine Flaw, and as a statement and declaration about what matters most, which pulls me back to my Core Values.

"Love a little more; hurt a little less." This statement reminds me that Success and Critic are related, just like love and hurt; they live next door to each other, in the very same neighborhood, and they're interacting with each other all the time. It helps me shift from rigid "all or nothing" thinking and it reminds me that big change occurs in small steps.

"Do the work I love with the people I love in the places I love." I use this one when trying to decide how to apportion my time. It reminds me to choose the task, project or assignment that incorporates my Flow moments, utilizes my Superpowers of helping to create conversations that fit statement numbers one and two above, and capitalizes on my Strengths of humor and compassion. It also prompts intentional choices about working with those who bring out the best in me because, after all, life's too long to work with people you don't like—as my friend Suzanne likes to say. Whenever I'm in the grip of those I.C. moments laced with "shoulds"—"You *should* do this work, *should* work with that person, *should* go to Munich and do that workshop"—this statement reminds me that if I do something because of *shoulds*, I'm likely *not* going to have a good time. Nor am I going to be at my best. This beauty is my personal, portable R.O.I. calculator!

Remember, there's no right or wrong way to write your Success statement. I'm not attached to what it looks like—it could be a Buddha bobble head bumping up and down on your dashboard or a placard hanging on your door that reads, "V.P. of Innovation, Creativity & Play." As long as it rings true for you, we've done our job together and that makes me very, very happy.

> **"**Being your true self is the most effective formula for success there is. —Danielle LaPorte, The Fire Starter Sessions

Update Your Story

In a perfectly reasonable but utterly lifeless tone, Richard told me that his goal was to become more visible so he could be cherry-picked for promotion. As is my custom (and yours now, too, I trust), the first thing I did was ask Richard to get more specific so we could arrive at a more personal and meaningful definition. It was crucial that we tap into some energetic emotions in order to stir Richard's passion, so I asked a series of questions, including:

- *Why* do you want a promotion?
- What does the promotion *represent* for you and what will it *mean* to you, both professionally and personally?
- What impact will it have on you personally?
- What impact will it have on your relationships, both professional and personal?

As it turned out, Richard's reasons for wanting a promotion had very little to do with the status of a VP title, the money and stock options that would come with it, nor the stability it would offer his family. While these are all valid reasons to want a promotion and are valid criteria for Success, they weren't Richard's.

He wanted to run a bigger business so he could nurture and mentor more people. Richard is at his best when he's helping people achieve their goals and creating a more positive work environment. He feels inspired, energized and *good* when he does this. Richard feels a huge responsibility for ensuring his team feels good about their contributions at work, because he knows this has a huge impact on how they show up elsewhere—that is, at home with their families and hanging with their friends. Richard wants the scope and authority that will allow him to create a business environment that fosters a positive *life experience* for his employees.

This desire became the heart and soul of Richard's updated authentic definition of Success: "I create business environments that allow people to thrive—at work and throughout their lives. My team's whole lives benefit from their being a part of a benevolent and successful business." Because he had connected to something deeply personal and meaningful, Richard could now pursue Success with confidence, throwing the entire weight of his passion, desire and intention behind it.

> **"** *It has been an evolution, but I am now a true believer in bringing our whole selves to work. I no longer think people have a professional self for Mondays through Fridays and a real self for the rest of the time. That type of separation probably never existed, and in today's era of individual expression, where people constantly update their Facebook status and tweet their every move, it makes even less sense. Instead of putting on some kind of fake "all-work persona," I think we benefit from expressing our truth, talking about personal situations, and acknowledging that professional decisions*

are often emotionally driven. —Sheryl Sandberg, Lean In: Women, Work, and the Will to Lead

Can you say the same about your statement of Success? Does it inspire you? Drive you? Fire you? Good! Share it with me. I'm serious. I want to hear your statement of Success as it exists in this moment. You don't have to feel like you've nailed it in order to share it. That's not the point; that's just the Perfectionist talking. Resist the temptation to save yours until it's exactly, perfectly right. In fact, lean super-far into allowing it be a little bit messy. It should be a living, breathing, growing organism—just like you are. I'm not the police or the matron of rules, I care more that it fits your unique life. I've adopted a line from the film, *Pirates of the Caribbean*: "It's more what you'd call guidelines than actual rules."

I'm your coach, I'm in your corner and I'm waiting to hear your authentic definition of Success—a definition full of your greatest assets and energy with a healthy dose of strategy for critic moments so you have plenty of resilience. I urge you to share it with me. Send it via email (stacey@innercriticinnersuccess.com) or pop it on our Facebook page (Connect Growth and Development).

I can't wait to be the first of many to read it. Yes, I said many. In the next chapter, we'll gather your Support Crew and personal Board of Directors. The agenda: Your Success!

11

Work Your Crew

Congratulations! You've done an amazing amount of work in the name of self-awareness, self-exploration and self-clarification. Not only do you now possess a living, breathing definition of Success that fits your Values, Strengths and Superpowers, but you also know your Inner Critics so well they'll have a really hard time taking you out. Having dug this deeply and learned this much about who you are and what drives you, inspires you and ignites you, there's no going back. Forgive me, but I've *got* to talk Matrix again (yes, I'm a total sci-fi geek): You've swallowed the red pill. The illusion (self-doubt and fear) has been shattered; you see things as they are, not as the Critic would have you believe. This doesn't guarantee an easier life, but it does guarantee an authentic one. Now, how do you *stay* aligned to your truth?

Throughout this book, I have consistently encouraged you to share your story with others. I've had you seek input and feedback in order to gather solid evidence, new information and a fresh perspective. In this chapter, I'm calling you to rise to the challenge of a whole new level of sharing.

As you begin to live out your new vision of a Success-filled life, it will feel both incredibly invigorating *and* a little daunting. To stay the course, you'll need the support of your very own A-team. This is where we turn from "Inner" to "Outer." One of the most essential tools in staying committed to the path of Success while continuing to tame the Critic is to gather the best people around you: your crew, your board of directors, your tribe, your counsel of elders, your posse, your peeps, your pack. . . . You get the concept, right?

In his book, *Adventure in Everything: How the Five Elements of Adventure Create a Life of Authenticity, Purpose, and Inspiration,* my colleague and friend Matt Walker, about whom you read in chapter ten, calls this Great Companionship. Explains Matt, "Without the enrichment that these positive relationships provide, it's nearly impossible to both go after our highest endeavors and enjoy the sense of fulfillment that accompanies such an undertaking."

> **"** *Human beings can't help it: we need to belong. One of the most powerful of our survival mechanisms is to be part of a tribe, to contribute to (and take from) a group of like-minded people.* —*Seth Godin,* Tribes: We Need You to Lead Us

My dear friend and colleague Jan Gelman and I have run Women's Leadership Circles for several years now. In these year-long programs, groups of women attend workshops and also meet once a month to build and nurture leadership skills. Using many of the same activities contained in this book, Jan and I help attendees find their own definition of Success, expand their view of health and wellness beyond diet and exercise and, perhaps most significantly, immerse themselves in a supportive, shared experience that cultivates deep and lasting bonds. These women often work in cultures that are predominantly male, and in which masculine leadership traits are prized and rewarded. In our Leadership Circles they discover a supportive space wherein they can feel free to be themselves and figure out what type of leadership feels true to them. Being allowed the breathing room to find their own way— free from fear of criticism or ridicule—is incredibly liberating for these women and fosters a fertile environment in which each is encouraged and motivated to bring her best self forward.

At the end of the program, many women cite this supportive circle as one of the key contributors to their Inner Success. Kelly, one of our recent program graduates, explained:

> I couldn't have come this far without the group. Hearing everyone's stories, their perspectives, their challenges and successes helped create an environment where I could explore my own leadership style. I was inspired by the trust, I widened my lens of what's possible and I gained more respect for different styles. I'll be sticking with this group long after our program ends. I need it for what I want to achieve.

In chapter ten, I shared that I'm one of Jan's tribe members. All it took was a phone call. One day, Jan called me up and said, "Okay Stacey, I'm going to be intentional about living a *joyful* life. And I'm going to need your help to do that. Here's the kind of help I specifically need . . ." Ever since that day, I'm part of Jan's crew and I always do my best to support her joy. Recently, Jan called me in the midst of being choked by her Inner Fraud Critic. "Who do I think I am to even consider taking two trips to Africa in one year, Stacey?" she asked. "It's ridiculous to spend this kind of money. Some people can't afford to pay their rent or put food on the table and I'm already going to South Africa in November. How can I even contemplate a trip to Rwanda as well?" Now, just to give you some context: The first trip Jan had planned was to South Africa to attend a professional workshop designed to deepen her capabilities in conflict resolution—with the added bonus of taking a safari in Zimbabwe to celebrate her 50th birthday with her husband. This second opportunity was to be part of a delegation that would visit Rwanda to learn about the incredible progress the East African country is making in support of women's leadership and empowerment.

Initially, I simply witnessed Jan, allowing her to name and claim her emotions. When they'd run their course, I helped her see a different perspective by reminding her that many aspects of the trip entailed *giving* and learning. Finally, I challenged Jan to have the courage to live her definition of Success. "Jan," I said gently. "You love Africa—the animals, the people, the culture, the adventure. When you even talk about Africa you are over-flowing with positive energy and lust for life, right?" In a quiet voice (and likely giving me the over-the-phone stink-eye), Jan agreed. "My friend," I continued, "this right here is a decision point—an important one: Are you going to have the courage, the guts, the will-power to live a *joyful* life? To say yes to the moments that seem almost too good to be true, that feel like more than you deserve and that will take you into more joy than you thought possible?" We both knew Jan's answer was yes.

Here's the deal, folks: when you start living that definition of Success you've taken the time and the effort to craft, some of your current crew—the people closest to you—may not be ecstatic about it. Some degree of change will be required as you become clear about what Values and Identities you want to live in alignment with and what fears and Critics you're no longer willing to put up with. And, as we've discovered, change makes people uncomfortable. Most people are happy with the status quo—even though you're not. Not anymore.

Charley began to encounter this reality as she shifted her focus to motivational speaking and from there to writing a book. She believed so strongly in her idea, she moved across the country so she could focus on it. When Charley left the secure job that sucked the life out of her, many of her friends thought she was crazy and her family was mystified as to why she would give up steady, well-paying work. One friend, with whom she used to commiserate over shared fears, could no longer handle hanging out with Charley as she focused her energy on what she wanted instead of beating herself up. Charley started to sense a seismic shift in her inner circle.

Brené Brown captured this phenomenon powerfully in an interview with *ORIGIN* magazine, telling interviewer Chantal Pierrat,

I can't be paralyzed anymore by the critics. My new mantra is, if you're not in the arena getting your ass kicked on occasion, then I'm not interested in your feedback. You don't get to sit in the cheap seat and criticize my appearance or my work with mean-spiritedness if you're also not in the arena.

Charley had set a new definition of Success that fit her brain, her body and her heart. She knew it was right because it *felt* right, and she needed to make some difficult shifts by gathering only the people who would stand beside her in the arena—those who were able to get behind her new vision of Success. She also recognized the need to reach out and foster new relationships that made rational sense for her goals but also *felt* right to her emotions and her body wisdom. Charley began building the tribe that would go with her into the arena—not judge her from the sidelines. She calls it stacking the odds in her favor!

Creating Your Board of Directors (B.O.D.)

Your B.O.D. represents the people with whom you will surround yourself in the days, weeks, months and years ahead. The criteria for selection is simple: anyone who will help you live this Inner Success life you've defined, support you in your Inner Critic moments, offer advice, help solve problems, weigh in on your Core Values, bolster your hopes and dreams, listen when you need a compassionate ear, and keep you honest and aligned to all these things. My B.O.D. is so integral to my life, they've become part of my definition of Success and one of my Core Values. I attend to these relationships as if the health of my spine, heart and lungs depended on them!

A recent study conducted by The International Consortium for Executive Development Research (ICEDR) (available to download at www.icedr.org) highlights the value of maintaining a personal B.O.D. in a business setting. Author Lauren Ready interviewed sixty top female executives across 20 different companies to learn more about their leadership techniques. My friend, colleague and former client, Erin Chapple, opened up about her B.O.D. in the report:

Once a quarter, Erin Chapple, Partner Group Program Manager in the Server and Cloud Division at Microsoft, gets together with a group of four women that she refers to as her Board of Directors. The women are all from Microsoft and were originally introduced over eight years ago by a Vice President at the company. Long after the VP had left the division, the relationship these women have developed keeps growing. They have been meeting regularly ever since. Erin explains how this board works: "The four of us are in similar places in our careers and personal lives and we have the belief that there is no competition between us. Each quarter we spend a day together. Usually we include a social activity such as dinner or the spa and we share ideas and do peer mentoring.

When I met up with Erin recently, she spoke of the importance of continually updating her B.O.D. to keep pace with new jobs, new roles and new life experiences. After Erin's beloved father passed away, she realized she needed to expand her board to help her process and learn from this personal situation and translate it into both her career and family plan. You can utilize this amazing resource in just about every area of your life. I've learned that belonging, relationship and growth are vital to my own essence, so I go green by using my B.O.D. energy as much as possible. And before you ask, no, none of them have ever felt like I ask for too much from them.

Here's just some of the many ways my clients have capitalized on the power of their crew:

- Before Paula took on a new leadership role in another division of her company, she set out to establish connections with key people within the new group to ensure she would have the support she needed in order to be successful.
- When Richard got promoted, he took a chance and asked a top leader—someone he'd long admired for his values and healthy work/life balance—to be his mentor (he got a yes).

- Maggie looked around her work group and found one person with whom she felt safe to open up and share her softer, more sensitive side. With a little encouragement from her mini crew, she began to let the walls come down and be less rigid and more approachable. Before long, she was cultivating deeper relationships at work, and even some friendships.
- Anna realized she had too many Type-A "doers" and "advisers" in her life, and began consciously cultivating relationships with people who could witness and support without feeling the need to "fix" her.

It's likely that you already have a board in place, but I'm betting many of your members were never actually voted in. For example, your mom might sit on the board and have a huge voice, but did you invite her to the table? Is it time to shift her to stockholder, whereby she gets to have a say—but you get to make the decision? I encourage you to think intentionally about who's on you B.O.D.

Decide what roles you need and then figure out who's *best* positioned to fill them. Pay particular attention to those functions you're not so great at. For example, you might excel in creative vision or start-ups, but lack know-how in finance or capital funding. Great! Make sure to select someone who's really strong in this area to advise you. In my case, I have a great head for business, but I'm less good at recognizing and respecting my own sensitivity. Thus, my friend Patty serves a very specific purpose on my B.O.D.—reminding me of and supporting me in strengthening my sweet, tender side.

Just as with your E.I. building tools, your B.O.D. should include a blend of the rational, emotional and physical:

1. Who do you need to serve the **rational practicalities** of reaching the goals that support your Success? A mentor who's successfully navigated start-ups and can guide you on your new venture? A connector who can help you meet the right people?
2. What roles do you need to support the **passionate, emotional** side of your Success? A friend and advocate who cheers you on and

helps you recall the amazing-ness of who you are when you're in the pits? A peer who shares the same passion and stokes your creative imagination?

3. Who possesses the **physical grounded-ness** to keep you centered in moments when you get too heady or heart-centric? A long-distance runner who can support you in staying physically resilient as you pace yourself for the flow of Success and Critic? A yogi who can remind you to slow down and breathe when life overwhelms you?

ACTIVITY: Elect Your Board of Directors

- What roles do you need filled on your board, based on your current definition of Success and your goals for the next one to two years?
- Who is currently on your advisory board? Make a list of everyone you turn to for advice on a regular basis. Include those who dispense advice without being asked!
  - Who helps tame your Inner Critic voices?
  - Who helps champion your Inner Success stories?
  - Who doesn't add anything of value?
  - Who actually devalues your Success and your sense of self?
- Who needs to retire? Make a list. And make a note to resist the urge to call on them in the future.
- Who needs to be recruited? Make a list of potential candidates. Crosscheck with the list of roles you need to fill. Have you covered every need? Do you feel good about everyone on your list? Great! Meet your new board!

How to Ask for What You Need:
Rock, Coach, Friend . . . and Fixer

Having a board or crew is important, but it becomes Superpowered when you pair it with *asking* for the specific type of support you need.

Was that a big sigh I just heard? An exclamation of, "But that is *so* hard for me!" Or the sarcastic, stink-eye and slightly resigned, "Oh sure, like they want to hear me whine." Cue E.I. Builder moment! Virtually all of my clients have some type of reaction when I ask them to tell their crew what they need: fear, anxiety, resentment, disappointment, and often surprise and wonder. It's almost always one of those Scooby-Doo moments, like I had when I realized I could break one of my Rules in Play. "Huh? I can ask for what I want? Really?" Yes sugar, you can.

Most of us, however, are not very good at this. We try to handle things all by ourselves (Perfectionists and Drivers), we don't want to burden others (Pleasers), we're afraid of what our crew might think (Comparers and Frauds) or we worry it will backfire horribly (Damn you, Saboteur). Forget the Critics! Let me tell you how I figured it out.

My friend and former co-worker, Samantha, and I would always take our lunch breaks together. As we talked about life and the challenges we were facing, we'd listen carefully and endeavor to help each other as best we could. However, we didn't always get it right. We wanted to help because of our mutual respect and regard for each other, but what we did or said didn't always hit the mark. So, we came up with a set of labels that would allow us to ask for *exactly* the right kind of help: Rock, Coach, Friend.

Rock: A fantastically great listener. Different from an actual inanimate rock that just sits there saying nothing, this type of rock actively listens and allows ample time and space for you to express everything you need to say and share (thinking, feeling and physical reactions). When you're sharing, a rock paraphrases back to you what they've heard so you feel like someone gets it. For example, "Wow, that meeting with your boss sounds like it tore you up. What he was saying to you really hurt. I hear you." A rock *acknowledges* what you're saying, as distinct from agreeing with everything you say. In a nutshell, a rock is there for you, period.

Coach: A coach offers some constructive help in addition to doing the job of a rock—that is, listening and acknowledging. A coach will remind you of your capabilities and ask questions intended to help you find your own answers and tap into your own inner wisdom. A coach helps you see other perspectives and sometimes this involves a little tough love—by which I mean a supportive type of honesty that helps you see something you hadn't before. It comes from a place of love, but it may be a little tough to hear. After listening and acknowledging, a coach might ask, "Did your boss make any points that might be true in some way?" With a coach you feel listened to, acknowledged and supported in finding some new perspective or potential enlightenment.

Friend: "Your boss is a jerk! You were totally in the right!" Yes, you get it. A friend listens and is totally and completely on your side. You turn to a friend when you need to vent—even if you need to take a side trip to crazy-town. Who cares? A friend goes to crazy-town with you, buys you a shot and then gets you both safely home. A friend is someone who listens even when you're being completely ridiculous, and still agrees with you. "You're right," he'll say. "They're all jackasses." You know he's not really telling the truth, he's just agreeing with you in the awesome way a loyal friend always does, and that's exactly what you need right now.

My clients *love* Rock, Coach, Friend but they felt something was missing. While in our leadership circles, as they learn listening and coaching skills with peers, they had to practically cover their mouths for the want to jump in, give advice and solve problems. I get it, in the business world it seems to be all about solving. It can drive my clients crazy to learn how to listen and coach. So, they asked to add a fourth role—the fixer.

Fixer: A fixer is the one you call when you want someone to *solve* the problem or tell you exactly what to do. While this is the one people believe they'll use the most, it's actually the "ear" least called upon. In my experience, the fixer is called upon in only about twenty to thirty percent of cases, those times when people actually want someone to tell them how to fix things. Most of the time they just want to be heard and be supported while they figure it out themselves.

"Rock, Coach, Friend, Fixer" is a fantastic tool not only for listening to others, but also for helping others listen to you. Most people want to be helpful—but they don't know how. So let them know. Tell them exactly how they can best assist you. Spell it out: "Here's what would be most helpful right now—can you please be a coach?"

Also, know that you get to change your mind. One day I reached out to my friend Mitch and told her I needed a coach. We met for a walk and as we talked I realized my emotional response wasn't relief, it was irritation. I didn't want a coach after all, what I really wanted was a friend. So I told Mitch I'd changed my mind and, being the amazing person she is, Mitch said, "OK, no problem" and switched to friend mode. I felt helped, supported and instantly better.

ACTIVITY
Stock Up on Rocks, Coaches, Friends, and Fixers

- Call to mind your current circle of supporters, both the first and second tiers. For each one, ask yourself: what's their primary role, or the one they adopt most frequently? Are they a rock, coach, friend or fixer?
- What do you need more of in terms of a support crew? What do you need less of? (Most people need more rocks, and less fixers!)
- How can you round out your support crew so you have enough of all four? Enough might mean having just one of each. That's totally fine; this is about quality, not quantity.

How to Build and Sustain a Good Crew

OK, you've thought about who should be part of your crew and what types of roles you'll need to fill in order to feel supported on your path. Now I want you to consider the how: how do you create the kind of relationships that will inspire, nurture and sustain you?

The answer lies in your own inner wisdom and past experiences. Reflect on the great relationships of your life, both past and present. What are the characteristics and traits common to all? In each case, consider what both parties bring to the table in order for the relationship to remain so insanely good. How does the dynamic keep pace with the changes and transitions in your lives? As with everything in this book, taking the time to bring clarity will allow you to be intentional and create a practice that is sustainable and solid.

Below, I share what I've learned from my own reflections on my most successful relationships—the insiders in my world who help me stay true to my Inner Success *and* get a grip during Inner Critic moments. There's so much to say here, but in the interests of clarity and focus, I've distilled it down to six essential elements:

Listen more than fix. As I shared in the introduction, I spent eight years in the high-tech industry prior to my current vocation. As I worked towards becoming a coach and leadership consultant, I had to undergo a fundamental shift in skill set: I had to become a listener instead of a fixer. I'm a fantastic problem solver and advice giver, and this is a prized trait in the business world. As a coach, however, my job is to listen and help my clients find *their* capacity. I'm not serving anyone if I simply dish out a task list because To-Do lists don't create real growth or sustainable change.

Much to my surprise, an interesting thing happened as I learned to become a better listener: it had a beautiful impact on all my relationships. I discovered that as a coach and friend, listening is almost always the best thing I can do to support another person. Think about your own experiences. When you've needed support, how helpful was it really when the other person shifted into problem-solving and advice-schilling mode? Not so helpful, right? Didn't it feel more distressing than soothing? Weren't you left feeling more edgy than before?

Therefore, my first and best piece of advice for building a solid and supportive crew or B.O.D. (or whichever term you'd like to use) is to become a great listener. Believe me when I say it will prove to be what you'll need most often, and when you become great at giving good listening, you'll be amazed at how magically and ease-fully it comes back to you.

Let others in. I'm a rock-solid pal to my posse but I have a hell of a time letting others help me, and I've come to see that this doesn't create the strongest, or the healthiest of relationships. The lesson struck home most deeply when I finally let my mom in. I've always loved her but we've also had our moments, which led me to erect pretty strong boundaries that served as barriers between us. We had a good enough relationship but I often didn't feel satisfied. My coach Kavita encouraged me to let the walls come down and allow my mom to help me, while allowing myself to depend on her, just a little bit. It took a long time, but I finally did and it's been transformational for me. Sure, it was a workout getting me over that hump. But the irony is that once I allowed my mom to care for me, I started to feel much more solid, confident and grounded. The lesson: Don't do all the nurturing; allow yourself to be nurtured. Fill up and you'll have even more to give.

Be yourself—all of you. Right on the fabulous stiletto heels (or wing-tipped Oxfords) of that last bit I want to add this: when you let people in, let them see *all* of you. Let them see the good *and* the bad. Let people love you both at your best and your sweaty, snotty-nosed, making-absolutely-no-dang sense worst. I don't necessarily love sharing my worst moments, but doing so has helped me learn and trust that my inner circle is there for me no matter how horrifying I look or sound.

The second and equally important part of this piece is to reciprocate: Find it within your capability to be with *other* people's good and bad. Foster enough trust that they feel safe to share their worst moments with you. Trust breeds trust. Have the courage to be the first to show up in all your messy, snotty-nosed splendor.

" *The strongest relationships spring out of a real and often earned connection felt by both sides. —Sheryl Sandberg,* Lean In: Women, Work, and the Will to Lead

Be honest about what you need—and speak it *out loud*. "Help me help you" is age-old wisdom and it's age-old for a reason: because it works! Help others help you by *telling them* what you need—they can't read your mind! We've all learned the hard way that it's no fun to get it wrong when all you ever wanted to do was help. It might feel a little embarrassing at first to ask for the kind of help you want but I urge you to get over it—what you may not know yet is that, when it comes to you, your peeps have a ton of bandwidth. They love you. Allow them to show it. Reach out, even at your most vulnerable, and ask for help. And on the flip side, reach out, even when you're not sure what to say to a friend who needs you and ask *how you can help them*. Ask them what they need. And when they tell you, give them exactly what they asked for—not what you feel like giving. Take risks. Make mistakes. Apologize. Above all else, be honest.

Nothing substitutes for time spent together. Oh, I can already hear you protest, "But there isn't enough time in the day! I can't do it all!" Yes, I know. I hear you. Every single one of us has to make hard, complex decisions about *how* we'll spend our time—but if you want solid, supportive relationships, ya gotta put in the time, sugar. If you're a parent, I highly doubt you'd ever say there's not enough time to spend with your children—because you know how important it is. Same goes for your most valued relationships.

Figure out who you want to invest your time and energy in and spend your capital there. I've had many clients and friends tell me they've consistently been there for people who never seemed able to reciprocate. That is a miserable feeling and a waste of your precious self. You don't necessarily have to give up these one-way relationships, but make a choice about how you want to spend your time and energy. Do you want to let them get sucked into a vortex or do you want to save your time and energy for someone who gives back? Make an intentional choice about who deserves a slice of you and make it a top priority to carve out time and space for those VIPs.

Try a little tenderness. This is a tough and complex life, which at times seems full of struggle and strife. We all get plenty of reminders of how we *don't* measure up. Be the one to remind others how they *do*. Remind your B.O.D. of their greatness, often. In fact, take on the cheerleading role way, way, *way* more often than you take the constructive criticism path. Most of us need more encouragement than we do reminders of how to do things better. Now, by this I don't mean be falsely sweet or have empty compliments, I mean *be honest*. Point out greatness where and as you see it, but point it out *often*. See the greatness in others and mirror it back to them. Allow them to mirror your greatness back to you. Generosity begets generosity.

The Perks of a Tight-Knit Crew

As I mentioned in chapter seven, I reached out to my tribe during the process of revamping my corporate brand. While brainstorming on my Core Identity and Strengths, I called on Patty. Not only is Patty a close friend, she's a rock, coach, friend and fixer, all in one. I shared what I'd written and asked Patty if it was pretty accurate, or had I missed anything. She helped me catch the two key Identities I'd missed:

1. I'm a savvy businessperson. This is a classic example of a Superpower—it's so ingrained in me I didn't even list it as a Strength. When Patty labeled this Identity "Business Mogul," my stomach clenched and I gulped nervously, and because she's crew I told Patty about my reaction to the word "mogul." Patty gave me the support I needed in that moment to hold me accountable to my capability and power. She ever so gently encouraged me to own my Inner Business Mogul.

2. The second thing Patty reminded me of is that I have a very tender, caring Identity that's an important aspect of who I am, both at work and in my personal life. I hadn't included it because I perceived it as a shadow side of me. I mean, if I talk about my tender side, I'll be perceived as weak, right? After all, I'm supposed to be a friggin' Business Mogul! Lucky for me, Patty knows to remind me that my sweet, caring side is what makes me so successful as a

coach. If I omitted it, I'd be omitting something really important, valuable and useful—essentially something Divine.

Bottom line: I needed my outer crew to help me do even better at my inner work. (Even if I did give Patty a dose of stink-eye in the process!)

I can't stress enough how important this outer practice is. In *Adventure in Everything: How the Five Elements of Adventure Create a Life of Authenticity, Purpose, and Inspiration,* Matt shares his five steps to achieving Great Companionship:

1. Be Authentic
2. Be Specific About You Want
3. Refine How You Give and Receive Feedback
4. Allow Shifts in Your Relationship to Happen
5. Reciprocate Great Companionship

I can say from experience that Matt walks his talk. When I decided to write my book, Matt was right there with me, sharing his own writing process, offering tips on how to publish, connecting me with people who could help. He was a constant champion of my effort, even when I was mired in the mud of writer's block. I'd like to take this moment to say, Thanks Mattie! Which brings me to my last point on the topic . . .

Pay It Forward

Never forget that the input of your B.O.D. is a gift—and always remember to treat it as such. Whenever your peeps share their time, talents and thoughtfulness, be sure to acknowledge their generosity. Express your gratitude—say thank you.

And then pay it forward. Help others see their Strengths, Superpowers and Successes. Whenever someone impacts me in a positive way, I'll tell them. It may sound a little silly, and feel a little odd at first, but believe me, every single person you witness and acknowledge will feel nothing other than deep appreciation. I mean, who doesn't like to be acknowledged? We all thrive on praise and appreciation. It costs absolutely nothing and the payoff is priceless. Why not share the wealth?

12

Cultivating Your Practice

In this final chapter, your goal is to develop a strategy for putting what you've learned into practice. While it's wonderful to educate yourself about a new subject, and to acquire new skills and tools, none of your newfound knowledge will have much of an impact until you apply it, practice it and live it. By now you will have read the book cover to cover, with the exception of this final chapter. You've completed all the activities and exercises—unless you're like me and you've saved some of the activities for last, in which case now is the perfect time to go back and complete any steps you skipped over. Your next step is to take what you've learned and translate it into meaningful change. In this final chapter, I'll share some practical and actionable suggestions.

First, Another Little Metaphor

What do you think of when I suggest you "cultivate a practice?" Using Merriam-Webster's definition of the word cultivate, it's likely your mind will conjure images of a well-kept garden or a golden field of wheat in its ripe, pre-harvest glory. When I think of the word, I see the time and effort invested by the farmer, which began in the previous season when he plowed the field, turning the soil over so it might become enriched and aerated with life-giving oxygen. I see the care he took to ward off noxious weeds or bugs that might choke the crop. He may have had to make the difficult decision to let the soil lie fallow for a season so it could refresh and replenish itself. And let's not forget his vibrancy and joy in seeing a field in its full flow, nor the happy feeling of harvesting one's own crop.

❝Cultivate

1 : to prepare or prepare and use for the raising of crops; also : to loosen or break up the soil about (growing plants)

2 a: to foster the growth of <cultivate vegetables>, c : to improve by labor, care, or study : refine <cultivate the mind>

3 : further, encourage <cultivate the arts>

4 : to seek the society of : make friends with

Cultivation—as I use the term in this chapter—asks that you commit to many of the same undertakings as the farmer. It asks that you be intentional about what you sow, tend your crops carefully throughout the seasons, and plan intentionally for that which you'll reap. It asks that you create an environment wherein your efforts will yield a bountiful harvest—resisting noxious thoughts and picking out creepy crawlers that eat at you (versus the beneficial ones that assist in your growth). And don't forget what all great farmers and gardeners know: cultivating crops is a process. It takes time, effort, attunement and adjustment. If you tried something and it failed (for example you planted chrysanthemums in a particular bed and they didn't get enough sunlight, water or fertilizer and therefore yielded a shallow crop of blooms)—that's OK. You now know what to adjust next season.

At the beginning of this book, I promised to share my experiences, expertise and strategies on how to diminish and tame the Inner Critic, see it from the volume-shrinking perspective of its relationship to what's so great about you (Divine Flaw) and gain clarity on what Inner Success means to you. Along the way I've inserted activities to develop and build upon your whole-person intelligence—that is, your rational thinking brain, your emotions and feelings, and your body responses and wisdom. Operating from my vocational perspective as a coach, I've offered help on how you call upon your own capability and wisdom, and posed questions designed to open up new possibilities and perspectives. I've asked that you share your story so that you might both learn from others and build the vital support crew needed to sustain a satisfying, gratifying, growth-oriented life. And now here we are near the end of this book—but definitely not at the end of this process. This process is something I hope you'll continue to cultivate with deep respect and care over the course of your entire life. After all, you are your most valuable asset and the key creator of an authentic and alive life.

Practice Makes Perfect (Kidding!)

Brené Brown, author of the book *Daring Greatly: How the Courage to Be Vulnerable Transforms the Way We Live, Love, Parent, and Lead*, admits that being authentic is something she works diligently towards every day. In her interview with *ORIGIN* magazine, she described her process to interviewer Chantal Pierrat:

> It has to be practiced. It's a practice for me every day, sometimes every hour of every day. It is an absolute practice. When I went into the research, I really thought that there are authentic people and inauthentic people, period. What I found is, there are people who practice authenticity and people who don't. The people who practice authenticity work their ass off at it. It was so scary to me. Oh my god, that's going to be a lot of work. I thought, You either have the gene or you don't. It was scary. But it was so liberating. I thought, This is not predetermined—I get to choose.

Brown's uniquely eloquent brand of "this is reality, honey" practicality and pragmatism is just one of many things about her that I love.

Now, I want you to consider how your practice will look, and how committed you'll be to constantly cultivating it. This practice should be attuned and authentic to you—the fabulous architect (and best asset) of your life. Much like your statement of Inner Success, it should be tailored to how you like to cultivate. In other words, it should feel good. As I wrote in chapter one, **the goal is not to find the answer—but to find your way**.

Staying Resilient In Success and In Doubt

You and I will be coming to a parting of the ways soon. And as you continue to move through this thrilling and (at times) tormenting life, you'll experience the rush of Success, the resonance of connection, the tightness of self-doubt, the softness of comfort, the bitterness of regret and the pain of mistakes. That's just life. The magic is in embracing all of it—the good and the bad—and having the courage to reach into the discomfort, knowing that it's all just information you can use to enrich and inform and adapt and enhance your experience. This is my long-winded way of describing Resilience. Merriam Webster's definition is "an ability to recover from or adjust easily to misfortune or change," but I think mine's prettier!

In *Search Inside Yourself: The Unexpected Path to Achieving Success, Happiness (and World Peace)* Chade-Meng Tan describes it this way: "Resilience is the ability to overcome obstacles along the way. Alignment and envisioning help you find out where you want to go, and resilience helps you get there."

Using Tan's definition, resilience is what will allow you to move towards embodying your personal definition of Inner Success while navigating the doubts, fears, failures and setbacks that will inevitably pop up along the way. Kind of like when the Yellow Brick Road took a detour through the dark and dangerous forest: resilience is what got Dorothy and her friends through to the other side.

Tan presents three methods with which to train yourself to become more resilient:

1. Achieve inner calm: "Once we can consistently access the inner calm in the mind, it becomes the foundation of all optimism and resilience," writes Tan. Meditation is of course a wonderful tool for quieting the mind, but if that's not your cup of tea there are other ways to enter a calmer mental state. For example, a moving meditation like yoga or running or an absorbing task or hobby like gardening or golf. Find what works for *you*. What enables you to bounce back from defeat? What keeps you grounded in the midst of chaos? What activities bring you back to your center fastest? Build them into your daily routine.

2. **Develop emotional resilience:** "Success and failure are emotional experiences," writes Tan. "By working at this level, we can increase our capacity for them." Having read this book and completed many if not all of the activities, you've significantly boosted your emotional intelligence and thereby your emotional resilience. Continue to build your E.I. by constantly checking in and asking: 1) What am I feeling? 2) What am I thinking? 3) What's my physical reaction?

3. **Build cognitive resilience:** Writes Tan, "Understanding how we explain our setbacks to ourselves and creating useful mental habits help us develop optimism." One of the best ways to develop optimism and an abundant mindset is to have a daily gratitude practice. This can be as complex as journaling at day's end on all the events, coincidences, surprises, synchronicities, etc., you experienced throughout the day or as simple as listing three things you're grateful for while brushing your teeth before bed. Or, take a leaf out of Alex's book and enlist your entire family by making gratitude a daily dinner table ritual!

The Order of Change: from Reaction to Choice; from Insight to Action

Change doesn't follow a linear progression, it's more of a line dance whereby you take two steps forward, one step back. One of the key pieces in that dance is awareness: gaining insight around your habits, beliefs and patterns. If you adopt the activities in this book as daily habits, you'll earn a Black Belt in the art of self-awareness, which will help give valuable and useful insight into what you do, why you do the things you do—and how you can do more of the things that are good and positive.

Cultivating self-awareness provides two golden opportunities:

1. With greater insight, you gain a wider range of choices around what you *can* do.
2. And from that wider range of choices, you can move swiftly from insight to choice to action.

Do you recall in chapter three when I asked Shandra to record her Inner Critic messages on Post-it notes and she had a freak-out moment because in her Type-A mind that didn't constitute action or change? Eventually, Shandra discovered the value and wisdom of an awareness practice: she couldn't change anything until she first became aware of *how* she was operating (her automatic reaction) and therefore what needed to change (insight and choice). Like Shandra, you'll discover that once you become aware of what you're doing, you'll have more choice about what you *can* change. From there, you'll move swiftly from reaction to awareness, from awareness to choice, and from choice to action.

The Science of Change

As an applied behavioral scientist, I've spent a great deal of time studying how people change—and how they resist change. "Change management" theorists use the change curve to explain the process in organizations. Adopted from Swiss-born psychiatrist Elizabeth Kübler-Ross' "five stages of grief"—which she outlined in her 1969 book, *On Death and Dying*—it describes the process and the path of change.

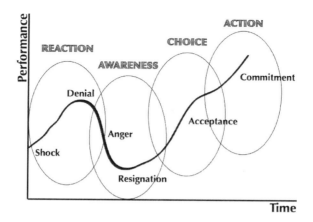

The graph shows a typical change curve for the average human being. (While your attitude and behavior around change might look very different from your neighbor's, everyone's change curve tends to follow the same trajectory.)

At this point in our journey together, you're at the mid-point where one of two things will happen: Either you're so resistant to change, you pop back down the curve—a phenomenon known as homeostasis—or you draw upon your resilience to push through and eventually pop all the way up the curve to the point where change has been adopted and implemented.

Homeostasis is the tendency to revert to our old habits because, as I wrote before, change is difficult. It requires dedication and commitment both on your part and on the part of those closest to you. You might find that your friends, family, even your coworkers try to entice you back into old ways. I alluded to this in chapter eleven when I warned that some of your old crew may not be ready or willing or able to support your new definition of a successful life.

Those trying to lose weight often experience homeostasis. What usually happens is the dieter will lose a certain amount of weight and then reach a plateau. At this mid-point stage, he will either a) push past the plateau as his body learns to operate at that new weight or b) he regresses, falling back down the curve and gaining some if not all of the weight he lost. Being surrounded by people who can support him and inspire him in his quest for a healthier lifestyle is crucial. As is his ability to feel and see himself as a healthier version of himself.

What you do from here on in will determine whether you pop up or down the change curve. In chapter ten you read about Mason, who incorporated imperfection into his statement of Success after being inspired by his young daughter. In order to realize his story of Success—to continue to contribute *and* create a more peaceful environment at work—Mason's number one goal was to stop over-reacting. In a coaching session to check in on his progress, Mason was beating himself up for failing, big time. "I've had what feels like a million misses," lamented Mason. "And it feels bad to miss. I feel bad for failing to notice and catch myself in the moment *before* flaring up. I feel bad for my harsh reaction. I feel even worse because the last time I railed at someone who absolutely didn't deserve it."

"I hear you my friend," I told Mason. "I really do. It's sucky to catch your miss just a moment too late. But the damnedest thing is that those misses are where we learn the most. You do know that, right?"

But Mason was in the midst of an amygdala hijack. It was time to back off, so I changed the subject. I asked about his weekend, and Mason instantly brightened as he told me what a great time he'd had teaching his daughter to snowboard. She didn't like all the falling down, Mason explained, so he told her that her job right now was just that: to fall down—a lot, and that the process of falling, getting back up and trying again was an information gathering process that would in time help his daughter become a good snowboarder (he's a quintessential engineer!). "You have to be committed to falling down a lot," Mason shared the message he'd told his daughter. As soon as he uttered those words, Mason stopped dead in his tracks. The room was silent as I allowed space for the words to resonate. It was a crystalline moment as Mason finally got it. He got it! He, Mason, had to be *committed* to those misses in meetings. He had to be *committed* to failing—a lot—in order to learn and in time get really, really good at succeeding.

Resilience also requires that you not only anticipate, but that you actually *plan for* making mistakes. You will get it wrong. You will fall back into old behaviors, habits and patterns. You will be tempted by the lure of homeostasis. You will find yourself in the grip of an amygdala hijack, hitting the giant red "nuclear" button as you spiral into DEF-CON-1. That's all right. That's to be expected. That's why it's important to have a plan. Like Mason, it's important that you build mistakes—and therefore, learning—into your goals.

The Practicalities of Change: Realistic Plans, Attainable Goals, Incremental shifts

Speaking of goals . . . Once I've helped a client determine their personal vision of Success and the goals they need to work on in order to move toward living their statement of Success, I then encourage them to narrow their focus to two or three goals at a time, depending on how big those goals are. She might brainstorm a list of 10 possibilities, but I'll have her pick no more than three to tackle first. This can be really hard for goal-oriented, Type A, high achievers (like me, too!) but the reality is, if you really want to learn, grow and change, the best way to do that is to direct intense focus, discipline and accountability to only a few objectives at a time. If you try to shoot for 10, you'll be spreading your energy and capability way too thin, which means you won't achieve as satisfactory a result. In fact, you'll set yourself up for failure. If, on the other hand, you direct all your energy towards two or three goals, you'll see a much bigger payoff and experience the rejuvenating thrill of achievement.

The other point I want to drive home is the importance of selecting goals that are *attainable*. For example, "I want to stop being a Perfectionist" is not a realistic, attainable goal. However, if you break it down into bite-size pieces, then you've got something tangible to work on. Using the above example, you could do that in one of two ways:

1. Figure out two to three areas where your perfectionist tendencies create the most problems or wreak the most havoc in your life; OR,

2. Figure out two areas where you'd see the most benefit in shifting *away* from your perfectionist tendencies.

For example, you might say, "If I stopped being such a perfectionist micro manager and started trusting my employees to do more stuff on their own, it would free up so much more of my time—and transform my relationship with my team." Now that gives you something tangible to practice, around which you'll see solid results.

In chapter three, I shared a mantra I use often: "Slow down to speed up." This is a perfect place to pause and remind you of it. The surest path towards Success involves solid, steady, incremental steps. By resisting the temptation to shoot for the whole enchilada, you'll actually gain a lot more ground in the end. I've worked with several clients on and off over the course of many years, which allows for a wonderful perspective on growth. One of these clients recently told me, "You know what Stacey, it always feels like it's taking forever to assimilate and integrate new learning. But then when we meet for our annual review, I'm always amazed at how transformational the previous year has been." Yep, exactly.

The Dynamics of Change: Behavior and Attitude

Another way to stack the odds in your favor is to break a goal down into attitude and behavior. Attitude is how you think about something; behavior is how you act in relation to it. Sometimes it pays to focus on changing one first—and allowing the other to follow.

Yuli had just moved to a new company and despite having a fantastic track record and stellar résumé, he was suffering chronic Inner Critic attacks. Yuli's Inner Fraud was inundating him with messages such as, "They don't think I'm worth it. The team can't believe they hired me. I'm just a heartbeat away from an epic fail." Needless to say, these negative messages were coloring Yuli's attitude a dull shade of depressing. Meanwhile his behavior was atypical of his former, successful self—he was subdued, withdrawn, failing to push for strategic viewpoints and fading into the background. Since Yuli was having a tough time changing his behavior, we focused on his attitude. Each time the negative critic thoughts came up, Yuli used The Truth Series questions to combat the gross and inaccurate generalizations. I also had him take his C.V. and use it to write a parallel story about why he was the best fit for his new company. In a short amount of practice time, Yuli's attitude began to shift. As it did, his behavior came back online, too.

The Practice of Change: Shower, Rinse, Repeat

As we progress through the ebb and flow of life, our circumstances change accordingly: we get older, we get married, we change jobs, we have children, we get hired, we get fired, we join a great team, we strike out on our own. . . . As you undergo all these transitions, it's only natural that your definition of Inner Success should change accordingly. And those rascally Inner Critic messages change along with it. The goal of this book is to provide you with activities and awareness exercises that will allow you to negotiate all of life's major (or minor) turning points. Change is inevitable and these processes are designed to help you gracefully navigate your way through the change process with ease and peace of mind.

Professional Change

Remember Richard? One of his goals was to get a promotion. Together, we worked through what Success (i.e., a promotion) would look like and how he would deal with the Critics that would surely surface along the way. Within a very short span of time, Richard got that promotion. However, his new role was not what he'd envisaged as his next step, which triggered some brand new iterations of his Inner Critic that he needed to deal with. Another side effect of Richard's transition was that in his new role, he needed to draw upon a whole different set of Strengths and Superpowers. In his book *What Got You Here Won't Get You There: How Successful People Become Even More Successful* Marshall

Goldsmith reminds us that as we climb the corporate ladder, it's often the case that what made us successful in our previous job doesn't guarantee success in our new one. Therefore, Richard made the worthy investment of going back to the drawing board in order to:

- Devise new strategies to deal with his newly mutated Inner Critic.
- Determine what Strengths and Superpowers he needed to amplify in his new role—along with pinpointing those Strengths that no longer served him.
- Update his Inner Success statement for the new role and avenues of influence—while continuing to have a positive impact on the people in his organization.

Personal Flux

The same can hold true in times of major life transitions—not just work-related flux. For example, a lot of my clients have aging parents and, just as Richard's role changed in his business organization, they're dealing with major role changes within their families as they step into the role of becoming caregivers to their parents. It's a very stressful situation so, naturally, they surf a range of emotions, which as you now know is a huge trigger for the Inner Critic. Together, we've talked through the I.C. messages that have surfaced during this major life-shift. Sometimes what comes up are self-critical thoughts that they don't spend enough time taking care of their parents, or that they should be more on top of understanding Medicare or Option B or Plan A.

My advice is to apply the very same processes you've learned in this book to times of personal transition. In other words:

- Identify what's triggered the Inner Critic attack.
- Delve underneath to determine what Values and Identity you want to hold as you start to take care of your parents (or whatever life situation you find yourself in).
- Identify what Strengths and Superpowers you can bring to this new way of functioning within your family.
- Create a statement of Success as it pertains to the situation. Yes,

really. Your definition of Success doesn't necessarily have to relate to your career or to your whole life picture. It can also relate to a specific situation you find yourself dealing with at a particular point in time. In this case, Success might be defined by asking: what would Success look like in the context of taking care of my parents? What Values are going to be important to me? And what Inner Critics are likely to come up?

Seasonal Transition

If you like to set resolutions or goals at the beginning of the year, make it a practice to re-visit this process each January 1. Ask yourself: what kind of Inner Success do I want to achieve this year? What challenges and Inner Critics am I likely to encounter as I move toward this new vision of Success?

Alternatively, you might align an I.C./I.S. check-in with your annual performance review at work or at any point in the year that represents a marker or milestone. In time, as you become adept at repeating this process, start to include the question: Where have I experienced growth in my learning, awareness and resilience as I've continued to use these tools? This will serve to remind you how far you've come!

It's really important to recognize your progress. If you're now at the point where your autopilot response to an Inner Critic attack is to think of your Divine Flaw, or if you go straight to "What's more or less true?", then give yourself a pat on the back! Recognize where you've grown and how you've made improvements when you do your annual Inner Critic/Inner Success review. Realize that these tools have gone from practice to habit, from something you've had to think about to something you just naturally do. Maybe you've mastered them to such an extent that they've become a Strength or Superpower? My clients often forget to recognize how far they've come and how much they've changed in their attitudes and behaviors around the I.C./I.S. Pausing to reflect and acknowledge and ground yourself in your growth is a powerful reminder of your capability and your capacity.

Coach's Closing Session

I opened chapter one with Kimiko's insights which she shared during our final coaching session together. Whenever concluding a coaching partnership—or a workshop or program—I ask a couple of closing questions with the intention that my clients review their investment and progress across our time together. I want them to have a whole-person experience (thinking, feeling *and* body) of what they've accomplished. I ask that they write "headlines" to summarize and articulate their experience. I also ask that they think ahead to how they'll continue to cultivate the practices on their own (without coaching or a leadership program). Since you and I have partnered together in this journey, I'm going to do the same thing.

I was designing the final session of a yearlong leadership program together with a colleague the other day. We brainstormed on the growth this group had experienced over the past eleven months in an effort to zero in on how best to help them encapsulate their investment and progress. I closed my eyes, calling to mind each individual, each session and the feelings this conjured. "I really want them to grasp the *distance* they've covered, both as individuals and as a team," I told my colleague. "I want them to know how incredibly awesome that progress is." I want the same for you.

ACTIVITY: Closing Session

While everything's still fresh in your mind, thumb quickly through the book and highlight the activities that resonate with you the most. These are the ones you'll want to revisit in times of upheaval when you know your critics and doubts will surface. It's also a good idea to notice if you're resistant to any activities. If so, flag these too as they'll prove worth revisiting.

Now, I want you to strategize specifically on which resources you'll use going forward:

- What ground have you gained having undertaken the processes in this book? What key learning stands out with the sharpest contrast and richest emotional undercurrent? What's irrevocably different for you now? Please add specific examples to help pull out all the valuable details (you know how I like the data!).
- What specific activities, reflections and/or exercises were most helpful in your progress, as mapped out above? Which ones were *instrumental* in helping you move forward and generate a shift in attitude and/or behavior?
- Of these, what are the *two or three essential resources* (meaning activities, reflections and/or exercises) you'll draw upon and adopt as ongoing practices in order to continue to grow and settle into this new version of yourself?
  - What structures will you put in place *as of today* to embed these tools in your day-to-day life (for example, carving out time in your calendar for journaling, capturing your Successes, Prouds or gratitudes, or making time for those activities that put you in flow)?
  - Who will you ask for support—this might include your Board of Directors; your Rock, Coach, Friend, Fixer (if different from your B.O.D.), a manager or peer with whom you'll share moments of triumph or doubt; your partner or family with whom you'll discuss prioritizing time for all of the above? Determine when you'll have conversations with all of the above and mark it on your calendar *now*.

These closing conversations often comprise my favorite coaching moments—I get to see a client's eyes light up when they share their accomplishments. I feel the energy flow through them as they realize they've got everything they need to maintain momentum; they'll have this easy, confident, comfortable posture about themselves. Is there ever angst? Yes, a little. Mostly it's positive angst about what's possible. And there's usually a hint of melancholy, mostly on my part—I love my clients. I've cheered for them. I've been with them in the fear, I've helped them fight the Inner Critic (brass knuckles and all), I've been privileged to hear about their dreams and their hopes and their goals and their glories and their new and inspiring vision of Inner Success. Each time I get to do this work is truly an honor and while endings are healthy and yield exciting new beginnings, it's never easy to part.

I wish I was sitting beside you right now to witness all of these changes in you. Thank you so much for allowing me to be your coach and partner. This is the work love of my life and it gives me great joy to share it with an even larger audience by way of this book. While I encourage you to come back to it during times of transition and challenge, it is my sincere hope you'll need to return less often over time.

And here are my wishes for each of you:

May your Perfectionist enjoy a sense of Peace through working your Core.

May your Driver meet the Delightful acquaintance of your Divine Flaw.

May your Pleaser receive great amounts of Pleasurable Appreciation.

May your Saboteur feel Satisfied and Satiated in knowing your Strengths.

May your Comparer feel the Contentment of your Successes and Prouds.

May your Fraud find trust in your newfound Freedom to share your authentic Story of Success.

May you be as committed to mistakes and learning as you are to succeeding. May you remain resilient in the face of Inner Critic doubts and fears. And may the triumphant story of your Inner Success exceed your wildest imaginings.

Notes

INTRODUCTION

Brown, Brené. *Daring Greatly: How the Courage to Be Vulnerable Transforms the Way We Live, Love, Parent, and Lead.* New York: Gotham Books, 2012, 65.

Rometty, Ginni. Fortune's "Most Powerful Women Summit." By Jessi Hempel. http://management.fortune.cnn.com/2011/10/05/ibms-ginni-rometty-growth-and-comfort-do-not-coexist/, May 10, 2011.

Tan, Chade-Meng, Daniel Goleman, and Jon Kabat-Zinn. *Search Inside Yourself: The Unexpected Path to Achieving Success, Happiness (and World Peace).* 2012. New York: HarperCollins Kindle e-book, locations 21, 348–350, 386–388.

CHAPTER ONE

Bradberry, Travis and Jean Greaves. *Emotional Intelligence 2.0.* San Diego: TalentSmart, 2009, 25.

Bradford, Harry. "Workplace Stress Causes I Million Americans To Skip Work." Last modified March 8, 2012. *The Huffington Post.* http://www.huffingtonpost.com/2012/03/08/workplace-stress-1-million-americans-skip-everyday_n_1332172.html.

Brown, Brené. (2010, June). Brené Brown (TED talk): The power of vulnerability. http://www.ted.com/talks/brene_brown_on_vulnerability.html.

Brown, Brené. *The Gifts of Imperfection: Let Go of Who You Think You're Supposed to Be and Embrace Who You Are.* Center City: Hazelden, 2010, 39.

Gibran, Kahlil. *The Prophet.* New York: Alfred A. Knopf, 1973.

Goleman, Daniel. *Working with Emotional Intelligence.* New York: Bantam Books, 2006.

Goleman, Daniel, Richard E. Boyatzis, and Annie McKee. *Primal Leadership:*

Realizing the Power of Emotional Intelligence. Boston: Harvard Business School Press, 2002.

Haidt, Jonathan. *The Happiness Hypothesis: Finding Modern Truth in Ancient Wisdom.* Cambridge: Perseus Books Group. 2006. Kindle e-book, locations 129, 240-243.

Sandberg, Sheryl. *Lean In: Women, Work, and the Will to Lead.* New York: Knopf, 2013. Kindle e-book, location 33.

Tan, Chade-Meng, Daniel Goleman, and Jon Kabat-Zinn. *Search Inside Yourself: The Unexpected Path to Achieving Success, Happiness (and World Peace).* 2012. New York: HarperCollins Kindle e-book, locations 21, 348–350, 386–388.

CHAPTER TWO

Matthews, Gail, M. "Impostor Phenomenon: Attributions for Success and Failure," presentation, American Psychological Association, Toronto, 1984.) Cited in V. Young, *The Secret Thoughts of Successful Women: Why Capable People Suffer from the Impostor Syndrome and How to Thrive in Spite of It.* New York: Crown Business, 2011. Kindle e-book, locations 268–269.

Young, Valerie. *The Secret Thoughts of Successful Women: Why Capable People Suffer from the Impostor Syndrome and How to Thrive in Spite of It.* New York: Crown Business, 2011.

CHAPTER THREE

Plato quote by J.D. Meier, Sources of Insight (blog), http://sourcesofinsight.com/emotional-intelligence-quotes

Tan, Chade-Meng, Daniel Goleman, and Jon Kabat-Zinn. *Search Inside Yourself: The Unexpected Path to Achieving Success, Happiness (and World Peace).* 2012. New York: HarperCollins Kindle e-book, locations 21, 348–350, 386–388.

CHAPTER FOUR

Goleman, Daniel. *Emotional Intelligence: Why It Can Matter More Than IQ.* New York: Bantam Books, 2005.

Katie, Byron, and Stephen Mitchell. *Loving What Is: Four Questions That Can Change Your Life.* New York: Three Rivers Press, 2003.

Seligman, Martin E.P. *Authentic Happiness: Using the New Positive Psychology to Realize Your Potential for Lasting Fulfillment.* New York: The Free Press, 2002. Kindle e-book, locations 1835–1836, 3141–3154.

CHAPTER FIVE

Carroll, Lewis. *Alice's Adventures in Wonderland.* Accessed May 10, 2013. http://www.goodreads.com/quotes/9467-alice-laughed-there-s-no-use-trying-she-said-one-can-t.

Chopra, Deepak, Marianne Williamson, and Debbie Ford. *The Shadow Effect: Illuminating the Hidden Power of Your True Self.* New York: HarperCollins, 2010. Kindle e-book, locations 87–88.

Collins, Jim, and Jerry I. Porras. *Built to Last: Successful Habits of Visionary Companies.* New York: HarperBusiness, 2004.

CHAPTER SIX

Kipp, Mastin. The Daily Love (blog), November 2, 2012, quoting Swiss psychiatrist Carl G. Jung, http://thedailylove.com/todays-quotes-what-you-resist-persists.

CHAPTER SEVEN

LaPorte, Danielle. *The Fire Starter Sessions: A Soulful + Practical Guide to Creating Success On Your Own Terms.* New York: Harmony, 2012, 62.

Phillips, Edward, M.D. "Build your core muscles for a healthier, more active future." Last modified December 28, 2012. Harvard Health Publications (blog). http://www.health.harvard.edu/blog/build-your-core-muscles-for-a-healthier-more-active-future-201212285698.

Sagan, Carl. Accessed June 3, 2013. http://www.quotationspage.com/quote/37684.html.

Stone, Douglas, Bruce Patton, and Sheila Heen. *Difficult Conversations: How to Discuss What Matters Most.* New York: Penguin, 2000, 113–114.

CHAPTER EIGHT

Achor, Shawn. (2011 May). Shawn Achor (TED talk): The happy secret to better work. http://www.ted.com/talks/shawn_achor_the_happy_secret_to_better_work.html.

Sandberg, Sheryl. *Lean In: Women, Work, and the Will to Lead.* New York: Knopf, 2013. Kindle e-book, location 33.

Williamson, Marianne, *A Return To Love: Reflections on the Principles of A Course in Miracles.* New York: Harper Collins, 1992, 190–191.

CHAPTER NINE

Buckingham, Marcus, and Donald O. Clifton. *Now, Discover Your Strengths.* New York: The Free Press, 2001, 124.

Seligman, Martin E.P., *Authentic Happiness: Using the New Positive Psychology to Realize Your Potential for Lasting Fulfillment.* New York: The Free Press, 2002. Kindle e-book, locations 1835–1836, 3141–3154.

CHAPTER TEN

Huffington, Arianna in Drake Baer, "How Arianna Huffington Defines Success" Fast Company (blog), March 13, 2013 (6:02 a.m.), http://www.fastcompany.com/3006902/how-arianna-huffington-defines-success.

Sandberg, Sheryl. *Lean In: Women, Work, and the Will to Lead.* New York: Knopf, 2013. Kindle e-book, location 33.

Seligman, Martin E.P. *Authentic Happiness: Using the New Positive Psychology to Realize Your Potential for Lasting Fulfillment.* New York: The Free Press, 2002. Kindle e-book, locations 1835–1836, 3141–3154.

CHAPTER ELEVEN

Godin, Seth. *Tribes: We Need You to Lead Us.* New York: Penguin, 2008. Kindle e-book.

Sandberg, Sheryl. *Lean In: Women, Work, and the Will to Lead.* New York: Knopf, 2013. Kindle e-book, location 33.

Walker, Matt. *Adventure in Everything: How the Five Elements of Adventure Create a Life of Authenticity, Purpose, and Inspiration.* Carlsbad: Hay House, 2011, 163.

CHAPTER TWELVE

Brown, Brené. Origin Magazine. By Chantal Pierrat. http://www.originmagazine.com/2013/05/25/brene-brown-interview-part-i-by-chantal-pierrat, May 25, 2013.

Goldsmith, Marshall. *What Got You Here Won't Get You There: How Successful People Become Even More Successful.* New York: Hyperion, 2007.

Acknowledgments

So many parts of my path, but particularly the trails that led to this book, can be connected like a constellation. I have to honor the many stars (people) in this constellation, although I don't tell the full story, I hope you all know it by now and your essential part in it

Patty Desrochers you are my sister in this life, and I'm sure in other lifetimes past and ahead. You've given me the nurturing and witness I've never felt before—the type of support and love that is so reliable that I just can't believe my good fortune sometimes, thank you. Jim Boneau my first wonderful friend at school, who gave me the courage to quit my job, who offered me my first real break into facilitation, and who continues to be a steadfast friend. Susanne Biro who gave me the first ever thanks in an Acknowledgement of her book—but more importantly the first person to make me believe I had a gift to give others, and to not wait, to just go for it.

I work with and learn from some of the most incredible colleagues—who I am very blessed to also call dear friends. Jan Gelman you are the consummate rock, coach and friend—you wonderfully helped create and support the full journey of ICIS, are the best partner to collaborate with, and have more generosity in your soul than anyone else I know. Thank you Mitch Shepard—from the first inspiration to the apprenticeship and to now, the most precious friendship. As well as Shelley Roberts, Zan Stafford, Cathy Gelb-Mobley, Erin Chapple, Matt Walker and Nancy Winship.

There are many important supporters, friends and influencers in my life—which is a particular blessing. I hope to catch them all. Jill MacGregor, Denise Stiffarm, Merrill Shattuck, the faculty, staff and cohorts at LIOS especially Pam Johnson for finding my Divine Flaw and helping me share it, the ladies in Bookclub (Jill, Kari, Megan, Natasha, Leslie, Rachel, Merrill), Kris Hendricks, Lynne Walker, Fiona Robertson-Remley, Terrell Cox, Tracy Burns, Caroline Simard, Deanna Davis, the writing group ladies (Jill, Piper, Kristy and Molly), Linda Sivertsen, Kavita Patel (amaze-balls love coach), Diane Chung, Lisa Martin, Colin Bodell.

I simply adore books, those for work and for pleasure, and I'm thankful for the many authors who have poured their hearts into the tomes I've read. Those who have educated, influenced and inspired my total geek-dom for this field include Brene Brown, Daniel Goleman, William Bridges, Danielle LaPorte, Chade-Meng Tan, Byron Katie, Peter Senge, Peter Block, Relly Nadler, Martin Selgiman, Shawn Achor, Irvin D. Yalom, Hal and Sidra Stone and Anne Lamott.

As I learned more about what it takes to put a book out into the world, I realized why in every book I'd ever read, whether fiction or nonfiction, had an acknowledgements list of as many people as they do—it takes a tribe, village, community, practically a nation of talent, desire, advice and help to get this tome into the readers hands. I, being fully naïve, fresh and new to this world had a tremendous community that were all very necessary and required. Any error, mistake, mistype in this book belongs solely to me—I'm stingy that way, I want all the credit for those bad boys! But let me focus on the perfection of this community.

Thank you and bless you Claire Coghlan, Editor Godmother, for diving as deeply as I did into this dream, you believed, encouraged, supported, worked like a mother, opened yourself fully, and then topped it all off with grace and beauty. Thanks and blessings to you Sarah Scherer for reminding me why I should consider you as Director of Operations—you were right of course. Your diligence, enthusiasm, persistence and spirit were exactly what I needed, I'm delighted God put you in my life. Thank you to our team of book beauty experts: copy-editor David B. Hare of SDG Associates, designer Dorie McClelland at Spring Book Design, and branding, marketing and book cover magicians, Tara and Kathleen, at Braid Creative.

These were the players along this specific path, but there are those most important players that have always been on every path I've taken my entire life . . .

The old-school crew—those friends who've known and loved me the longest and therefore have gone through the "trashy and tiara" moments. Samantha Britney, solid, lovely Canadian-American, flipping-me-off first friend at MSFT. Missy, a.k.a. Amy Condon—I love the wild beauty of who you are and how you never fail to make me laugh. And to The Jennie, Jennifer Greve, the BFF. Laughing and silly from age 14 to now—you, my first and favorite redhead, are the oxygen—and damn funny too.

And so much love and thanks to my family, my incredible, unique and loving family. Thank you Bella-girl, Belly-fulla-Jelly, Bella Luna— yes, I know you're a dog—but you make me smile, laugh and play every day, and while I didn't get kiddos of my own, I know God gave me you to take care of and I'm pretty happy with it. Thank you Sean, for always being my big brother—which means you consistently tease me AND have my back in all things. And thanks to my kick-ass sis-in-law Kathy who is solid and steady. Thanks to my niece, the incredible, wonderful, couldn't ask for anything better Heather SugarBean—you bring light to my life. Thank you Daddy, for being such a solid and steady presence— you encouraged me to live my life for me, were always satisfied and supportive of anything I did, from grades in school, to job changes, to buying a house, even to quitting a perfectly good job. This gave me such a sense of freedom, trust and love. And for bringing Nel to our family who has the biggest heart of love for us all, who shares her faith, her ideas and her humor with me. And thank you Mom—there aren't words to adequately thank you for it all but I will highlight a few that stand out as I write this. You didn't just tell me, you showed me that a woman could be successful, could grow and take risks, could fall and get back up even stronger, could be her own person and be loved for that, I'm so glad you did it all so that I could watch when I wasn't quite ready to always listen. You believed so completely in this book and what it would do for me, and for others—I loved that faith. This wonderful family of ours is my very greatest blessing of all. I love you.

About the Author

Stacey Sargent is an inspiring, energetic and authentic facilitator, coach, speaker and author—and the CEO of Connect Growth and Development. She is an advocate of bringing humanity back into the workplace. Stacey's approach is about Whole-Person Intelligence—partnering the logical with the creative, the rational with the emotional, our brain and our body. She helps people make the connection between their inner and outer selves so they can bring all their superpowers to any endeavor—in work and life.

Stacey and the team at Connect deliver programs for new-thinking organizations and leaders who "get" that the well-being and success of their people lead to the success of their business. Connect provides leadership and culture programs, facilitation, coaching and workshops for clients like Microsoft, Amazon, Raytheon, Expedia, Bungie, Moz and BigDoor—and through open events. She has enjoyed being a speaker at over 30 events in the last three years.

Stacey paired her degree in Business with a Masters in Applied Behavioral Science to create the "work love of her life." Join the conversations at www.ConnectGD.com's blog, Facebook page, or email us about the book at stacey@innercriticinnersuccess.com.